Dubai, 1 City 2 Different Tales

Northern Empress

NORTHERN EMPRESS

Library of Congress Control Number: 2016903074
CreateSpace Independent Publishing Platform, North Charleston, SC

Copyright © 2016 Northern Empress

All rights reserved.

ISBN:
ISBN-13: 978-1511644877
ISBN-10: 1511644877

NORTHERN EMPRESS

DEDICATION

This book is dedicated to my spouse for all his encouragement as I took on this complex project. I further dedicate this to my brand new grandson Emerson. May he grow up to travel the world and see things as they are.

NORTHERN EMPRESS

CONTENTS

	Acknowledgments	Pg # 6
	Introduction	Pg # 7
1	The City Of Dubai	Pg # 8
2	Rules And Laws	Pg # 18
3	The Maids	Pg # 25
4	Children, Abuse & Rape	Pg # 45
5	The Babies	Pg # 70
6	Relationships, Sex & Rape	Pg # 81
7	Oh Dear!	Pg # 112
8	Beverages	Pg # 123
9	Cops	Pg # 128
10	Physicians	Pg # 136
11	Laborers	Pg # 148
12	Paws-N-Claws	Pg # 152
13	Jobs	Pg # 158
14	Wheels	Pg # 162
15	Customer Service, Etc.	Pg # 169
16	Food And Shop	Pg # 176
17	School, Youngsters & Pampered	Pg # 183
18	Over The Top	Pg # 194
	References	Pg # 205
	About The Author	Pg # 206

NORTHERN EMPRESS

ACKNOWLEDGMENTS

This book is in honor of the women and men less fortunate who often end up as abused victims. The multitude of abuse taking place around the globe is staggering. Many helpless innocent children also fall prey to cruelty and sometimes ruthlessly murdered by the hands of family and friends. I want to offer my admiration to the housemaid I knew for telling me about her painful life. My spouse who was the constant rock receives a huge thank you as I devoted every waking moment of every day working. Further, my respectable friend who read the evolving manuscript and offered advice. In addition, a talented friend who extended his hand in making this novel prevail.

INTRODUCTION

The stories within this book are all true. United Arab Emirates is home to many thousands of female maids. The physical and sexual abuse a lot of them endure is deplorable. I firmly believe in sharing these short stories after listening and seeing the pain of a housemaid I knew. This is however, an opportunity to see both sides of the coin since within are narratives on how the maids are not so innocent.

The novel also focuses on abandoned babies, child abuse, bizarre murders, relationships, pet abuse, policemen, physicians and so many more. Knowing what I know, I believe the only thing that truly shines in Dubai is the sun.

Torture

A 45-year-old Emirati woman is on trial for torturing her maids. She beat them regularly, forced them to drink bleach and locked them in a bathroom. She even made two of them strip naked so she could take pictures of them and then threaten to publish them. This abuse became known when one maid died. They found pesticide chemicals in her body, and she only weighed 81 lbs.

The other Filipina maid only 29-years-old said that it began when the first maid started working in the home. She explained that her boss locked the kitchen door so she couldn't prepare food for herself. She is only allowed one piece of bread, small drops of water and a cup of tea for the entire day.

The employer, was once unhappy how the maid cleaned the bathroom, so she forced the maid to drink a small cup of detergent with bleach. She was beat continuously until she drank it.

When the second maid arrived a month later, the abuse didn't stop, and they were given even less food to eat. The maid said her co-worker was so hungry that she went through the trash to look for food. The Emirati employer caught her and didn't give her anything to eat for five days. A few days later she died.

When the paramedics arrived they didn't think her death was due to natural causes, and they called the police. The surviving maid explained to police what had happened. In court a friend of the defendant said she saw the woman beating both of the girls with a metal bar throwing one of them down the stairs.

The Emirati woman denied the torture that led to the death of the maid. Her 42-year-old Emirati husband is on trial for criminal abetting and said his wife has psychological problems. They both pleaded not guilty. No further information available.

CHAPTER 1
THE CITY OF DUBAI

I would like to present these incredible true stories I have gathered while living in Dubai, United Arab Emirates with my spouse. I am passionate about sharing this insight as nothing is what it pretends to be. There is a recognizable harsh distinction between how the twinkling city and pleasing lifestyle is being portrayed versus, the reality of how it truly is if you don't have money or are not local. The arrogance hovers over the city resembling fog from a science fiction film as expatriates are looked down upon. If you are foreign and unfortunate enough to have ended up in court, you will likely be hammered over the head with a gavel.

I am blessed to have come from a country that shines with so many freedoms. We can say what we wish and do as we want, but just as important, we have an equal and impartial court of law. Plenty of regions appear to not have the same mindset as we do, nor do they have any consistency in fairness, even though they are living in these current times within modern cities.

These factual narratives are on torment, sexual assault, bizarre murders, abandoned babies, relationships, pet abuse and many more. You will notice the injustice, suffering and cruelty that takes place each day, along with a few unusual and downright humorous ones.

First off, let me tell you about the flashy city of Dubai, and the steps we had to take just to live together as man and wife along with what it took to get a resident visa. To start, I needed a resident visa. I had to gather up a marriage certificate because living together unmarried is illegal. You would think that proving you are married ought to be an easy practice, but actually it wasn't.

I started by going to the office of our Local State Department to get our marriage certificate and have it notarized. I then took it to the County Clerk to have it signed and dated. Next I was off to the State Department again to have them stamp and sign it, authenticating the County Clerk's signature. I then mailed it off to the U.S. State Department in Washington, D.C. Hillary Clinton, who was the Secretary of State at the time stamped and signed it. The document was forwarded to the U.A.E. Embassy in Washington, D.C. so they could sign it.

After it came back I then had to send it off to my spouse who by now was in Dubai working. He took it on to the authorities so they could stamp it. After this was done and proven that we were legally married, my spouse hand carried it to a typist. He "typed" up the application which enabled me to get a resident visa. Finally, the application, along with the other paperwork was taken to the Dubai Immigration Authority to apply for my visa. I won't even get into what we went through to take our little dog with us!

Upon me arriving and part of the visa procedure, my spouse and I immediately had to go to a clinic. We were required to take a "medical fitness screening." We tested for HIV, tuberculosis and leprosy. Depending on your occupation, you could be tested for syphilis, Hepatitis A, B, C and given a pregnancy test. If you fail any of these tests, you will be denied a visa and deported back to your home country.

Dubai lies directly within the Arabian Desert which occupies 900,000 square miles. The desert features everything from red dunes to quicksand. It is on the Southeast Coast of the Persian Gulf or what the locals refer to as the "Arabian Gulf." They are part of the United Arab Emirates. The U.A.E. consists of 7 Emirates or you could say "states," with Dubai being more open and relaxed than the rest. The other 6 Emirates are: Abu Dhabi, Ajman, Fujairah, Ras Al Khaimah, Umm Al Quwain and Sharjah where they are deeply conservative.

The capital of the U.A.E. is Abu Dhabi. They are exceptionally conservative and only an hour car ride from Dubai. Abu Dhabi is referred to as the "big brother" to the "wild child" Dubai. It is the headquarters for the president of the state, the cabinet, ministries, the federal institutions, foreign embassies, broadcast tv and most of the oil companies. They completely bailed Dubai out of a financial crisis in 2008/2009 while they were spending like crazy.

The population in Dubai as of 2014 was roughly 1.78 million. As a comparison, in 2014 the United States population was roughly over 318 million. There are 150 different nationalities and only 10-15% are local Emiratis. Approximately 100,000 are British. The biggest expatriate [a person who resides in another country other than their own citizenship] group is the South Asian population. They make up 58% and this fully includes India.

The people in Dubai are young with the median range in the neighborhood of 27-years-old. Most everyone can speak English, at least a little.

Dubai's temperature isn't only hot, but believe it or not, very humid. It is the "hottest" holiday destination in the world. There are really only two seasons, summer and winter. The summer starts in April and lasts until October with extreme heat and humidity. We have every year experienced temperatures of 129^{0}F with the heat index. April will see above 91^{0}F. May and June is the time sandstorms hit the city. June to October regularly sees 104^{0}F. In November and December, Dubai experiences an autumn sense and the start of the rainy season. This is also known as "BBQ" season. The temperature remains above 68^{0}F throughout these months. During this time tourists begin to arrive. January through March is winter, but the temperatures can still reach 86^{0}F with the lowest dropping to 59^{0}F.

Wintertime, Dubai is packed with visitors in-spite of it being the full on "rainy season," 3.7 inches annually. Because the rain is so little, the government does something known as "cloud seeding." This method is done by flying airplanes above the clouds to drop chemicals in order to make it "artificially rain." A very expensive undertaking.

Dubai is considered a star-studded city with Hollywood and Bollywood stars frequenting the place. Gold, money and fancy skyscrapers are looming everywhere. They currently hold a world record for having 73 "completed" skyscrapers that stand at 656 ft. and this includes 18 that stand at least 984 ft. This is by far more than any other city.

One iconic building is named the Burj Khalifa and is the tallest building in the world standing at 2,722 ft. The structure is skinny and sometimes referred to as a "needle in the sky" by the residents. You can often see it sticking up through the clouds.

Inside is the Armani Hotel designed by Giorgio Armani himself. There are restaurants, shopping and a 12,000 square foot spa in the hotel. You can also buy tickets to the Observation Deck on the 124th-floor.

According to data released by Emporis, Burj Khalifa does not hold the record for the fastest elevator, in-spite of what has been said. It comes in third. Even though, it still travels over 1,968 ft. per minute. Essentially you go from the ground to the 124th-floor in one minute with dazzling lights and music inside. Once you get to the top, you may not see a thing, more times than not, the visibility is always very poor.

It is worth mentioning that the Burj Khalifa holds the record for the fastest "double-decker" elevators in the world. It carries passengers the longest distance possible in an elevator.

The decision to build the Burj Khalifa came from the government when they wanted to change from an oil based economy to one that is service and tourism. The skyscraper is surrounded by hotels, the Dubai Mall, residential towers, restaurants and a large artificial lake where each night they display the "world's largest" fountain show. It is coordinated with music and is precisely like the one in Las Vegas, Nevada but bigger. The Vegas Fountain was built first, and the same people were hired to build the one in Dubai.

There are 5 world records right at the Burj Khalifa. The fountain show as I have just mentioned, the largest mall, the thickest aquarium glass, the tallest building and last but not least the fastest double-decker elevators.

The Burj Al Arab is another iconic luxury hotel. This dramatic shape looks like the sail of a ship. It is the third tallest hotel in the world. It has been referred to as the world's only "7-star" hotel, but technically only 1 to 5-stars are given out to classify a hotel. The 7-star rating was given by a British journalist there on a pre-opening press trip. He was so amazed with the hotel that the term stuck.

Impressively, the resort stands on an artificial island 920 ft. from the popular Jumeira Beach. It is connected to the mainland by a private curving bridge. The spectacular building towers at 689 ft. above the ground. There is a helicopter pad near the top to boot. This is where celebrities played golf, tennis and a Formula 1 race car was lifted to the pad by a helicopter. An Aston Martin Vanquish was also lifted to the top.

In 2012, the Royal Suite at Burj Al Arab was listed as the 12th most expensive room in the world, topping out at $18,716 a night. This resort is unquestionably popular with the Chinese market as they made up 25% of the total bookings in 2011 and 2012. The inside decor is nothing short of exquisite. If you are a tourist and decide at the spur of the moment to go to the hotel, you will not be allowed in. Reservations are paramount and need to be booked in advance for either the hotel or restaurants.

Everything at the Burj Al Arab is pricey and the cheapest reservation is for "High Tea." The cost is $100 per person, and that includes finger sandwiches. It is well worth it since the inside is stunning, and the sunset views are breathtaking. The price tag to build this skyscraper comes in at $650 million. Unfortunately, the building doesn't come without critics. In a nutshell, one critic had said: "This extraordinary investment in state-of-the-art technology is largely due to the power of wealth." The other criticized the hotel and Dubai by saying: "Both the hotel and city are triumph over money and practicality."

Gorgeous yachts are everywhere in Dubai. The Ruler had his parked at his private island right next to the Palm Jumeira and just along the street where we lived. It measures over 508 ft. long. From what we saw, it never moved. Occasionally a helicopter flew in to drop off guests for lunch.

There is a man-made marina district filled with spectacular yachts and is really an artificial canal city. It is dug out along a two mile stretch of the Persian Gulf shoreline. It has nearly 5 miles of pedestrian walkways that wrap around the waterfront lined with yachts, restaurants, coffee shops and a grocery store. The first phase is finished, but when fully completed they claim it will be the "world's largest" man-made marina. Many expats live in the vicinity since it is so striking, and a fun place to walk around and grab a bite to eat.

The malls are enormous with every world renowned store in them. Dubai is home to an annual "Shopping Festival" where once a year many come from around the globe for the 1 month event. From my experiences, the price tags are good, but not too much of a big change from what I have seen during the rest of the year. The only real difference is constant raffles which allows you the chance to win cars, gold, trips and other prizes.

Dubai Mall is the "largest mall in the world" having more than 1,200 shops and is expanding. The size is equivalent to 50 football fields and has won 5 different awards. Inside is a city giving you the choice to do whatever you choose. With the relentless heat, people need to stay occupied as being outside is not possible. The mall has 22 cinema screens and 120 restaurants and cafes.

If you go to a movie, you can choose a V.I.P. experience. Inside, the seating is limited and private with reclining leather chairs, blankets, pillows and your own butler service. A ticket is pricey and well above the normal price. This really though is an excellent way to go to the movies, that is if the rest of the people watching are respectful. Occasionally, you see wealthier young men come in to do nothing more than play on their phones and in the end, fall asleep. They miss the entire movie and the noise from the snoring is unbearable! If a show is deemed unsuitable in any way, or the language is poor, the movie will not be shown.

At the mall is an aquarium and underwater zoo. The aquarium has the "world's largest" viewing acrylic panel around it. It measures over 107 ft. wide, over 27 ft. high, 2.5 ft. thick and weighs 540,132 lbs. The aquarium holds 33,000 marine animals. In 2010 a leak caused a partial evacuation of the mall and a brief shutdown.

A mall isn't a mall without an ice rink. This one can hold up to 2,000 guests and uses refrigeration plant technology. It can produce 1.5 inches of ice bed, that is two times the thickness of an NHL Olympic size rink. SEGA Republic, an inside theme park offering 150 amusement games can also be found. If visiting the mall, don't overlook Candylicious, the "world's largest" sweet shop that extends over 10,000 square feet. The Dubai Mall has 14,000 parking spots with most being inside a garage. They offer valet and have a system set up to find your car if you lose it.

In 2015 more than 100 foreign laborers protested in front of the mall causing disturbance to traffic. The guys did not receive a paycheck with their "correct wages." I believe they didn't get paid at all. The country will not tolerate any kind of demonstration. If this scene reflects earlier instances, I can assume these individuals are kicked out and not in the U.A.E.

Another grand mall is named Mall of the Emirates. Inside is Ski Dubai, an "indoor ski resort and snow park." Ski lessons are provided, and they have a Cafe named the Avalanche, halfway up the slope. Incredibly, this mountain presents an overwhelming theme. The resort with sub-zero temperatures stretches over 73,818 ft. with actual snow the entire year. It also houses the "world's largest" indoor snow park covering over 9,842 ft. The man-made mountain measures over 278 ft. high and includes 5 different slopes with the greatest run at over 1,312 ft.

The snow park has sled and toboggan runs, an icy slide, soaring towers, giant snowballs to roll around in and an ice cavern. To add even more excitement, penguins were imported. That caused a stir among the animal activists since penguins should be in their natural habitat. There are three different options of tickets to view the penguins. The least expensive is $41 with views up close. The most expensive is the V.I.P. that goes for $232, and provides a full on experience.

In the Mall of the Emirates, and straight in front of the ski resort is a 393 room luxury hotel named the Kempinski. If staying at this hotel, guests can choose an Aspen Chalet and watch people skiing through the window in their room. They can jump into the elevator, eat or shop never leaving the building. The mall won an award for the world's leading new shopping mall. Employees at all of the malls are migrant workers bused into work. Typically a western teen will not be seen working in any mall as they do in other countries. These jobs are reserved for the migrant worker with lower pay, excessive hours and often have passports taken away until contracts are fulfilled. It is very difficult for a teen to get a part-time job to earn money.

Five-star resorts are located everywhere and most are on Palm Jumeira. The palm is a man-made island composed of sand in the shape of a palm tree. This is one of several artificial island projects Dubai is working on to finish. Special plans were designed for Palm Jumeira so the streets didn't "mess up the look of the palm tree." For people wanting to visit the resorts, regular city bus service is forbidden to run on the palm. However, a monorail station is situated at the foot of the palm which goes straight down the middle arriving at the Atlantis resort. You can also choose to take a taxi if you prefer not to drive.

My spouse and I lived on Palm Jumeira and in 2013, we watched a "Guinness World Record" of 500,000 fireworks being set off in 6 minutes. On one hand the display was spectacular, but the organization of the entire event was an absolute nightmare. Transporting the public to the event was a fiasco. Thousands ended up walking on the roads trying to get to the places where they paid large sums of money to reserve spots and tables.

Two other larger palms are started, but not finished. Palm Jebel Ali which has no infrastructure was to house 250,000 people. The other is Palm Deira which changed names back in 2013, and will now be Deira Island and no longer be shaped like a palm tree. The island is going to have 1,400 retail units, a hotel, and amphitheater. This haven will primarily be used for entertainment.

Shoreline, is an apartment complex where my spouse and I lived. This complex is beautifully landscaped with enticing private beaches comprised of swimming pools, restaurants, cabanas and a particular stretch had beach butlers. Bunches of chatter took place saying the city is making plans to cool the sand on the beach, so the residents didn't have to walk on the hot ground. The plans did not progress while we lived there.

This is the only privately owned area that serves alcohol not connected to a hotel or resort. The law to serve alcohol in Dubai states that a club or restaurant must be connected to or inside a hotel or resort. Any sports organization is also allowed to serve, such as the Country Club.

Just up the street from our apartment was the Atlantis resort. Two exist, the other is in the Bahamas. What sets this one a part from the other one is that gambling is illegal. This 1,500 room vacation place is nautically themed and infused with Arabian flair that turns out to be jaw-dropping. The 110 acre, 5-star resort has attractions for children and adults including the main one, Aquaventure Water Park. It encompasses 42 acres and a 1.4 mile river ride with cascades, tidal waves and rapids.

Episodes from reality television shows were filmed at this water park and scenes from movies filmed at the hotel. Inside the Atlantis, the Lost Chambers Aquarium exhibits 65,000 fish and sea creatures. The Ambassador Lagoon, a marine habitat that holds 3,000,000 gallons of water is featured. This retreat includes Dolphin Bay where the guest can swim with the dolphins and a stretch of the beach is covered with over 700 sun beds. While inside, shopping along "The Avenues" is popular.

The grand opening of this sanctuary back in 2008 was extravagant. Festivities attracted many guests from Hollywood. As part of the ceremony, a light show of moving images illuminated onto the building. Custom made shells shipped in from around the globe. Roughly 100,000 fireworks blasted off, which was seven times more than Beijing had at their 2008 opening ceremony of the Olympics. Fireworks discharged from 716 firing locations from around the island, including 400 balconies at the resort. The 3.1 mile sweep lit up the entire Palm Jumeira Island and Atlantis resort.

Dubai has a project known as the "World Islands," these are man-made islands 2.5 miles off the coast of Dubai in the Persian Gulf. When looking downward from the sky, the image looks like a world map.

These islands are made of sand dredged from Dubai's shallow coastal waters and 386 million tons of rock. The 300 archipelago is not finished because of financial trouble stemming back to 2008. In 2014 a different investment group announced the project was well under way.

The first series will be Europe, Sweden and Germany. They range from 150,000 to 450,000 square feet, with distances between islands averaging about 330 feet. The whole development covers 3.7 by 5.6 miles and is surrounded by an oval breakwater island. They created 144 miles of shoreline. Very impressive from the air.

During the time my spouse and I moved out of the country in 2014, an "underwater hotel" named the Hydropolis is being developed. This becomes the world's first underwater hotel. The original plan is estimated to be over 65 ft. underwater and to cover over 642 acres, equal to Hyde Park in London. The hotel has 3 segments, first is a land station to transport people out to the hotel, then a "noiseless" train and the hotel.

There will be 220 underwater suites, said to go for a cool $5,500 per night. The hotel will host restaurants, a spa, a cinema, a ballroom and bars. This extraordinary place expects to greet 3,000 visitors a day.

Dubai sure loves record breaking adventures, but they relish their cars! I'm not talking just any average car, these are often custom made for the owners and imported. Nothing is unusual when seeing multiple top of the line Bugattis, Ferraris, stretched limos with hot tubs racing around the city. The police department is no exception, riding in style using BMW's, but are often seen in many other high dollar vehicles.

Dubai is known as the "City of Gold" because a major part of the city is based on gold trade. Hundreds of tons of gold are imported per year and is the fastest growing gold center in the world. Quality is well known as is the impressive variety of stylish jewelry designs. The quantity of gold in the jewelry far exceeds the standard in the United States. Free trade makes this one of the cheapest places in the world to buy gold jewelry and you can haggle. Plus, no sales tax.

The famous Gold Souk [Souk means an open air market], is a window to the Arabian world with narrow alleys lined with fresh spices in sacks and barrels. There you will find a fish market, traditional wooden archways and old wooden dhows [boats] that have one or more masts. Dhows are lined up one right after another and are still in use today to carry heavy items such as water, fruit and goods.

The Gold Souk is one of the largest retail gold markets in the world. There are over 400 retail and wholesale units that covers a 1/4 square mile. This place is popular with the tourists as 95% of total visitors will end up buying gold and 76% of residents in Dubai already own gold. Many vending machines sell "gold bars" and are displayed around the city in the airport, malls and resorts. The gold is often bought as souvenirs. The vicinity is not only known for tons of gold but diamonds and other precious gems too.

One year during Christmas my spouse and I drove to Abu Dhabi, the capital to visit an exquisite 5-star resort called the Emirates Palace. In the lobby stood a 43 ft. Christmas tree decked out in jewelry worth $11 million. The tree was fitted with gold, diamonds, rubies and other precious stones. Watching over the tree, just 2 security guards.

This hotel received criticism from around the world saying the tree does not represent Christmas. It was never to be displayed again. The resort said they wanted to bring cheer to their guests and told how it was not for any publicity stunt.

What the Emirates Palace really has to offer is extravagance. For $1 million, you can receive a 1 week package that includes: jet-setting around the Middle East, a "bath caviar," $15,000 cognacs and real Albino Caviar. Just over 13 lbs. of this caviar is produced per year, and the going rate for 2 lbs. is $46,354. The hotel has a little over 4 lbs.

The majestic resort sits on the top of a hill. When entering, opulence is the theme and for $15 a customer can buy a 24K gold flake cappuccino. The hotel has 302 luxury rooms with 6 different styles to choose from and 92 suites. In all 302 grand luxury rooms are 52 in. plasma screens and a square footage of 592. The bedrooms range from 1 to 3 rooms.

In each of the 92 suites are 61 in. LCD screens and a 24-hour butler service. A body-guard and a touch screen pad that controls each service are a few more things included. Sizes on these suites range from 1,184 to 7,319 square feet. A single suite costs $16,400 plus a 20% service charge per night. Gold and marble are throughout all the suites. The top floor is for royalty and dignitaries and has 6 Rulers Suites. This floor is reserved for only the elite.

Inside the palace you will find 114 domes. The center is dominated by a jaw-dropping grand atrium over 196 ft. high and over 130 ft. wide, topped with the largest dome in the world. This is said to be higher than the one in St. Peter's Basilica in Rome.

The dome has 13 different colors of marble to show the many hues of the desert and has over 19,816 ft. of gold leaf. There is so much gold inside the resort, people say the South African production was washed-out for a full year. This "entire" hotel is dominated by gold, marble, silver and glass mosaics. The chandeliers are made of Swarovski crystal and there are 200 fountains.

This resort is so large that the staff needs golf carts to navigate around while dropping off fresh towels. Many celebrities and presidents frequented the place and performed there too. The hotel appeared in films and is the second most expensive hotel in the world to build, topping out at $3 billion.

We have always said Dubai is wonderful to visit, as long as the tourist has a plane ticket home. There are so many extravagant things to see, more than any country in the world.

Even though Dubai isn't as strict as the rest of the emirates, the rules still need to be followed or the visitor could pay dearly. Most people don't have problems, but there are those who do. The biggest mistake many tourists make is getting caught up in all the bling and fanciness which can very easily make a person forget where they are.

At last, with all the glitz in place it's time to move onto the stark reality of what it is like living in Dubai, U.A.E. and what happens when the lights go out.

CHAPTER 2
RULES AND LAWS

Before getting to the stories, this chapter is important as it goes over the rules and laws in the U.A.E. This will help you better understand the narratives and give you an overall picture of what you can and can't do in Dubai.

Rules and Laws that Expatriates Must not Break

1. **Illegal Satellite TV:** The fine can go up to $13,612 for an unauthorized satellite television connection. Those providing the services can face jail and deportation.

2. **Storing Alcohol at Home:** 6 months in jail and a fine of $1,361 if you do not have a liquor license. There is no consuming, transporting, possessing or selling.

3. **Employing Domestic Help Illegally:** This fine could go up to $13,612 if you hire someone without a proper visa. Also, if they are sponsored by someone else and you hire them. Over a thousand people were on trial for recruiting maids illegally.

4. **Littering:** This penalty goes from $136 to $272 even if you throw a cigarette butt out of the window or spit. There are 700 inspectors and residents allowed to impose fines on the spot. Several thousand people are fined for throwing waste and spitting in public.

5. **Jaywalking:** $54 is the fine, and several thousand people each month have to pay.

6. **Washing your Car on the Road, Pouring Water on the Road or Letting Water Drip from the Air-Conditioner:** A $27 fine and hundreds pay.

7. **Using Phone Cards that are Illegal:** You're subject to a jail term, fine and deportation. Cards are often made on a home computer.
8. **Sharing an Apartment or Having a Live-In:** A fine, detention or both with the possibility of deportation. Under Sharia law, unmarried and unrelated people of the opposite sex are prohibited from living together.
9. **Sex out of Wedlock:** Anyone who engages in consensual sex other than a husband and wife will get at least one year in jail. Expect a fine, jail and deportation, but it depends on the judge's discretion.
10. **Public Display of Affection:** You can expect up to 6 months in jail and deportation. This means no kissing or hugging in public if the person is unrelated to you. I'd still use caution even if you are related.

Other offences you should not be caught doing is taking pictures of any sensitive buildings and locations or people, especially women without their permission. This can be considered "sexual harassment."

To swear or show "the finger" is prohibited. Common in road rage and plenty of that around the city. It's best to not even raise your hand as that can be used against you. It could be said you showed "the finger," and it will be up to you to prove your innocence. Talking or texting while driving is another offence, but is common in the west.

Most people know the Middle East can be stern with areas being downright severe for not obeying their rules. I talked to many people who have the same question. Do western women need to wear a Burqa [a loose garment covering the face and body] while in Dubai? The answer is no. We could dress how we wanted as long as it was modest and not provocative.

During the holy month of Ramadan, a month of praying and religious worshipping, Muslims and other people living in the country are expected to dress extremely conservative. No music is to be played either. Fasting is a very important part and goes from sunrise to sunset for the entire month. We as expats, are forbidden to eat food, drink water, chew gum or smoke in public. The one exception is for small children and the elderly who can "possibly" be exempt.

During Ramadan some of the hotels will have at least one restaurant opened during the day where you will find a limited food choice. Food is to be eaten behind a black curtain, out of view of other people. All the other restaurants are closed until sunset with a few donut outlets and coffee shops open. These few establishments gained a government permit to stay open during the day for "to go" orders only. The bags are "stapled" shut, even if you order just a cup of coffee. Expats can consume these items in their home.

The government is more lenient with western people for eating in the privacy of your own home. Plus, harder for them to watch and enforce this law inside your house.

The British Consulate is warning tourists and residents to either show respect or face jail time. An officer from the British Embassy gave a series of speeches to teenagers on the do's and don'ts in the United Arab Emirates. They are also told of cases the British Consulate handles. Such cases include alleged murderers, victims of murder, suicide, forced marriage, drugs and alcohol.

The British Embassy said: "Substance abuse among young people of different nationalities in the Emirates is a problem. Drinking is one of the biggest headaches for the embassy and not because British nationals misbehave. Sometimes it isn't clear to everyone what you can and can't do." For my spouse and me, it was very frustrating not to have clear and consistent rules. You will never get a straight answer to a question simply because no one really knows. It has been said when a person does their best to abide by the customs and practices, there isn't a problem. Where it goes wrong is the "unwritten rules" Dubai has that are enforced and expected to be followed. Most times, you don't even know what they are.

An expat couple came to Dubai to visit two of their friends working there. They all went out to brunch, and on the way out, one of them "accidentally" tripped and bumped into an Emirati lady who was not happy about it. The expat couple, and two friends are arrested and held in jail for 2 days. What the offense was is not clear. Was it the tripping or the bumping?

Consistency is definitely a problem. A 16-year-old boy "whipped" for consuming alcohol, but what about the people of different faiths or young men who frequent the clubs and restaurants consuming alcohol? The punishment is never the same.

My spouse and I were walking our little dog. We saw a drunk expat man walking across the street. An Emirati guy driving down the road slammed on his brakes trying to stop so he would not hit the drunk man. The expat became angry at almost being run over, so he walked up to the Emirati man's car. The man rolled down his window, and the expat punched him in the face. A fight erupted in the middle of the road.

A neighbor of ours jumped in to break up the fight and just then, the police arrived. The police handcuffed the expat who was drunk and was ready to take our neighbor away too. An Emirati who saw the incident, stepped in to let the police know that our neighbor was trying to defuse the situation. Both would be in jail if it wasn't for the Emirati witness. The drunk expat did his time in jail and was deported back to his country.

The traffic lights on that street are very dangerous as they go from green to red then back to green again. There is no yellow light. Due to the design of these lights, many drivers don't realize when they have a red light, they need to stop on a dime so they don't hit a pedestrian who immediately has a green light. This creates a deadly situation.

Another hot point of what you can't do is dance. Who thought dancing in public could cause a problem? A big problem according to the U.A.E.

authorities. One example is of a woman who filed a rape claim only to have a CCTV footage of her dancing in public used as evidence against her. The prosecutors said that dancing "showed" that she wanted to have sex. Dancing is allowed only in the privacy of your own home.

There is also a proposed bill for the demand to crackdown on public display of affection and wearing unsuitable clothing. Many, many U.A.E. nationals complain and are upset over people wearing skimpy outfits while shopping. They are angry at couples being intimate in public places and the overall behavior of expats and tourists.

If this proposed bill passes, the goal is to educate and inform people of the modesty law and the possible punishment you can expect if broken. Brochures at the malls and airports are handed out advising people of the laws and customs. There are also signs on the mall doors to cover up.

An Emirati official was at a mall with his children when he became outraged. He saw a man putting his hand down the back of his girlfriend's jeans as they walked. He said many local people were shocked. They walked up to him and said, "Do you see what he is doing?"

A spokesperson from the Center of Cultural Understanding said: "Modesty for us is about not showing off the gifts that God has given you—wealth, health and your beauty. To do so can cause feelings of inferiority and intimidation. When everyone dresses modestly, it is a way for everyone to be equal, regardless of their wealth or their background." What is Dubai if not a show off of wealth?

Laws regarding checks say you can't write a check without having the funds in your bank because it is illegal and is considered a criminal act if the check bounces. When you buy a car, home or whatever you may try to get a loan for, you go to the bank for the loan. They make you write one check for collateral in the full amount of the loan. Depending on the bank, you could write multiple checks for each monthly installment for which you have agreed. The bank then holds onto the check or checks, and they give it back to you when you paid back the loan, or they will destroy it.

When we purchased our car, the bank said we had to write one check in full. A statement on the check said it was not to exceed the outstanding balance of the loan. Muslims are "prohibited" to charge interest on a loan per Sharia law. For them to get around the interest law is simple. You agree to pay the car dealer [for example] $30,000 for a car, that is what the bank pays the car dealer. The bank then makes out the loan in the amount of $36,000 and that's what you pay back to the bank in monthly installments.

This is what we call interest, but because we wrote a check to cover the full purchase price, there is no loan and no interest paid, just monthly payments. If for any reason you fail to honor your payment, they will cash the check for the full purchase. If you do not have the funds to cover the check, more than likely you will end up in jail.

There are practices followed by banks when a stop payment is requested by the customer. Many of the banks follow their own internal policies that vary from the law. The customer cannot easily stop a payment. If you move forward with a stop payment, you need to get a letter from a "competent court." If there is a dispute between you and the person you wrote the check to, the bank still will not accept the stop payment. Because again, a "competent court" is necessary.

If you quit your job or get fired in Dubai, the law says your employer has to inform your bank. If you have any outstanding debts that can't be covered by your savings, then your accounts are frozen and you are forbidden to leave the country. A person can find themselves on the street and in jail.

The law does not have a bankruptcy clause so, it makes it impossible for you to carry out your debt through personal bankruptcy. This is why after the financial meltdown in 2009 there were scores of cars abandoned throughout the city. The residents couldn't keep up with the payments and ultimately skipped out of the country.

Many years later, we still saw a lot of deserted cars. Inside our parking garage at our apartment, a very nice Range Rover sat unattended next to our car for the 3½ years we lived there.

A Small Sticker Dangerous and Illegal

A resident took their car into a government inspection facility, what you need to do before selling it. They are informed that the tiny 3 in. by 1 in. sticker of a country flag on the back window was illegal. The facility insisted that the sticker be removed so the vehicle can be certified as safe.

This person questioned why it was illegal. He probed the legality of the cars being driven with blacked out windows from the tint on the vehicles. He points out the oodles of pictures of the Rulers' plastering windows on National Day [a holiday that somewhat resembles July 4th in the United States]. He even mentioned car dealership stickers on windows, baby on board stickers, but no explanation can be given. Ultimately he needed to remove the sticker. This is common, some people are allowed to do things while others can't.

When my spouse and I went to sell our vehicle just before moving back to the U.S., we pick up a "for sale" sign from our home state. We brought it back to Dubai to put it in our car. We read in the paper much later, after the car sold, that placing a sign that says "for sale" inside your car is illegal. This could have resulted with the police impounding our car and a fine to get it out. Who knew?

A Park Brawl over the Hijab

Some years back 3,000 visitors on a Muslim tour came to the United States and visited an amusement park. Disputes broke out when the women are told to remove their hijabs [a veil that covers the head and chest]. They are told that this is for their own safety.

Further explaining the veils can become tangled in the mechanical parts and choke the riders or fly off and land on the tracks of another ride. The visitors are even offered a refund, but that wasn't enough as they argued and fought to wear their hijabs. Two park security employees were injured and hospitalized during this argument.

The rules are the rules, and foreigners too must obey them, whether they are in the United States, or other countries.

My spouse and I visited the Grand Mosque, a popular tourist place in Abu Dhabi. A Muslim guide said: "The religious dress code for women requires them to dress modestly, the color black and white is modest. There is no religious requirement that women have to cover up fully. The need to cover up fully came from the men's interpretation of what modest is. The men also had a certain jealousy towards other men looking at their women, so they wanted their women covered."

Emiratis Warned While Traveling

The government tells Emiratis to follow local laws while visiting abroad. The end of June and beginning of July are popular times for Emirates to travel. A campaign is launched reminding Emiratis who are traveling abroad to follow the local laws. This is true with places that ban the face veil like in France and different cities in Italy. Belgium too is considering banning the face veil. The authorities said they don't want it to lead to "embarrassment for the families."

Emiratis are also warned to know the country's minimum wage for maids, since many locals travel with them. The authorities said: "This would avoid trouble from them running away to human rights. When you treat people, you have to not be arrogant, especially at the borders and at government buildings. Don't forget you are not in your country." It sounds as if it's ok to be arrogant in your own country, but other countries may not take to it.

Thousands of flyers are handed out to Emiratis with information on how to get a travel visa, along with how to handle airport body scanning. They are cautioned too when carrying large amounts of cash at the airports.

I believe women traveling for the first time out of the Middle East will be in for a big surprise. They will find other airports [especially in the West] don't have a "separate room" for women to go into for a security pat down, as they do in that region.

A Witness to a Wedding Must be a Muslim

Two witnesses to a marriage are rejected by a judge because they were not Muslim. A Filipino woman with a 2-month-old baby stood before a judge. The judge said he can accept two Muslim men, OR one Muslim man and two Muslim women as a witness. This is because her husband-to-be was a Tunisian Muslim.

The Filipino woman who is getting married was doing so because she wanted to get a birth certificate for her baby boy. Every single document is always filed under the male. She didn't have a birth certificate because she wasn't married at the time she gave birth. She presented a written testimony from two of her friends, but got rejected since they were Christian.

A court official later said: "A man's testimony is considered more reliable than a woman's, as women may not give objective evidence. Women are considered to be emotional in their thoughts, more likely to decide issues from the heart."

Ladies' Day, no Boys on the Beach

Women are urged NOT to bring their boys over "4-years-old" to the Mamzar beach on Mondays and to the Jumeira beach on Sundays and Wednesdays when it's "ladies' day." The public park announced that ladies' day made sure the women are comfortable since no men are allowed, and this idea is part of respecting the culture of the U.A.E.

CHAPTER 3
THE MAIDS

The housemaids or nannies are in everyone's lives in the U.A.E. These women clean the house, cook, wash clothes, iron, walk the dogs, take care of the children and go with the "ma'am" on errands. Sometimes, but not very often they will go by themselves.

In the city of Dubai you are always addressed as "ma'am" or "sir" by the migrant workers. If you are with your spouse it is combined, "ma'amsir." As agitated as individuals get with constantly having to be called this, not much you can say or do that will change it.

The maids can work for a cleaning company that is endless work for 6 long days with the 7th day being a rest day. They work for numerous households. Like many local companies, the service takes their passport away from them and holds onto it until their contract is satisfied. Most of the cash passes to the business, with little going to the maid. Often they can go months without getting paid.

Many of the girls live in housing developments, or "accommodations" for migrant workers. These places are poor and run down. They are usually in places far away from the razzle-dazzle of the city. Many of the men live in areas known as "camps."

The small apartment or room with squalor conditions will sometimes house 10 women. This is how most of the migrant workers live in other occupations too.

Villas and apartments have an extra room built in for a housemaid or nanny. If they choose to stay in the home, they also have their passports taken away. They are always held by the "family" who is the sponsor for the nanny's visa. The sponsors pay a large sum of money to buy these visas. Again, the contract needs to be fulfilled before the nanny gets possession of her passport.

Like working for a cleaning company, they usually only have 1 day of rest. The pay varies per month, it can be $381 or sometimes $190 apart from toiletries. Still better than what a cleaning service pays, but a bigger risk since they don't know the family. "Typically" just the food and room is supplied by the family, but sometimes more is given than just that.

The maids take a big chance when coming to the country. They either live with a family whom they don't know, or work for a foreign cleaning service who may or may not pay them. Often they are misinformed by unscrupulous agents before arriving in Dubai and don't work as a maid.

Many times after they arrive, they are abused, beaten, raped, taken advantage of, mistreated or even killed. A few examples of this abuse is when a woman was on trial for beating her housemaid to death over an "untidy" home. She said: "I only beat her up because I wanted her to do the housework properly."

Yet another employer in a separate case is on trial as well for the murder of her maid. She poured boiling water on her body and threw pepper in her eyes. This is how slaves have been treated up through the ages. It is common for people who think they are superior, to beat others who they believe are inferior.

There are so many stories in this chapter that have common threads of beating, torture, severe mistreatment, restricting personal freedom of movement and even death. The level of cruelty is staggering. This not only happens in the U.A.E., but other parts of the world too.

It is difficult for these maids to show proof of their abuse, and that they are being held prisoner since they are so isolated. The threats made by the employers instills much fear into these young women, by telling the maids they will be put in jail. Sadly enough, the maids feel there is no way out, and end up jumping out of tall buildings. Many times they are encouraged, or helped along by their employer.

A 35-year-old Filipina maid is facing a "lifetime" ban in the U.A.E. She claims she fled after being beaten. Her employer has filed a charge against her for running away. When the maids run away from their employer, and if they get caught they will go to jail, face fines and deportation. The employer will usually press charges against them. Since their passports are held by the employer, they can't escape out of the country, but yet they can't endure the beatings by staying.

This is mostly always a double-edged sword for the maid. When terrible conditions are involved, the only choice for the maid is to run if they choose not to commit suicide. However, they are more inclined to stay with their employer because of the threat of being blacklisted or jailed. The maids that run are banned from working in the U.A.E. for 6 months, sometimes for life. If a maid is banned for life, she has no legal recourse.

Maids will also put up with abuse so they can keep their income, and a lifetime ban can become devastating to them. The Ministry of Labor does not cover domestic staff issues. Home country embassies are the ones who advocate their rights which makes it difficult to enforce since there are no federal laws to protect them.

Dubai Naturalization and Resident Department is there to approve contracts between the maids and employers, and they can arbitrate for any complaint. They are clear in saying that if a maid runs away, they have waived their rights by default.

The system is broken, and it's a catch-22 for the maid. If the maid never leaves the house, how does she make the complaint? She will have to run, so now in the eyes of the law, she is a runaway, and she waived her rights.

When the maids decide to file a case against their employer, they often are charged for their visa, which the employer paid. The employer counter sues for the cost of the visa, this in retaliation for the claim against them. The maids will often drop their claim because of the threat of having a criminal charge filed against them. Sometimes charges are brought against them even when the maids contract is up, and they shouldn't have to pay.

Often when a woman becomes pregnant and not married, the woman serves a jail sentence and then is deported. The baby can end up behind bars with the mother and then placed in a "center" or orphanage, while the mom is deported back to her home country.

A real tragic story is of a housemaid I knew. She no longer worked for her employer as a nanny, for reasons unknown and ran away. The maid is sweet, honest and caring. She appeared to be young and shy as she softly spoke to you in broken English and seldom looked you in the eye.

I listened as she told me she came from a very large family and were poor, in the Philippians. The maid had been married with 1 child. Her husband was an alcoholic who spent much of his time chasing other women and often beat her to no end.

One evening, he took a broken bottle and hit her over the head and knocked her unconscious. She woke up in the hospital not remembering what happened. I saw the terrible scars left on her head. She ultimately divorced him since she could no longer take the abuse.

I listened as she spoke of her brother who was doing well for himself and working in the Philippians. He was so proud when his company told him he will be promoted to a supervisor. When the rest of the men at his company found out, they became jealous and shot him in the head, killing him.

One year just before Christmas, her mother became extremely ill and a devastating typhoon came through her home country. Her family's house sat on top of a hill and it was demolished, they lost everything they owned. I remember getting the chills as I watched the horrible after effects on tv. Tragic as that all sounds, there is much more to her story which can be classified as modern day slavery.

She took a job as a nanny for a Korean couple who lived across the street from us. The Korean woman appears to be nice and works as an attorney. A classic case of a sheep in wolf's clothing. The woman and family is cruel to the girl on all accounts.

The maid worked up the courage to ask them for a bath towel, and they told her to take the towel she uses to wipe the floor. Her sleeping arrangements consisted of an ice cold floor, and she was only given a sack of rice to eat. They never allowed her to talk on the phone, listen to music, watch television or go outside unless she cleaned the balcony. She was only allowed to go down the hall of the apartment to throw the garbage away. She felt scared and trapped, but convinced that things will get brighter.

One month passed, and she never received her pay. The Korean woman told her they are still examining her work, yet she remained hopeful she soon would receive her money. A few more weeks passed and the couple told her they were going back to Korea to visit family for a week and she needed to take care of the children.

The couple gave the housemaid strict orders what she can and can't do while they were away on their vacation. Just before the pair left to go back to Korea, the woman stocked the kitchen with a variety of food for the 2 children and only rice for her.

The couple was gone and the housemaid was left alone with her thoughts. Day after day the children come home from school and went straight to their bedrooms without speaking to her. Each night after the kids finished eating their dinner, they left the table to hide in their bedrooms again. She had absolutely no contact with anyone for fear the couple will find out. They threatened her so much that it scared her into doing exactly as they said, and she never once disobeyed them.

Every week the couple called and said they are staying 1 more week, lying to her each time. She spoke of how lonely she was as she cried to them on the phone, and how each day there was nothing left for her to clean. The woman told her to clean her friend's apartment who lived upstairs from them. She was to do the cleaning only while the children were in school.

Shocked at how filthy the friend's apartment was she knew it would take many days to clean. Much of the laundry had not been done in a long time and sat in large heaps on the floor. The clothes to be ironed were in a pile that climbed halfway up the wall. The exhausted housemaid worked hard each day trying to clean the apartment but never received pay from the friend either.

After a month of the couple being gone, they finally returned to Dubai. When the housemaid asked about her pay, the Korean woman picked up the phone and called the police. Within minutes she was being arrested for running away from her former employer. The police slapped her in the face and threw her in jail for what turned out to be 3 months. She was finally released and deported back to the Philippians. She was told she could never return to the U.A.E.

Some of the short stories you are about to read do not always contain the sentencing or punishment given out by the court simply because it is unknown or pending at the time. What's important is the severity of these cases and how frequent they happen.

Torture

A 45-year-old Emirati woman is on trial for torturing her maids. She beat them regularly, forced them to drink bleach and locked them in a bathroom. She even made the two of them strip naked so she could take pictures then threaten to publish them. This abuse became known when one maid died. They had found pesticide chemicals in her body, and she only weighed 81 lbs.

The other Filipina maid only 29-years-old said that it began when the first maid started working in the home. She explained that her boss locked the kitchen door so she couldn't prepare food for herself. She is only allowed one piece of bread, small drops of water and a cup of tea for the entire day.

The employer, was once unhappy how the maid cleaned the bathroom, so she forced the maid to drink a small cup of detergent with bleach. She was beat continuously until she drank it.

When the second maid arrived a month later, the abuse didn't stop, and they were given even less food to eat. The maid said her co-worker was so hungry that she went through the trash to look for food. The Emirati employer caught her, and didn't give her anything to eat for five days. A few days later she died.

When the paramedics arrived they didn't think her death was due to natural causes, and they called the police. The surviving maid explained to police what had happened. In court a friend of the defendant said she saw the woman beating both girls with a metal bar, throwing one down the stairs.

The Emirati woman denied torture that led to the death of the maid. Her 42-year-old Emirati husband is on trial for criminal abetting and said his wife has psychological problems. They both pleaded not guilty. No further information is available.

Acid Poured on a Corpse

The police claim a husband poured acid on a maid's corpse after the wife killed her, and then tried to cover it up. The body of an Ethiopian woman was found wrapped in a sheet with her fingers burned. She was beaten and assaulted.

The Arab national was tracked and found, but denied any wrong doing until the evidence was brought forth. The husband confessed that his wife and the maid had gotten into an argument.

She beat the maid with a stick until she died. He said he tore off her clothes, and poured acid on her trying to "wipe out her features." After that he wrapped her in a sheet, and put her in a suitcase. They drove to a sandy place to dump the body. The wife was later arrested at a hotel where she hid. She was afraid of getting caught if she went back to her home.

The sentencing is unknown, but the police department is working with social support centers to care for their 2-year-old child. The couple's 8-month-old baby will stay with the mother in jail.

Tortured Maid was Burnt and Skin Ripped off

This story is horrific and about torture which did not happen in Dubai but in Saudi Arabia. A 23-year-old Indonesian maid is covered in injuries from head to toe. She was stabbed, finger fractured, iron imprints from being burned and pieces of skin missing from her scalp and lips. The maid had only been in Saudi and working for the family for 4 months.

Many of her injuries were inflicted by using scissors. The woman of the house, along with her daughter used an iron to burn her. Both of her legs were almost paralyzed from the burns. Portions of her scalp had been removed, the skin on her lips ripped off, her middle finger fractured and a cut was located near her eye. She was also stabbed and had marks from older wounds on her body. The maid miraculously survived and was hospitalized for a month.

The Indonesian Consular of Citizen Protection is saying they want "justice." It had been reported to the Saudi police, but at the time they had yet to respond. In Saudi the woman was found guilty, and could have faced up to 15 years behind bars, but instead she received "only" a 3 year sentence. The Indonesian Foreign Ministry said justice had not been served. An appeal was filed by the maid's attorney. No further information.

Warning not to Abuse Domestic Staff

A police official gives a warning to employers. He said:

> *Treat your staff fairly and don't abuse them in order to reduce the risk of crime. When you treat people poorly, abuse them and delay payment, this causes a desire for revenge and encourages the workers to abuse children or commit serious crimes against the sponsors. This problem is affecting our society. Don't push them too hard, treat them with respect, but don't trust them 100%. These people are from poor societies, and it's a problem if their salaries are late. If a maid feels mistreated, she might use sorcery*

such as putting strange materials in food and drinks to improve the situation. Some of them steal, remain vigilant.

The official gave an example referencing a working mother who found her 2-year-old son bleeding from the nose. A maid claimed that he had fallen from his bed, but later confessed she assaulted him out of revenge for her boss treating her poorly.

The official also said: "Families must not be easy with the staff and not let them meet others alone, because they can know other people who can lure them to escape for better jobs [sic]." There has been backlash over the words chosen by the police official, and the message it sends. There doesn't seem to be any simple human decency.

In a matter of just one year 1,258 complaints were reported by the employers against their staff. Most of the complaints were for running away and working for someone else, but there are also sexual offences, illegal affairs, betrayal of trust and theft too.

A Runaway Caught

A maid was ordered by a court to pay $1,497 to a wealthy Emirati businessman who owns a series of fast food restaurants. She will pay the businessman the money to cover the costs of hiring her. The maid who worked 20 hours a day, tried to flee from her job.

The maid worked for the businessman for more than 6 months before he demanded she work for other family members. She was ordered by her boss to work at his sister's home, which is where she fled from. She ran straight to the Philippine Embassy to seek help. Meanwhile, the businessman filed an "absconding" or runaway case.

In court, the maid was given 1 week to pay up, or she will go to jail. The businessman at first tried to get $3,539 from her, but is awarded only the cost of a visa and employment agency fees. While the court proceeded, the Filipina maid did not get a chance to explain to the court she had not been paid in six weeks. She also wanted to say she worked 20 hours a day.

In response to the maid not being able to speak in court, the Appeal Court said, "She filed too late" and refused to hear her. She doesn't know how she is going to find the money.

Maid gets 100 Lashes

A pregnant Filipina maid is found guilty of having an illegal affair and is sentenced to receive 100 lashes.

When her Emirati boss found out she was pregnant, the maid was afraid she could be turned over to the authorities because of her unwed pregnancy. The next time the family left the house, she saw her opportunity to escape from potential prosecution for her unwed pregnancy. But, before she fled she stole cash from her Emirati boss.

The employer came home, and found the maid gone, and realized the money in the bedroom has disappeared. He called the police and reported her missing. He reported her pregnancy and the money she had stolen too. According to the police, the search for her turned into an extensive "manhunt."

The maid was caught, and she confessed. She admitted to taking the money to cover the costs of having the baby, and said that she was afraid her boss would turn her in for being pregnant.

Besides the 100 lashes, the maid was sentenced to 3 months in jail for stealing, and will be deported after her sentence is served. It's unclear what will happened to the baby.

Boss Defends Working Hours

A housemaid ran away after allegedly enduring 3 years of mistreatment from her employer. A female employer stands strong on not giving her staff a day of rest.

She said that she treated the maid well, giving her what she needs. The employer said the maid watches her babies, and she made her part of the family. She wants to know why the maid needs a day off, and where will she go? She said: "When some people give their maid a day off, the maid will bring men back to the home. That causes a problem because they then become pregnant and blame it on sir [employers husband] when it's really the boyfriend's baby. It makes problems for everyone [sic]."

The maid claims she endured "excessive control," verbal abuse, no days off and never allowed to go out of the house. She started out with a 2 year contract, but renewed it for 1 more year before giving her notice. The boss did not accept the notice without payment from the maid for $1,633.

The employer claims she saw a change in the maid's behavior after two years. She's angry all the time, shouting at the children and shouting at the other 3 maids she has for cooking and cleaning. She said she didn't know the maid wanted to leave.

The boss let it be known that her detached villa is closely monitored by CCTV. She said it's there to make the maids afraid, not for her to watch them all day. She encourages the staff to treat the property as their own home. The employer said: "I treat all of them well, they are not animals."

One of the other housemaids was interviewed and said she is treated well, but has no friends in Dubai. She expressed: "Having an occasional day off, if madam would allow, I would like it [sic]." The outcome of the court case is unknown.

Deadly Beating Made to Look like a Suicide

A female Emirati employer was arrested for killing her maid. At first she denied the accusations. She claimed it was a suicide, and her sister who is a policewoman, corroborated the story and said, "The maid had killed herself."

The Emirati boss claimed they found her in the bathroom dead after she had beaten herself to death. They said: "The maid often cut, mutilate and hit herself." It was determined after an autopsy, she suffered a fractured skull, bruising to the legs and arms and broken teeth.

The Emirati confessed and said she often beat the maid with a wooden cane. She claimed the maid was lazy, and she had to beat her to make her work. The woman remains in custody. The victim's family will likely be awarded $54,455 in "blood money," money paid to the next of kin for an untimely death of a person. If the next of kin accepts the blood money, the punishment can severely be reduced.

Employer Claims Death was Natural Causes

An Emirati woman is charged with illegally hiring an Asian maid then killing her. The maid was beaten up badly by the woman, and suffered a fractured skull and severe wounds to her body, consistent with a ruthless beating.

The woman denied the charges and claimed, she returned home and found the maid dead. She said, "She died of natural causes." The case was adjourned.

Maid Attacked and Raped

A 35-year-old Ethiopian housemaid was attacked and raped by a carpenter inside the home where she lived and worked. His colleagues had been working on the grounds during the attack.

The maid was startled to find the carpenter in the home. He dragged her into a room and ripped off her clothes then raped her. She said that she was shocked and afraid and wasn't able to overpower him since he was so much stronger. She later identifies him from a lineup. The outcome of the court case is unknown.

Maids Locked up

Twenty female Filipina hotel maids are locked up in a villa for 1 month by 3 Indian men who worked for the hotel. The women are only allowed to go to work.

The men claimed it was to prevent sexual harassment, and for their own safety from single men in the area. A driver drove them to work in a bus and then drove them back to the villa. The main gate to the villa compound was barred and locked, and so is the main door. The bus driver and a guard monitored the women.

Once a month they were taken to the market to buy supplies, but closely watched. The maids said that they were never physically abused, but just prevented from leaving. The maids accepted the conditions because they were lead to believe that is the way things are done in Dubai. They thought the orders came from the hotel management and they acted within the law. They didn't complain since they desperately needed to keep their jobs. The 3 men pleaded guilty, and the court was adjourned.

This is an example of young women from poor places, lured into the country with a promise of a great job and end up being enslaved. Most likely their passports taken away too.

Rape Case Dropped

A Filipino maid accused her Iranian boss of raping her, but police dropped the charges due to lack of evidence. The woman tells how her boss brutally raped her while his wife was out of the house. She quickly called the Philippian Embassy asking for help. A staff member from the embassy accompanied her to the police station to file a complaint. The maid filed the rape claim and was then arrested.

Soon afterwards the boss showed up at the police station and claimed she ran from the house that morning. The boss was allowed to leave the police station while the maid was held in prison for several days. After the investigation, she was released with no charges against her.

The maid left Dubai since she was afraid of her boss pursuing the runaway claim. She is now back in her home country. This is an example of a woman filing a rape claim and finding herself to be the one locked up.

No Pay

A Filipina housemaid filed a complaint with human rights stating, she worked for 4 months without getting paid and worked tirelessly for the family. She said that her employer's children are beating her. The maid says not only was she severely beaten, but never allowed to leave the house.

The employer told a court she had no problem with the maid, and she wasn't aware that her sons beat her. Authorities made sure the maid was paid, and they gave her the choice of canceling her visa and leaving the U.A.E. or staying. The maid left the country.

Facebook Plea

An abused 23-year-old Filipina housemaid sends a plea for help on Facebook that had gone viral. The maid had been working in the house for eight months. She said her boss slapped her and continually try to rape her, but she fought back. He threatened her with prison if she ever told anyone.

She sent her family in the Philippians a message informing them of the attempted rape. They contacted the Overseas Filipino Workers Facebook Group who posted a photo of the maid with a plea for help. The post was shared 5,207 times, and it read: "She's helpless. Her employer attempted to rape her. Her employer threatened to abuse her even more if she fights. He threatened to kill her." The post went on to say: "She's scared to use her cell phone to ask for help. To all overseas Filipino workers in the U.A.E., please help us notify the embassy."

The welfare workers received calls in Dubai and acted. They sent a message to the maid informing her they were outside the home, and it was safe for her to come out. She was traumatized, but in stable condition. The maid doesn't want to press charges and just wants to go back home to the Philippines.

The Philippian Consulate responded by saying: "She is one of the lucky ones that escaped just in time. We have seen much graver cases. Victims come in with bruises and marks after they have been raped or physically abused. The number of cases we see varies, but there have been times where we have even received five calls a day."

Killer's Family Unable to Make Payment

An Indian man hid outside where a Filipina housemaid worked and waited until the family left the villa. He then snuck into the home and tried to rape her.

The man pinned the maid down when he attempted to rape her, but she resisted. As she fought back, the man then strangled her, and she choked on her vomit and died.

The killer was convicted, and the maid's family accepted the $54,461 in blood money. This will mean a lesser sentence for the killer. But, the problem is the killer's family is having a very difficult time coming up with the money. The sentence is unknown.

Boss Ready to Sell Maid

A Filipina maid is set to be sold by an Emirati family for $2,450. The maid is in court trying to receive her unpaid wages.

The maid stated in court that she left the family because they stopped paying her. Her contract showed she is supposed to receive $408 a month, but she only received $272. Eventually she was not paid anything.

Her female boss then tried to sell her to a British family with the negotiation being made over the phone, but the British family could not afford to pay.

The Emirati boss has a brother in the U.A.E. army, and he did not pay his maid her wages either. That maid is in court as well trying to collect her money. Both Emiratis filed a criminal case against their maids for running and stealing money from both of their houses.

The maids are willing to drop their wage case so that the criminal cases against them will be dropped; they want to go back to the Philippines. The outcome of the court case is unknown.

Maid Trapped

A 44-year-old housemaid who had been in the business for more than 15 years left the home of an Emirati woman. She had worked in the home for 3 years. She could no longer take the lengthy 18 hour shifts, verbal abuse, no day off and no freedom. The employer viciously told her that she's "just a maid," and "she couldn't doing anything." She knows she's just a maid, but in her heart she also knew she was good enough to teach the employer's children and take care of them. Her boss said she can't leave unless she paid her, money she doesn't have.

Calling from the villa's cellar with a hidden phone, she pleaded with the Philippine Embassy to help her. She told how nervous and fearful she was because she needed to keep working. She also realized that by leaving, she was taking a tremendous risk. The housemaid had not been out of the house alone for 3 years!

Before going, she left behind a remorseful note for her boss saying she could not endure the treatment anymore, and was sorry. She was terrified, and her heart pounded as she took off when the Philippine Embassy suggested she run. She left the home wearing a pink pajama style uniform that the madam insisted she wear.

The maid who is a mother herself with one child said she didn't dislike being a housemaid, and she isn't unwilling to work hard. Still confused and frightened she said she is a human being and doesn't know why she is being treated so badly.

According to the Philippine Overseas Labor Office, they were uncertain at this stage whether the maid could remain and work, or be deported. There is a lot of red tape such as forms that are required to be filled out due to running away besides, an investigation.

This girl is one of the multitude of women who enter the country each year hoping to start a new life and work for a good family. Some of the women do well with the families, others do not. Many are subjected to this kind of abuse.

Don't Film Us

The maids are coming forward asking not to be filmed on CCTV, but they prefer to be trusted instead. Many cameras are installed in homes to watch the hired help. The maids are saying in a sarcastic way they love to show off and want to know if a camera will be installed in the bathroom and bedrooms next?

They said if you don't trust anyone, then you might as well not hire anyone. They say it's humiliating and sad to know that their employers don't trust them at all. On the bright side, they are hoping the authorities look at the footage so the employers behave, and don't abuse the maids.

Maid Abused by Disabled Woman

A disabled 59-year-old Emirati housewife in a wheelchair is accused of beating her 28-year-old Indonesian housemaid.

The maid who worked for the woman for 5 months said that her boss was angry with her all the time, and assaulted her many times. A neighbor saw the maid had injuries and asks her where she got them from. He then helped her escape, and contact the police.

The Emirati woman denied she had ever abused her, but she stated that she had many bad stories about the maid. The outcome in court was unknown.

Maid Jumps to her Death

A 32-year-old Lebanese woman had frantically called the police. She reported her 27-year-old Filipina maid was getting intimate with the maid's boyfriend, inside the family home. This caused the maid to jump to her death from an apartment building.

The female employer who has a 1-year-old, saw that the maid had become "negligent" in her duties and decided to "search the maid's belongings." During the search she discovered contraceptive pills and confronted the maid. The boss pulled the maid's hair, and threatened to call the police if she didn't tell her the truth about where she got the pills.

The maid confessed and said she had gotten them from a neighbor's maid. She explained she was having consensual sex with a 34-year-old Pakistani man who drove her to work, and admitted having sex in the employer's apartment.

The Lebanese boss said she couldn't stand the fact that the man was coming into their home. She called her husband to tell him and then called the police. The maid cried and became sad when the boss told her the Pakistani man is married and has children. Walking to the balcony, the maid sat on the edge. Reaching out, the woman and her husband tried to connect with her, but she jumped.

Police received another call in a separate incident, where a housemaid jumped from a 4th-floor building after falling in love with someone she met on Facebook. The man said they had sex one time in an apartment. It is unclear what happened, but the man is serving a sentence for illegal sex and then will be deported back to his home country.

Caught in the Bedroom

An Emirati boss caught a man from Nepal in the bedroom of his Indonesian maid. The maid had admitted to letting the boyfriend into the house. The man said: "I had been at the house before and knew it would be good to stay away from the boss." He said that the boss became very angry when he found him in the bedroom.

Both the maid and the man met when he had gotten her number from a friend. They talked on the phone many times. Soon the friendship they had developed into a relationship. The man appeared before the prosecutors, but the charges were not yet known.

Gang Rape

A housemaid said she was raped by her Palestinian boyfriend and two Emirati men near a road. The woman said the men asked her to have sex with them and she refused. All the men undressed her and then rape her. The guys claim it was consensual. Having denied charges of sex outside of marriage, all four men are on trial.

Kissing in a Car Lands 2 Couples on Trial

A couple in the front seat of a car were caught by an Emirati policeman kissing while the couple in the backseat were having sex.

The policeman saw a car with tinted windows near a beach, rocking. When he went to investigate, he couldn't see through the windows, so he knocked on the glass. When no one acknowledged the knock, he opened the door and saw a naked couple in the backseat, along with a couple sitting in the front.

A 28-year-old housemaid sitting in the front admitted to police that 2 days prior, she had sex twice at a villa with the Bangladeshi man. The Bangladeshi man said his friend invited him on a trip and told him to bring a female. He says they only kissed, and the housemaid said: "I was tired and sleepy, we just exchanged kisses, but the others were having sex on the back seat [sic]."

The kissing couple had not entered a plea, but the other couple who had sex in the backseat is being prosecuted for an illegal affair.

Jailed After Losing Baby

A 30-year-old Filipina loses her unborn baby, and is arrested after admitting to having sex and not being married. She said her boyfriend dropped her off at the hospital. Later when she tried to reach out to him, he changed his number and wanted nothing to do with her. She has an 8-year-old back in Manila, and her family did not even know that she had been arrested.

The staff at the hospital said she had complications with her pregnancy and she lost the baby. The hospital did everything possible to find proof she was married, but she had misled them. They even contacted her embassy, but they could not find any documents saying she was married.

No help could be given to her since the hospital has a policy of not interfering in morality cases. They couldn't even offer legal help because she broke the U.A.E.'s ban on sex outside marriage. The hospital had no choice but to turn her into the police. The sentence is unknown.

New Mom Deported

A Filipina housemaid will be deported back to the Philippines with her 6-month-old baby since she could not show she was married.

The maid had spent 1 month in jail while trying to get documents to the prosecutors.

The maid claims she was married in the Philippines, but didn't know she had to prove the marriage when she arrived in the U.A.E. She said that she was 2-months pregnant when she arrived in the country. She agreed to be sent back to the Philippines, but will likely spend another week or two before being deported.

The prosecutors are "allowing" her to keep her baby girl. Usually in a case where an unwed female becomes pregnant, the mother is deported and the baby is placed in an orphanage.

A Filipina Maid who Ran away was Arrested at a Hospital

A Filipina woman who had a miscarriage, was charged for having an illegal affair. An Emirati employer found his maid bleeding heavily in their villa so she was taken to the hospital. The maid had suffered a miscarriage, and as a result was arrested at the hospital.

The maid is married, but her husband was living in Bangladesh. She had an affair with another Bangladeshi man who worked at a villa nearby her place of employment. The man confessed to having a sexual relationship with the maid so he will be brought before the court for having an illegal affair.

The housemaid who was 3-months pregnant when she had the miscarriage, is expected to plead guilty. It had been 7 months since she last traveled back to Bangladesh to see her husband.

Maid gets Support from Employers

A 27-year-old Ethiopian housemaid gave birth just 3 days after starting work for a new family. She complained of stomach cramps so they took her to the hospital, only to find out she was in labor, and going to give birth.

She has a husband, and a 4-year-old daughter in Ethiopia and can't wait to get back to them. This is going to take a while before the mom can bring her baby back to her country. The birth certificate needs to be produced before the passport can be issued to the baby. In order for that to happen, the hospital needs a marriage certificate proving the mom has a husband. The hospital needs to know the child is not a result of an illegal affair.

Since the mom is from a rural area in Ethiopia, the husband will have to send the marriage certificate to her. In the meantime, the mom and baby are with her employers. The family was supportive and paid the hospital bill.

The following stories tell of maids who are not always angels. There are people out there that say the housemaids and nannies aren't always the good guys and portray themselves as the victims all the time. However, others say that when the nannies kill babies and children, for whatever reason, it's the employers fault, and the maid committed the crime out of despair.

Maid Laced Family Food with own Blood from Menstruating

A Filipina maid worked for an Emirati family. One night just before dinner, a child of the employers found a "napkin" with blood stains on it sitting in a cooking pot in the kitchen. It is believed to be the Filipina maid's menstruation blood.

The maid was arrested, and an investigation launched to find out what prompted the maid to do this. The woman will be referred to a criminal court.

Housemaid and Boyfriend get Death Sentences

An Asian maid who worked for a 42-year-old handicapped Emirati woman for 2 years ended up killing her boss. The maid waited until the woman's brother and his family left the house for a wedding. Then with the aid of her boyfriend, ran into the woman's bedroom and tied her up with rope, and strangled her with a headscarf. She then took $5,445 and jewelry from the bedroom before leaving the scene.

When the Emirati family returned from the wedding, they found her tied up in the middle of the floor. She was dead with the headscarf that the maid wore, wrapped around her neck.

The maid and boyfriend are captured. The maid admitted to the murder, but claimed she did it because of constant quarrels and clashes with the Emirati lady. The maid and boyfriend are sentenced to death.

Dubai Housemaid Sentenced to Death, by Firing Squad?

This brutal murder happened in the emirate of Ras al Khaimah. A 23-year-old worked for an Emirati family for just ten days before she brutally murdered her female boss, by stabbing her 117 times.

The maid was cutting vegetables in the kitchen when she argued with her boss. During the argument the boss threatened to deport her. The maid became angry and stabbed her in the head, back, torso, lungs and kidneys. She then put the body in the bedroom where the family's 2-year-old daughter was sleeping.

Next, she cleaned herself up, and put the blood stained clothing into a bag. She stole jewelry, gold, money and a cell phone that belonged to the victim. Then set the bag on fire with the bloody clothes inside and threw it into the bedroom where the toddler was.

Fire spread and the toddler died of smoke inhalation. The entire apartment gutted. Suspected of the crime, the maid is found living in another emirate with a female friend. She confessed to the crime, but explained that her employer was abusive. She had only been in the country for 20 days and worked for two other Emirati families who both dismissed her.

The court found her to be of sound mind, and able to stand trial. The distraught Emirati husband had no interest in sparing her life by accepting blood money. He wants to see justice served through the death penalty and as soon as possible.

The method of death for the housemaid is unknown. It is being suggested she die by firing squad.

In order for the death penalty to go through, a panel of three judges must agree, and the ruler of the emirate must sign the death sentence. The last execution in Ras al Khaimah before this incident was back in 2008. Five men sentenced to death for smuggling drugs, and an Emirati killed by a firing squad for a double murder.

Maid Attempted to Kill Co-Worker over Boyfriend

A 28-year-old maid from Nepal claimed her 32-year-old Sri Lankan co-worker ran off with her boyfriend. She tried to kill her. The maid sprayed the victim with pepper spray and muzzled her mouth. She then dragged the Sri Lankan woman into an elevator where the maid stabbed her three times with a knife and beat her. The co-worker had escaped before becoming unconscious.

In court the 28-year-old maid is given a sentence of 7 years in jail.

Housemaid Killed with a Skewer

An Ethiopian housemaid is recovering in a hospital after being in brutal fight. She killed her friend with a skewer. The 2 housemaids locked themselves up in a laundry room to duke it out and settle their differences once and for all. The specific reason behind this brutal fight is unknown.

When the police arrived, they found the two women in a pool of blood and one dead. The Ethiopian stated that she was trying to defend herself when she stabbed her friend with a skewer and killed her.

The maid is undergoing treatment in a hospital for injuries to her throat. A police officer stood by the bed since she tried to commit suicide. She regrets the incident. The housemaid is being prosecuted, but the outcome is unknown.

Maid Charged With Practicing Sorcery

In the Emirate of Ras Al Khaimah, an Emirati man said that his Asian maid practiced sorcery and endangered the lives of his 2 small children. He found amulets [an object that protects owners from danger or harm] and talismans [an object believed to have magical or sacramental properties that offer good luck or protection from harm] in the closet of his two children.

The Emirati thinks the sorcery could have resulted in the death of the children. The maid explained to the officers that a friend helped write hieroglyphs [ancient Egyptian formal writing] on the objects. Her friend said that the talismans could help control the children.

The woman is charged with practicing sorcery and the sentence is unknown. Police are warning about an increase of sorcery in the emirate.

In an unrelated case, three Moroccan waitresses are arrested at their home where they practiced witchcraft. They are accused of luring men into the cafe by use of witchcraft, so the men would pay for indecent activities.

The cafes are operating 24-hours, and the residents are fearful that the women may hurt the young children in the neighborhood.

Indonesian Maid is Arrested for Urinating in her Bosses Cup of Tea

A 34-year-old Emirati called the police when his Indonesian maid brought him a cup of tea. The maid worked for the Emirati for 5 months. He said he asked for tea and it took 30 minutes to prepare.

Before taking a sip, he smelled something nasty such as urine. When the boss confronted her, she became scared and confused so he called the police. In her statement, the maid said: "I did not put urine in the drink. A friend who was a maid gave the liquid, and it was a secret potion made of a red substance used in sorcery. The other maid told me if I put the liquid in the tea and serve it to my boss, the family would treat me well and even give me a pay raise."

She says she wanted to be treated decent and did not intend to endanger lives. She told how she never did anything this terrible before. The maid is sentenced to 3 months in prison.

A 37-Year-Old Sri Lankan Maid Spiked the Family Tea with Drugs

A 37-year-old Sri Lankan maid drugged a couple and their daughter with spiked tea to make them fall asleep. She then opened the front door to let 3 Sri Lankan accomplices in to rob the villa.

The next morning they woke up feeling dizzy. The housemaid is nowhere to be found. They discovered they were missing $408 in cash, cell phones, jewelry, Indian rupees, laptops, cameras and other goods.

The maid is tracked and found a few days later by the police. After being interrogated, she confessed to the robbery and explained she mixed a drug with the tea, but pleaded not guilty. The two other suspects are apprehended and pleaded not guilty. The third suspect is still at large. The case is adjourned.

A Maid Faces Execution

A death sentence is handed out to an Indonesian maid after beating a 4-month-old baby girl. She slammed the little baby's head against a wall out of frustration. The maid is caught on camera lifting the baby from her crib, throwing her on the floor and bashing her head against the wall. The baby had a fractured skull and severe brain damage. She spent just about 2 weeks in a coma before dying.

The maid at first blamed a Filipina co-worker for the attack on the baby. Later confessing she resented the other Filipina maid whose job was to care for the baby and brother. Her job was to clean and care for a sick grandmother.

An attack was captured on camera as the maid assaulted the Emirati mother and Saudi father too. The family has said that they are angry and will not accept blood money. The maid is ordered by the court to reenact the murder so the court can decide whether they will keep the death penalty by firing squad.

At the Appeals Court, her lawyers will try to show "severe psychological problems." They will try to prove she is insane, but will accept a life term.

U.A.E. law states that a defendant convicted of a murder may have two separate appeals.

Maid is Jailed for Attacking her Boss with a Hammer

An Indonesian housemaid learned that her 33-year-old Jordanian female boss was going to replace her with another maid. The boss was sleeping in her apartment when she felt someone come into her room. She thought it was her husband but felt lots of pain on her head. When she opened her eyes, she saw the maid with a hammer. The woman tried to scream for help but couldn't since her jaw was broken. She took the hammer away from the maid and subdued her.

The woman's husband returned home to find his wife covered in blood and holding down the maid. The woman is convicted and given 1 year behind bars.

Maid Kills her Baby

A Filipina maid gave birth to a baby boy in her bathroom at her employer's house in Abu Dhabi. She killed the baby by wrapping underwear around the baby's neck. She then rolled him up in a plastic bag and dumped him in her closet. After killing the baby, she checked herself in at the hospital. In the meantime, her boss found the newborn in the closet.

In court, the maid said she used her underwear to wipe blood off the baby's neck after giving birth. She claims she then passed out so that is why she had the underwear in her hand which she admitted to. But, the forensic report stated that there was a knot in the underwear and that it needed to be cut off the baby's neck with scissors. The maid received a life sentence.

Housemaid Suffocated her Newborn so Boss Wouldn't Find out

An Ethiopian maid kept her newborn baby a secret from her Emirati employers, so she wouldn't be fired. She said they had "no idea" she had gotten pregnant after an illegal affair.

The maid told the court how she had given birth to a baby boy that day and hid him in her room. She said she loved her baby and only covered his mouth to stop him from crying. The Emirati family discovered the dead infant that evening. They said she had been working for them for just a few months and did not realize she was pregnant.

The maid continued by saying she had been dating her Ethiopian boyfriend for a few weeks when she became pregnant. She said before becoming pregnant he promised to marry her, but disappeared out of the country once he found out she was with child. She is sentenced to a 5 year jail term and then will be deported back to her home country.

Maid Tried to Kill Boss with Kitchen Knife

In the emirate of Fujairah, a 23-year-old Ethiopian housemaid claimed her female Emirati boss attacked her with a knife at the home. She wrestled the knife away but was stabbed. She didn't plan to hurt her boss, but once she had the knife she stabbed her multiple times.

After the stabbing, the maid fled to Abu Dhabi in a cab. But, could not pay for the taxi ride so the driver called the police to report her for not paying for the fare. The police tracked her down and arrested her due to the taxi driver calling.

The woman in Fujairah survived the attack, and the housemaid denied the attempted murder charge. She told the court that her boss mistreated her and beat her up daily. The case is adjourned.

Premeditated Murder

A group of 6 Bangladeshi women and 1 Filipina strangled a Bangladeshi sex recruiter. He forced them into the trade in the U.A.E., and they could now face the death penalty.

The Bangladeshi women are recruited and then lured from their home countries with promises of good paying jobs as maids. They are told they will work in homes and hotels.

After arriving in the U.A.E., the recruiter took their passports away, locked them up and forced them to sell their bodies. The recruiter promised them money if the women slept with his male clients, but he kept all the dough to himself, and their frustrations grew.

The women enticed the recruiter with a massage, so he became vulnerable and they could tie him up and strangled him. One woman stated in court she was just the "lookout person," and the other six had killed the man. But, forensic evidence of blood, fingerprints and hair samples pointed to an "unknown" person who was present at the time of the killing. No further information is available.

Jewelry Found in Baby Milk Containers

A Sri Lankan housemaid was caught and arrested trying to leave the country when security officers at an airport discovered gold jewelry worth $22,325. The jewelry was inside a metal container with powdered milk given to babies. Security located the container inside a suitcase.

The maid confessed to robbing her employer while they were away on vacation. She said two other Sri Lankan maids helped steal the jewelry and encouraged her to leave the country before her employer returned.

The outcome is unknown, but the police are warning employers to be extra cautious when leaving domestic staff alone while traveling.

Nanny and a Set of Twins Fall out of a Moving Vehicle

A van entering a roundabout traveling at high-speed caused a back sliding door not shut properly, to open. The 3-year-old twins and nanny sitting in the backseat were ejected out of the van, no seatbelts on. Parents of the twins, who were not in the vehicle were notified. Minor fractures and scratches are found on the twins, while the nanny was not so lucky, she is in the hospital in critical condition with severe head injuries.

CHAPTER 4
CHILDREN, ABUSE & RAPE

Rapes are common in different areas of the world and not looked at as a serious crime. It is not always frowned upon and often considered cultural. The minimum legal age for consensual sex in the U.A.E. is 14-years-old.

There are few orphanages for a child to go to in the emirates and only two in all the U.A.E. One is in Abu Dhabi, the capital and the another in the emirate of Sharjah. These two facilities will take in youngsters that are sexually abused and suffer from domestic violence, or any other form of abuse. Dubai announced they have the green light to open one in 2016.

The children are cared for until adopted, but the rules are rigid. "Only" Emirati families are qualified to adopt. These families have to show they are financially set and have a stable home environment. An individual is denied if they have failed medical checks for diseases, or has proved positive for HIV. A "good conduct" document is demanded from law enforcement. If accepted, the family must inform the youth at an early age he or she was adopted.

In regards to discipline, many parents often fail to teach their children to respect elders and teachers. In Islam, the way to discipline a child is through soft words, and when they reach 10-years-old, the parents may spank them if they choose.

You will often see these children doing whatever they want. Screaming at the top of their lungs, and running wildly inside of stores knocking over clothes racks, but also refusing to wear seatbelts on airplanes causing delays on flights. They jump on top of tables at restaurants and grab food off customers' plates while dining.

My spouse and I have had balls and straws thrown at us while we ate out. A friend of mine had a child grab onto her purse and swing on it while she was out shopping. There is no limit to what these children do, and I personally have never seen any "soft words" spoken to the kids to calm them.

Race is another issued not often discussed with children. A mother voiced her opinion and said that she is so surprised at how children are not taught to be more open-minded. She was playing with her 1-year-old child when a group of children between the ages of 4 and 5-years-old came up to play with her child.

The mom heard one boy say leave him [the woman's child] alone, he doesn't like brown people. The child then asked the woman if she was the mom because she is Latin with a darker complexion, and her child has blond hair and blue eyes. She said the kid was very "surprised" when she answered yes.

Often when children go to school in the U.A.E., parents take a big chance when their child gets onto a school bus. This is because background checks on bus drivers are flawed and prove to be difficult to get. A lot of the drivers come from countries where records are sparse and there is inadequate record keeping.

Student Lashes out

A teacher had been tutoring a local family for over two decades without incident. The teacher asked a female student to write the "incorrect" answer 5 times. Lashing out, she said, "I'm not afraid of you." The tutor was in shock at the behavior and suddenly she gave him a "hard blow." He called out to the mother while the girl came from behind again and hit the tutor.

After the tutor told the mom what happened, he walked out, never to return. Commenting on the incident, the teacher said: "Money isn't everything, parents have to train our children right from the start."

Death Penalty Demanded for Assaulting 5 Children

A 39-year-old Arab man lured children between the ages of 8 and 10-years-old of many nationalities to go with him, so he could rape them. The man waited for the children to leave their homes, and then befriended them by talking to them, and asking their names and how old they are.

Next, he offered them money, and then invited them to look at the birds he was caring for. He brought them to the rooftop of a residential building and raped them there. Several parents complained that their children had been sexually assaulted by a man. A forensic report confirmed bodily fluids on the kids, and the DNA matched his.

The man was arrested, and prosecutors are seeking the death penalty.

Five Laborers Cleared Of Raping a 4-Year-Old Boy

A 4-year-old Emirati toddler went missing from his home. His nanny, who was out looking for him heard screams coming from a labor camp nearby. When she entered the camp, she said the toddler was naked and said the men "molested" him.

The 5 Bangladeshi men were cleared as the judge said there was no medical evidence to suggest the toddler had been raped.

8-Year-Old Girl Molested

A young 8-year-old girl was in an elevator in her apartment building when an Indian neighbor who apparently was under the influence of alcohol, touched her inappropriately. She came crying to her father and told him what had happened. The dad tracked down the neighbor and called the police. They found him and he was arrested, but denies the molestation charge. The case is adjourned.

23-Year-Old Male Caught with a 13-Year-Old Girl

A 13-year-old girl was introduced to a 23-year-old Emirati man by her parents. They spoke on the phone before agreeing to go on a date to the mall. They sat in the mall parking lot and kissed in the car, and then he took her to a hotel room where they had "consensual sex."

The girl was under the age of "14-years-old" so he was charged with molestation, but never showed up in court. The case is adjourned.

11-Year-Old Girl Assaulted at the Mall

An 11-year-old Arab girl was walking at a shopping mall alone when a Bangladeshi man in his 20s stalked her. He waited until she reached an isolated corridor then attacked her. A security guard saw the incident happen. He ALSO witnessed the man doing the same thing to the same girl on a different day. This time he decided to inform his supervisor who then notified the police.

Watching the CCTV footage, the police saw the molestation take place. The girl was previously attacked by the Bangladeshi man one year prior, on two separate occasions.

The man denied the sexual assault charge. He was given 1 year in jail and then will be deported back to his home country.

Mom Loses 6 of her 8 Children, Sexual Assault by her Brother

After a divorce, an Arab mother was granted custody of her 8 children all under the age of 10-years-old. In court, the woman demanded that her children be with her, and her husband needed to pay for rent, furniture allowance, 2 maids, a car and a driver.

The woman moved into her father's home with the children. Three of the boys talked to their father and told him that while they were at the grandfather's house, their uncle raped them many times. Their mother knew of the rapes, but warned the children not to tell their father. The father then filed for custody of his 8 children.

In court they ruled that the 6 oldest children live with their father, and the 2 youngest children are to stay with their mother. A judge said: "One child is 8-months-old, and the other is 2-years-old, they need the mother's care since they are so young." He ordered the dad pay his ex-wife $1,089 each month for rent, and $272 for each of the 2 children. The woman's brother is awaiting trial on rape charges of his 3 nephews.

A 16-Year-Old Kidnapped and Raped?

A 16-year-old Emirati boy said he was at a gas station when he met a 19-year-old Yemeni man and his 25-year-old Omani friend. The teenager who loves dogs said the men promised to take him to see the dogs. When he got into the car they said there were no dogs and they are going to have sex with him. He claims they raped him, and threatened him with a sword.

The defendant's lawyer claimed the teenager was a glue sniffer, and he was high during the incident. He said: "I want the police to check the car because it has evidence that the two had sex with a woman one hour before the boy claimed they raped him. How could my clients have sex with him if they just finished having sex with a woman?"

The 2 men were charged with having an illegal affair with the woman, and not rape because evidence proved the teenager agreed to have sex with them. One defendant was jailed for 1 year and the other for 6 months.

12-Year-Old Sexually Assaulted by Air-Conditioning Guy

A mother called a company to send someone to come and fix the air-conditioning unit in her daughter's bedroom. The woman's daughter was left alone in the bedroom with the 29-year-old Pakistani man, and he allegedly molested her. Scared and hurt, the child ran to her mother in tears, telling her how the man touched her "sexually."

In court, the Pakistani denied the charges and is awaiting a verdict.

A Cleaner Allegedly Molested a 7-Year-Old

A young 7-year-old Indian girl played with her friends near her home. A Bangladeshi man, cleaning up the yard, came up to the girl, and hugged and kissed her. She pushed him away then told her parents. The man has denied the charges against him. The case is adjourned.

Driver Accused of Molesting a 7-Year-Old

A 30-year-old Pakistani driver was alone in a car with a 7-year-old boy. He was driving him to school. The man allegedly touched the boy's private parts. Later that day the boy's mother could clearly see that something was bothering her son, so she questioned why he was upset. He told his mother what happened that morning and that it happened on 15 other occasions in the last month. The boy's driver denied the charges, and a verdict was pending.

Security Guard Accused of Molesting a 14-Year-Old Girl

A 14-year-old Emirati girl was walking to her father's home to visit him because her parents are divorce. A Nepalese security guard grabbed, kissed and hit her. She got away and ran back to her mother to tell her what happened. She was too ashamed to tell her father.

The mother immediately contacted her ex-husband who then called the

police. The security guard denies the charges. No further information is available.
A Bangladeshi Man Jailed for Raping a 5-Year-Old Child
A 5-year-old Pakistani boy and his friend were taking Quran lessons at the friend's house. They were being taught by a 24-year-old Bangladeshi man. Two months into the lessons, one boy informed his father he was being sexually abused. When sternly confronted, the teacher confessed to the father, and the police were called.

The teacher was given a 15 year jail sentence and then will be deported back to his home country.
12-Year-Old Lured by a Bangladeshi Man
A 12-year-old boy was praying at a mosque near his home. He met a 37-year-old Bangladeshi man who chatted with him. The man wanted to show the boy toys, but he refused to go with him. He then grabbed the boy and dragged him to a building which was nearby. He pushed him into a room, and threatened him to not say a word.

While raising a knife in front of his face forewarning to kill him, the man forced him to take off his clothes. The boy was raped twice then escape through a bathroom window.

He strongly denied the charges, but DNA shows the man raped him. Prosecutors were asking for the death penalty. The Bangladeshi man was convicted and given life in jail.
Teen Molested a Young Boy at a Pool
A 19-year-old Emirati teenager approached a 12-year-old Egyptian boy in the changing room at a community pool. He asked the young boy to be his friend. When they reached the showers, the teenager undressed him then tried to rape him. The boy ran to get help. The outcome is unknown.
Uncle gave Niece STD after Molesting her
A 7-year-old girl reluctantly told her mother that her uncle took her to his bedroom, held her down and took off her clothes. He threatens to beat her up if she ever said a word to her parents, or if she didn't follow his orders. The 29-year-old mother questioned her daughter when she noticed that her genitals were inflamed. She took her to a clinic but was sent back home.

After a week she saw her condition became worse so she went back to the clinic for more thorough testing. This time the results came back saying she had gonorrhea.

The Emirati uncle was given a sentence of 10 years in jail, but for unknown reasons the court cut his jail term to 1 year without revealing why.
Father Rapes his 14-Year-Old Girl
A couple was living in a studio apartment with their 14-year-old daughter and 3 sons. One day when the brothers were not home, and the mother was out begging, the Moroccan father who is an alcoholic raped his

14-year-old daughter.

When the mom came home, the daughter told her what happened. She said that this was not the first time and that he has raped her more than 20 times before while the family was out of the home. The mother contacted the police and reported her husband.

Testing showed she had been raped often, and traces of blood from her father was found on the child's underwear. The dad denies the charges. No further information available.

A Laborer Accused of Molesting an 11-Year-Old Girl

An 11-year-old Indian girl was dropped off by a school bus outside her apartment building. The 41-year-old mother spoke to her daughter on the phone and inform her that the elevator in their building was broken, and she had to use the stairs.

Ten minutes later the mom received a call from her daughter who was crying. She said a stranger followed her then hugged and kissed her and told her he loved her. The following day the mom found a folded up note in her daughter's school bag from the suspect. It had a name, phone number and he asked her to call when she was at school but to not tell anyone. The mother called the police.

The Indian man confessed and said he had a girl her age back home and she passed away. He said: "When I kissed the girl, I felt like I was kissing my dead daughter." The outcome of this case is unknown.

Professional Soccer Player Commits Immoral Acts with a 12-Year-Old

A 12-year-old boy met an Emirati soccer player on Twitter and exchanged messages. Soon after, the family notice a change in the boy's behavior. The soccer player was accused of "immoral acts" with the boy, but the athlete denies it, only admitting to exchanging messages on Twitter.

At first he was convicted and given a 2 year sentence, but after an appeal the sentenced was "increased" to 3 years. The court said: "The athlete had exploited the young boy's admiration for him."

Child Porn

A Sudanese man was using social media online to share files of nude pictures and pornographic movies of children. Police traced him to an apartment, seize his computer and arrest him. The outcome of the case is unknown.

11-Year-Old Boy Raped

An 11-year-old boy met a 33-year-old Nepalese man in a parking lot. He showed the boy pornographic pictures and videos, then raped him on two separate occasions. The parents found footage of the assaults on the boy's cell phone. A 10 year jail sentence was given to the man.

Mid-Air Assault on a Teenager

A 15-year-old girl was on a flight from her home country Morocco to Dubai to visit her sister. Five hours into the flight, a boozed up 36-year-old

Indian blacksmith went to sit next to the 15-year-old. As she watched a movie, he touched her chest.

The man was convicted and sentenced to 6 months in jail and fined $272.

Peeping Tom Spies on a Teenager

An Arab man in his 20s lived directly across from a teenage girl. He could see from his kitchen window when she was getting ready for bed. For a closer look, he leaves his home and looks through her window. The man watched her change into her pajamas. One night the sister noticed the man peeping at her sister through the window and told her parents, who then called the police.

The Arab man is arrested and charged with indecency and invading the girl's privacy. No sentencing information available.

Stepdad Raped Girl for 3 Years

An Emirati man raped his stepdaughter multiple times over a period of 3 years. The girl who is now 15-years-old, said the rape started when she was 12-years-old. It always happened when her mother was out shopping.

When the mom saw how withdrawn her girl had become, they sat and had a long discussion. This is when she told her what had been going on in the last 3 years.

The Emirati was given a 10 year jail sentence for the rapes. The court also found out that the man had been driving recklessly and fined him $2,722. He had been caught drinking alcohol too so he was given 80 lashes.

A Girls Age is Questioned in a Rape Case

A girl told a court she was raped by many men who she met online. The girl said that it was 4 Emiratis, and a man who was stateless. Which means a lack of any nationality, or not recognized as a citizen in any state.

The lawyer of one man accused is demanding the prosecutors present "hospital documents" [birth certificate] to prove that she is over the age of 14-years-old. Again, the law states rape if you are under the age of 14-years-old. No further information is available.

16-Year-Old Rapes a 13-Year-Old Girl

A 13-year-old girl met a 16-year-old Emirati boy on the internet. He asked for her home address and then showed up at her house. The girl said she was scared so she opened the door. He raped her in the bathroom. The girl's sister-in-law knocked on the door, the boy fled pushing her to the floor.

He is charged with forcing his way into a home, raping a 13-year-old and assaulting her sister-in-law. The teenager denied the charges. No further information.

A Salesman Molested a 6-Year-Old

A 6-year-old Chinese girl and her mother went to the mall to help the mother's husband who runs a shop there. The little girl went off to play with a friend but came back yelling "bad man." The girl explained a man had touched her private parts.

She then pointed him out to her mother who confronted the 42-year-old Bangladeshi salesman working in his store. After being challenged, he said that he was only "adjusting" her clothing. The man denies the charges. No further information available.

Father Tortured 2 Daughters and Killed 1

A 29-year-old Emirati man and his 27-year-old Emirati lover were given a 1 year prison sentence for having an illegal affair. They could be given the death sentence if convicted of torturing 2 children and killing one of them.

The man's 7-year-old daughter confided in her uncle. She said she had seen her father carry her lifeless 8-year-old sister out of the home. The little girl who suffered from serious injuries and torture, told the uncle that she thought her sister was dead.

After talking with his niece, the uncle was convinced something was absolutely not right, so he contacted the police who uncovered a horrific scene. The police found stun guns at the home used to torture the girls. The surviving daughter said: "They used wire, bars and a stun gun to torture us. They use to throw boiling water on us and even used a heated iron on my skin for no reason. They use to lock us in the bathroom and tie our hands up." She says they were made to eat their own feces.

The children were locked up for many hours without food or water. They were burned with cigarettes. It is believed that the torture went on for 6 months. After the 8-year-old girl died, the couple took the body and buried it in the desert. She was not found until 3 months later.

In court, the now 6-month pregnant girlfriend claims a different story. She insisted on taking the blame for the torture by saying she has "psychological problems," and her lover had nothing to do with it. She admitted to physically assaulting the girls, and helping her lover bury the child's body. But, her story contradicts the story of the 7-year-old and details uncovered during the police investigation.

The girl's father claims he had nothing to do with the torture. He stated that the stun guns found in the home didn't even work, and there were no broken bones or signs of strangulation on the child that died. He says the injuries found on the surviving 7-year-old is from a botched medical procedure done at a hospital when she received treatment for a broken arm.

The father admitted to burying the child's body in the desert and said: "I made a mistake when I buried her." The man told a police officer he beat the girls because they were laughing and he believed they were possessed.

Explaining to the court he only confessed to the crime early on because he was protecting his unborn child. He didn't want his baby to live and be raised in a prison if the mother was convicted. He said to a prosecutor: "I took responsibility and confessed to allow my son to live outside the bars.

Don't tell me I don't love my children, I do love my children."

The couple both face charges of abusing and torturing an 8 and 7-year-old, causing a death and illegally burying a body. The father was originally given the death sentence but on appeal, is serving a life sentence. His girlfriend received a life sentence and is in jail with her baby boy. But, is given 4 more months for assaulting a police major and corporal when she wanted her baby moved to be with his father. Previously, she received an additional 1 month for an assault on a policewoman when the officer commented about her clothing. Prior to that, she was fined $272 for attacking a prisoner over a bag of potato chips.

Sex Attack on a 4-Year-Old Girl Riding a School Bus

The mother of a 4-year-old girl suspected that her daughter had been assaulted. Being afraid, her husband was reluctant to report it to the police. They took her to the hospital to have her checked, and they found evidence that the girl had been molested, so they turned it over to the police.

Her parents claim it was the bus driver, supervisor and a "cleaner" who were on the bus. The "education providers" said that the school was not made aware of the incident until "2 months later." They said once they were informed, they contacted the bus company. The company then suspended the bus driver, supervisor and a cleaner pending an investigation.

The company whose bus the assault happened on, transports 44,000 students every day. They have put out a statement saying they added CCTV on the buses to beef up their security.

Dubai Roads and Transport Authority [RTA] published a school transport manual one year before the incident. Guidelines say every school has the responsibility to keep a supervisor on the buses that carry children, under 12-years-old. The RTA says it is the bus companies responsibility to carry out the background checks on their drivers, but the background check is "not needed." No further information is available.

Sex Assault Clip Sent to Boy's Classmates

A 13-year-old Emirati boy was raped, molested and assaulted with a knife at a school bus stop by 7 teenagers. Two boys 15 and a 16-years-old didn't just rape, but filmed it with a cell phone.

Five other boys ranging from 13 to 15-years-old had molested him. He confided in a Palestinian teacher that footage was going around of him touching the private parts of one of the seven boys. The teacher brought it to the principal's attention when the video "showed him looking sad and crying."

In court, the boy stated that a month after telling his teacher had gone by, more students joined in to molest and beat him. They were taller and stronger than he was so he could not fight them. He said they laughed at him when he cried, and he begged them to stop.

It is not known how the assaults ended, or who contacted the police, but we know the Emirati boys have been charged. All defendants denied the charges. The case was adjourned.

Restaurant Worker Jailed for Molesting a Girl

A 25-year-old Indian restaurant delivery man delivered a meal to a home of an Algerian family but had no change. The mom sent her 7-year-old daughter with the delivery man back to the restaurant to retrieve her money. He molested the Algerian girl twice in the elevator.

The man was convicted and will spend 3 months in jail for molesting the girl.

Teenager Cut with a Razor Blade

A fight broke out among 10 teenagers at their school. What started off as a joke, escalated into a full brawl amongst rivals. One student mocked another student, and then one boy pulled a razor from his pocket and slashed his rival on the shoulder. The wound was so bad that the teen needed stitches.

Six out of the ten boys have been arrested. Two students age 15 and 17-years-old showed up at the local prosecutor's office with their legs in shackles, escorted by a juvenile prison officer.

The attorney for the two boys said he will fight for them. He says: "The dispute was just a small thing between boys that got out of hand. The boys have not been charged and we're still to know [sic] if any charges will be brought. They're not the ones who caused the major trouble. This was just a fight between boys until the boy was cut." No other information is available.

Teenager Molested

A 32-year-old Sri Lankan man pretended to be lost when he stopped to ask a 19-year-old Chinese girl for directions to a train station. The girl who had been walking said that she agreed to guide him there and jumped in the front seat on the passenger side. He then touched her inappropriately.

The man denies the charges. No other information available.

Youths Accused of Kidnapping

An Emirati man had been shopping at a mall when 5 youths threatened him with a knife in a mall elevator. The youths drove him to another city where they demanded $4,083 and tortured him. The boys took his car, and forced him to "transfer" his vehicle into one of their names.

One defendant who appeared in court had denied the charges of kidnapping. No other information available.

Two Men try to Abduct a Girl from a Grocery Store

A young girl was at a grocery store shopping with her mother. After a short time in the store, two Asian men grabbed the daughter and ran towards the exit with her. The mother screamed and darted after them yelling to let go of her. This caused such a big scene that the men dropped the girl and took off running.

The grocery store is located very near to the girl's school. The mom informed the police and the school. An email from the school went out to parents and staff informing them of what had happened. The school said: "Even though Dubai is recognized as a relatively safe environment, high levels of vigilance is required from everyone." No further information available.

Janitor Fights the Death Penalty

An Indian man working as a janitor at a school is accused of sexually assaulting a 9-year-old girl in the school's kitchen. A teacher said she had the girl in her classroom later that day, and her behavior seemed normal.

An Arab teacher testified for the defendant. In court she had said her daughter has attended the school for six years. Stating she would never have allow her to go to that school if she had any suspicions it was the janitor. She told the court he has a good reputation and she has known him for 9 years.

She said: "It was impossible since there is a large glass window in front of the small kitchen viewable from the outside. He surely would have been noticed." Another Arab teacher had testified and said: "There were always parents and teachers going in and out of the kitchen."

The man confessed to abusing his position to touch the girl when he was alone with her. The court sentenced the janitor to death. His family is pleading for DNA tests to be carried out.

The authorities said: "Legal action will be taken against the school management as the law stipulates that private schools are responsible for children's safety."

Pupils Molested by Tutor

A couple took out a newspaper advertisement seeking a private math tutor for their 2 daughters age 8 and 13-years-old. The couple hired a 58-year-old Egyptian tutor. He had only been in the house for an hour when he is accused of kissing the two girls during their math lesson. He touched the thighs of the 13-year-old girl.

The mother was in different room when the older girl came crying to her and he fled. The mom called her husband who was away at the time to come home. An investigation is conducted by the police, and he is arrested.

The tutor tried to hide his identity by showing a copy of his "friend's ID." He was convicted a year ago in another molestation case and deported. He returned to the U.A.E. by sneaking through one of the country's ports. The man denied kissing or molesting the children. No other information available.

Tutor Assaulted a Boy

An Indian tutor was hired by an Indian woman to tutor her 14-year-old son in Arabic. The tutor come to the home regularly. While he is teaching, the mom slept in another room. He took advantage of the mom not being there by stripping and raping the boy. After 2 months of this abuse, the mother walked in and saw her naked son being raped by him.

The man denies the rape charges. No other information available.

Teacher Made Sick Threats to Girls

A 43-year-old man is hired to tutor 4 young Emirati girls between 7 and 11-years-old in their home. This man had been teaching them for 3 years.

The youngest girl ran to her father saying she is being abused by the tutor, and he took off her trousers and molested her. The dad called the police who then arrested the tutor. All the girls are questioned and said they were assaulted often.

In court, the father said: "The tutor threatened to cut them all into pieces and feed them to the dogs if they ever told us what happened to them." The Emirati mother indicated that while the tutor is teaching her daughters, he is saying romantic things to her and even asking her to marry him.

The tutor denied the charges, but the man remains in custody. His lawyer said: "The only evidence is the little girls' stories, and you can't rely on that." No other information available.

Girls Lured into Cars

Schools send out warnings to parents to make sure kids are extra careful. There have been reports of strangers trying to lure girls into cars near colleges. On two different occasions in the same week, a motorist drove up to girls and asked them to go for a ride.

A 17-year-old had just gotten off a school bus when she is followed by someone in a red vehicle. The man asked her if she wanted to go for a ride, but she refused and he drove away. Later that day a 16-year-old girl left her college and is approached by someone in a white car. She refused to get in the car, and he drove away too. She said that she has been repeatedly approached. Both girls are very shaken. No other information is available.

Teacher not Guilty

A South African teacher lived in a teachers housing accommodation on the school grounds. A group of children dared each other for fun to run up to her door, and ring the doorbell. The teacher is then accused of slapping an 8-year-old Jordanian girl for ringing her doorbell.

After the court watched the surveillance footage that was located outside of her corridor, the teacher is cleared.

Coach Guilty

A former Romanian coach said he had to personally pay for his teams football shirts because the club could not afford to pay. The man is found guilty of defaming the club with the statement saying they could not afford to pay for their shirts. For that, he is given a 3 month suspended sentence, and a fine of $10,890.

He is acquitted on a separate charge of defamation which arose from other comments he made on social media.

Death Sentence for Teen Killer

An 18-year-old Asian youth took the rap for his brother to save him from the firing squad. The troubled teen is just 17-years-old when police found him at the crime scene holding a kitchen knife. He had allegedly just stabbed his cousin to death. He is sentenced by a lower court to serve 7 years for the crime, and then be deported back to his own country after he serves time in jail.

The prosecutor appealed the light sentence and the Appeals Court, after reviewing the case agreed with the prosecutor. They said the sentence is too lenient, and has now sentenced him to death based on his original confession to the crime.

The teenager withdrew his confession and said his brother and cousin had gotten into a heated argument over the sale of a car. One wanted to sell it for the parts and the other did not. The disagreement turned into a fight, and the older brother stabbed his cousin to death. He says he saw the crime being committed.

After he was stabbed, and laying there in a pool of blood, the brothers discussed whether to call the police but decided they had to report it. The older brother then convinced the teen to take the blame. He said that the death penalty will not be given to a 17-year-old. He would go to a Juvenile Detention Center where he will serve a few years. The youth agreed to support his older brother.

In court the young man said his brother cleaned up the murder weapon to get rid of fingerprints. He convinced him to take the knife because it will show he carried out the crime.

The court did not believe him, and a judge said there is no evidence to back the teens claim. There also is no hope that the victim's family will ever accept blood money which could have lessened the penalty. The youth is tried under Sharia law which says a fellow is seen as an adult when pass puberty. So, he is convicted as an adult and handed the death penalty.

The older sibling who could have carried out the homicide, left the country by the time of the younger brother's arrest.

Teen Ordered by Mother to Help Commit Murder

This story lacks material, but I still elected to mention it. A 14-year-old boy arrived home from school one day. When the boy entered the kitchen, he saw his 42-year-old mother trying to murder someone who is lying on the kitchen floor. She hesitated for a minute then calmly ordered her son to "finish the job" as she handed over the weapon. He seemed to have no problem continuing the grisly act. His mom watched, sipping her afternoon tea as he finished the horrific crime.

Neighbors are in shock and disbelief that the mother could convince her teen to help her commit this crime. The police investigation showed this is not the first time as he has aided his mother in similar crimes. No other information is available.

Teen Arrested after Wedding Death

An Emirati teen who attended a wedding accidentally fell with his gun. The gun went off twice hitting a 37-year-old Emirati man who died. The teenage boy is arrested. No other information available.

Gunman Shoots Boy

A gunman tried to kill a boy for reasons unknown. Instead of killing him, he ended up leaving him disabled. The court found the man guilty and set the damages at $205,552. The mother appealed and filed a lawsuit for $694,142.

There is no mention of a jail sentence attached to this case or what the woman is actually awarded in damages.

Husband Kills Wife in Front of School

An Indian man who worked as a bus driver at a school stabbed his wife to death. The wife worked at the school as a bus attendant. This happened in front of the staff and children at the school and then he slit his own wrists.

The husband is taken to a hospital and watched by a police officer. He would have been arrested for the murder of his wife, but he died from self-inflicted wounds. There is no clear motive.

This couple leaves behind 2 children in India, age 10 and 12-years-old. The school hopes to give the children "relief money" after "management clearances" are finished.

Teen Teetering at the Top of a Tower

An Arab teenage girl was staying at one of the high-rise hotels in Dubai. She made her way to a helicopter landing pad 27-stories up and threatened to jump. When the emergency staff approached her trying to help, she told them to stay away.

A policeman handed her a cold bottle of water and she took it. A psychologist is called to the scene to talk to her from the ledge. While he is talking, the policeman gave her more water, and as she reached for the bottle, he grabbed her and pulled her away from the edge.

The girl is taken to a hospital and the staff said she is suffering from heat exhaustion. The teenage girl is placed under arrest and charged with attempted suicide.

Teen Stabbing at School

Two Emirati boys, age 14 and 15-years-old were taking a test in the school's examination hall. They got into a heated argument that turned into a fist fight. The 15-year-old pulled out a small knife and allegedly stabbed the 14-year-old in the stomach. It is unclear what caused the fight.

The 15-year-old Emirati will be referred to public prosecution. No other information available.

Student Dies over Fight About Money

A 19-year-old Kuwaiti student is brought to a hospital by his roommate in critical condition. He is taken to the emergency room where he passed out. The doctors saw signs of assault with many injuries on the teen's body. The student later died, and the hospital informed the police of his death and suspicious injuries.

They questioned the roommate. He stated that they were at a cafe when his friend fell to the ground and became unconscious for no reason. He then took his friend to the hospital. The roommate is pressed by police, confronting him with the suspicious injuries found on the victim's body.

Finally, he confessed. He told them he and another Kuwaiti friend assaulted him for 3 days over a money dispute. He said they used their hands and feet to kick him. They wanted to severely punish him over personal and financial problems.

The two young men are charged with assault leading to death. No other information available.

Teens Attack a Taxi Driver

Five Emirati teenagers are taking a taxi home at 2am. A 19-year-old sitting in the front seat starts harassing the 32-year-old Bangladeshi driver. He brandished a knife while interfering with the taxi driver. He turned on the windshield wiper fluid and put the car in neutral. The driver who is too afraid to say a word, pulled over and stopped.

Yelling at him for stopping, the 19-year-old then tried to stab him with the knife, but he stopped him. Four of the other teens then joined in the assault, and kicked him. An off-duty policeman driving by saw the teens attacking the cab driver, and shouted at them to stop.

The boys took off running, but not before taking $95 from him. Cops took off after them, but the boys got away. Officers called for backup, and shortly afterwards the 19-year-old is tracked down and arrested along with his pals.

Instigating the incident, the 19-year-old pleaded not guilty to assault and theft in court. The other four who are younger, will be tried in a juvenile court. No other information is available.

Fake Driver's License Sold to Minors

An Arab man sent text messages to young people saying he could get them a driver's license from a neighboring country. He said it is legal to drive there at a young age. The legal age in Dubai is 18-years-old. The man claimed that the license is approved by the authorities in the U.A.E. This is all done in exchange for cash.

The police found out about the scam when an 18-year-old Arab showed up at the Traffic Department to replace his forged license with a U.A.E. version. He is then arrested. He explained to police he had gotten a message on his phone saying that if he wanted a license, he will have to pay $2,178.

Seven others teens are caught purchasing an illegal license.

The fraudster is arrested, but denied issuing a license or communicating with the teens. No other information is available.

Girl Dies as she Steps off the School Bus

One day a mother of a 17-year-old Emirati girl became concerned when she did not come home from school at the normal time. So she left her home to go and get her. When the mother got to the school, she found out that her daughter stayed late, but she had just taken the school bus home.

The bus stopped near the girl's house to let her off, and the girl walked behind the bus to cross the street. An Emirati woman ignoring the stop sign and lights on the bus ran over her. She was taken to a hospital where she later died.

Prosecutors are questioning the Emirati woman and Pakistani school bus driver before they decide whether to press charges. The bus driver has been suspended pending the investigation. No other information available.

People are outraged over the fact that in Dubai, no one ever stops when the lights on the school bus come on, and the stop sign comes out. Everyone speeds around the bus to avoid having to stop.

Teenager Runs over American

An 18-year-old Emirati admitted to running over an American man's leg, but said he did it to save him from being hurt. The teen said he was driving along when he spotted two Americans fighting with each other on the side of the road. The teen drove towards them to calm them down but said both Americans swore at him.

He drove away when he noticed one man hitting the other man's head on the pavement. The teen went back to stop them from hurting each other and drove towards them again to scare them off, but "accidentally" ran over the American's leg. The case is adjourned.

Hit and Run Teen

A 16-year-old Emirati boy without a driver's license allegedly is speeding. He lost control and rammed into two vehicles, and badly injuring two people on the road. The injured are taken to a hospital, and the teen who sustained minor injuries had fled the scene.

The police are searching for him. No other information.

Student Fined over Girl's Death

A 22-year-old Pakistani student is fined for running over a teenage girl and killing her. But, witnesses say she was trying to commit suicide because her boyfriend had broken up with her. They said she closed her eyes, and walked into the road.

The student's attorney said: "My client was groundlessly charged with running over the girl and killing her." The 22-year-old is fined $2,178, and ordered to pay $32,670 in blood money. He is banned from driving for 3 months.

Six Teen Drivers Busted

Six underage boys are caught driving their parents' cars on major roads without a license. The boys are between the ages of 14 and 17-years-old. They insisted that their parents allowed them to drive.

None of the teens are punished by the Traffic Court, but they ended up fining only one parent $136 for allowing the boy to drive. The court then handed the boys over to their parents. The vehicles are seized by the police.

Eight Boys Car Racing Help Friend Flee

Eight boys between the ages of 17 and 24-years-old are arrested. They helped their friend get away by blocking a police car during a high-speed chase. The police spotted a boy fixing a puncture in his tire, and they became suspicious that the car was used for illegal races.

When the police pulled up, the car sped off without the tire being fixed. The chase was on, but the boy called his friends and told them where to go so they could block the police. All six removed their plates from their cars and kept the police at bay by blocking them with their cars.

The boy is eventually caught, and all nine ended up in court. No further information available.

Two other boys in a separate case were in court. They didn't report damage to their cars [which is required]. The damage was due to high-speed racing and stunts.

Keep your Seedy Services Away

A mother complains that every morning when she gets into her car many "calling cards" are tucked into the car windows. These cards are advertising seedy massage services, and personal at home services from very attractive young women. She says she has to quickly grab all of them so the children won't become curious about what the lovely ladies are selling.

She wonders [as all of us expats did] why this business is not heavily regulated in Dubai, and prefers not to be solicited in this inappropriate way.

This is a huge problem for everyone. These cards are not only on your car, but you can come home and find three or four of them slipped under your door.

Doctor Sells Medicine to Young Children

An Arab doctor working for a private clinic is caught selling prescription medicine to young children. The doctor gave out "psychotropic" [mood altering] drugs that include "tramadol" [Oxycodone]. He gives them the medicine without a doctor's prescription after they pay him money.

The criminal has been referred to public prosecution. No other information available.

Stores Selling Narcotics to Kids

A 16-year-old Emirati boy is caught with a tobacco based drug called *Paan. When his mother confronted him, he confessed being hooked on the illegal substance but wanted to quit. The boy is scared that his father will find out.

The family contacted the authorities. While talking to the police, the boy said: "Plead for me before my parents so they could forgive me as I would never use the banned tobacco again."

The boy agreed to take the officers to the shops that sold the drugs to him. He said they are selling these drugs to both school children and Asian workers along with a similar narcotic drug called *Naswar. The police had seized 88 lbs. of Paan from a vehicle that supplied the shops and 40 lbs. from inside the stores.

*Paan is called betel leaf and is traditionally chewed in South Asia. It can include tobacco and spices. *Naswar is a tobacco containing calcium oxide and wood ash. Both drugs are highly addictive, and are banned for causing health risks. It's been said environmental damage can also be caused from spitting the tobacco out since it leaves red stains on the ground.

Mystery of How Women who Drive can Still have Babies

A Dubai resident responds to a claim made by a Saudi psychologist. He says, "Driving damages women's ovaries and pelvis." The angry resident wondered if the Saudis think that all women are complete morons who need no evidence or facts.

She wants to know how the human race produces such excellent offspring with a damaged pelvis and ovaries. She said so many women in the world are driving.

Court Blames Child for Drowning

A 42-year-old Indian father said he dropped his 9-year-old son off at a birthday party. The party is hosted by a 37-year-old Indian mother. The woman called the father one hour after dropping off his son telling him something is wrong, and he needed to come back.

When he arrived, he saw the paramedics carrying his son. They told him the boy had drowned. The father is "unaware" this is a pool party and is told by one parent that his child followed the other kids in the pool and drowned. The father said that his son doesn't know how to swim. He said if he knew it was a pool party, he never would have taken him there.

In court the father claimed that the mother giving the party is negligent for failing to watch the children while they were swimming. An Egyptian "safety expert" testified and said: "The pool had all safety procedures in place, but there was no lifeguard. The boy was with his friends in the pool, but they went deeper and he drowned." The court found the defendant innocent and blamed the boy for going into the pool without knowing how to swim.

Blood Money for Drowned Girl's Family

A 4-year-old Egyptian girl fell into a swimming pool at a hotel and drowned. There was no lifeguard on duty. The girl's mother left for a few minutes to get "biscuits" thinking her daughter was playing with the other children.

When the father went to check on the girl, he found her floating lifeless in the swimming pool. The hotel, and two employees said the child should never have been left alone and denied any negligence.

A lower court ruled for the family to receive $27,226 in blood money from the hotel. This is "half" of the blood money that would have been given if the victim had been a boy. On appeal, the court ruled for the full amount, $54,452 [the same as a male] plus $27,226 for psychological trauma. The total comes to $81,678.

Blood money can differ between male and female as men are expected to provide for their parents and family when they make money. Here, the family argued their daughter could have supported them.

Teen Insults Policeman then Stabs him

A 20-year-old off-duty policeman walked into a cell phone store with his 18-year-old brother. They went to trade the officer's phone so he could upgrade to a newer one. A 19-year-old boy and his friend followed them inside to cause trouble.

The 19-year-old confronted the policeman and said: "You only want a new phone because only the son of a prostitute sells his used phone." he repeated this twice, then the cop asked him why he said that. The kid then turned to the officer's brother and punched him.

He pulled out a knife and fought with the cop, stabbing him in the shoulder. Running out of the shop, the policeman tried to call the police. The boy followed and stabbed him again. Police arrived and arrested the defendant.

The brother of the policeman said, "Something was sprayed in my face" and confirmed he was beaten up by the defendant and his friend. The 25-year-old Indian cell phone salesman also verified the fight. He states he asked them to leave and they did.

In court, the teen has been charged with attempted murder. No other information available.

Mom and Daughter Beat up a Tenant

An Arab woman had sublet a part of her home to an Arab man. The woman and her daughter insulted, and assaulted the tenant by hitting him with sticks. The reason is unknown. They grabbed his shirt and pushed him to the ground. The man sustained bruises on his face and injuries to his body.

The woman and her daughter have been fined $136 each for beating up the tenant.

A Daughter Reclaims her Home

A court ruled in favor of an Arab women whose mother unlawfully sold a home that the daughter inherited from her father. She is young when her father passed away. Her mother sold their residence without ever informing her. An Arab man purchased the house.

When the daughter grew up, she learned the home was sold. She then sued the man who purchased the house for "unlawfully" buying the home and won the case.

Three Young Men Beat up Stepdad

The father of 3 young Arab men passed away. Their mother remarried so the new husband could look after her and the 3 sons. The men, in their early 20s are unhappy the mom married so soon after their father died and saw it as a betrayal. They confronted the stepdad and then beat him up leaving permanent damage to his hearing.

The men received a jail sentence of 6 months but is reduced to 1 month. They are ordered to pay $12,251 to the stepdad for psychological and physical damages. The court also canceled a deportation order for the defendants.

4-Year-Old Killed

An Emirati mother killed her little 4-year-old girl. She starved her for many days. The mother beat her up, put her in a "dust bin" and locked her in "laundry baskets." The little girl died in a hospital of a brain hemorrhage caused by consistent beatings.

When police confronted the mother, she said she was only trying to discipline and teach the child good manners and intended no harm. The mom showed no remorse. Prosecutors suspected the couple are not the child's biological parents, but DNA proved they were.

The mother received 10 years in jail for torturing and another 3 years for abusing the child, causing death. This came to 13 years in prison. The father received 3 years for failing to report the abuse.

People are shocked, not understanding the sentencing in the country. The woman received 13 years in jail not just for murder, but torturing the little girl day after day. Some say it would be better to whip her every day for 13 years.

Siblings Abused by Dad and Stepmom

Two Pakistani sisters age 20 and 25-years-old have filed complaints against their father and stepmother for assault. The 20-year-old claimed that her parents denied her insulin while being a diabetic. She showed up at a hospital to get medicine and reported the incident to the staff.

She said her father hit her many times and locked her in a room. The stepmother once accused her of cooking when she shouldn't be and then dragged her by the hair and threw plates at her. She says: "The fights were always for silly reasons. In some cultures, it is very difficult to disobey a parent and leave home like that, but if you are in a dangerous situation, you should leave" The 20-year-old ran away to her sister's home. The 25-year-old filed a complaint about the father earlier in the year. Those charges are unknown. No other information available.

Secret Love Child

A 42-year-old Emirati man and a 29-year-old Russian had a love affair for 12 years after meeting at a nightclub. The woman became pregnant, and the couple delivered their baby girl at home using a big pot and scissors. They kept the child's existence hidden for 8 years.

The 8-year-old girl has not attended school and is not vaccinated. When the child becomes ill, the father gets the medicine himself without a prescription because the girl has no legal ID papers, and they could not take her to a doctor. This would have triggered an illegal affair and jail. The woman begged him to marry her, but he refused. He lied to his family saying they were married.

The couple are arrested after someone informed the police about their child, and illegal affair. They admitted to having an illegal affair, but denied endangering the welfare of the child. No further information available.

In Dubai, you can walk into any of the countless pharmacies sprinkled throughout the city and buy many types of medicine without a prescription including, any kind of antibiotic. If you are not good at diagnosing yourself, the "migrant worker" behind the counter of the pharmacy will assist and give you "what they think is best!"

3-Year-Old Dumped at a Hospital

A young 3-year-old girl was found at a Kuwaiti Hospital in Dubai by a woman when a "stateless" father left her there. The child was tortured and burned. A relative of the girl said: "The father always threatened to throw the little girl on the street. He did not want her to live with her stepbrothers from his first marriage." They arrested the father at a "resort" when the police used social media to spread the word about the crime.

Due to hard times, he admitted to getting rid of her [yet he is at a resort] and not being able to care for her. The child's mother moved back home to Ethiopia. Since the child had no ID documents, the mother could not take her daughter. She asked the dad to take care of her. The father thought she will have a better life if dumped at the hospital.

DNA tests were conducted on the child and father. The investigation is ongoing.

Parents Sell Kids for Sex

A 44-year-old Arab man and his 45-year-old Arab wife had forced their "presumed" daughters age 17, 20 and 27-years-old into prostitution. They also made their 23-year-old daughter-in-law, housemaid, a niece as young as 12-years-old and other relatives perform illegal sex acts. The 25-year-old son helped keep things in line.

For many years this has been happening. The couple forced the girls to strip dance at private parties and have sex with various men who paid the couple. When the victims refused to please the men or have sex, the couple threatened to deport them as they received a beating.

An anti-trafficking organization set up a trap to catch the couple after receiving a tip. Learning through DNA, they had 1 biological daughter, the 17-year-old. They forged documents on the other 2 girls to make it look like they are the parents to keep a tight hold on them in the prostitution ring.

The couple is referred to public prosecution on charges of human trafficking and abusing young girls. No other information available.

Teen Lured to the U.A.E. for Trafficking

A Pakistani couple are in their home country when having met a 16-year-old girl. They invited her to come to the U.A.E. and become a housemaid. The couple meet with the girl's father and discuss the proposal. He agreed to let her go because the family is struggling for money.

When the 16-year-old arrived, they forced her into prostitution for 10 months before a customer helped by calling the police. No other information is available.

Teens Virginity Sold by Parents

A 17-year-old Pakistani girl arrived in the U.A.E. After being there for ten days, the father took her to a hotel and handed her over to a stranger. In court, the girl says: "He took away my virginity and paid my father $4,356." She is very emotional and told how her dad did not speak to her when refusing requests to sell her body.

A month later the couple brought their daughter to another hotel. The parents said: "Remain with the man the entire night and have sex with him." The girl said there are two men in the room. One is in traditional Pakistani dress, and the other wore casual clothes.

She heard her dad telling one of the men not to cause any harm because she is young. Her father agreed to accept $2,722 for his daughter. The men, are undercover police who received a tip by one of the girl's customers. It is unclear how many men the parents forced her to have sex with before being caught.

Police investigated a brothel and found 5 prostitutes. The parents had many dealings with the Pakistani couple who owned the brothel. They closed it down and confiscated money and a laptop where the business was being advertised on their website. They also found a long list of prostitute names, prices and preferred hotels.

All the defendants are arrested. The second Pakistani couple appeared in court on charges of running a brothel, abusing women and creating a website with photos to advertise the prostitutes. They denied the charges.

The 38-year-old Pakistani father confessed to asking his daughter and 35-year-old wife to both be hookers and says the daughter agreed. The wife denied ever working as a prostitute. He said he told them their financial status is in shambles, this would make them rich.

A 36-year-old customer appeared in court and denied charges of having sex with the teenager. The hearings are ongoing.

Father Accused of Abuse

A divorced Emirati man has been accused of attacking his 14-year-old daughter. He pulled her hair, pushed her to the ground, kicked and hit her when she disobeyed him.

The wife has received custody of their daughter and her sister, but the father is given visitation rights. The man is denying the charges.

Brothers Forced to Care for Mom

Four Emirati men in their late 20s and early 30s are forced to care for their Asian mother. She ran out on them two decades earlier. The woman abandoned her sons after their father passed.

The oldest boy was 12-years-old when his mom moved back to her home country. The young children are left to live with relatives. Their mom eventually married another man from her country, but he died in a house fire.

The boys never saw their mother until she returned to the U.A.E. and filed a complaint ordering the men to take care of her. She told the boys how the second husband died in a fire, and how it left burns on different parts of her body.

The mom said she needed shelter and treatment and asked for their forgiveness. She explained that her "traditions" forced her to go back to her home country as a young widow and remarry. She claims that it was her husband who would not allow her to go back to the U.A.E. to visit her children.

The boys are angry at their mom for leaving and refused to listen. A judge issued an order "forcing" the sons who both work, to look after their mother.

Woman Left 5 Kids with Maid for 10 Months

An Emirati mother who worked as a police officer was divorced and won custody of her 5 children. The kids are between the ages of 2 and 10-years-old. When becoming debt ridden, she ran away for fear of being arrested. She owed $217,808 in bank loans which included one car.

Her children are left with 2 housemaids. The mother would sneak back to the home for visits but never saw the children. The maids are ordered to "lock the 3 boys and 2 girls away" when she visited. It is unclear where the woman was staying.

A friend of the officers went to visit because she had not seen her in a long time. The friend couldn't believe she fled the home, so she reported it to the police department. Police thought the friend was lying and are totally shocked when finding out she isn't.

The department said: "The 2-year-old girl liked a policewoman who was visiting them and considered her as her mother." The children's father said he had been paying for the children starting in 2009 but had not seen them very much because he remarried and moved away.

In court the mother received a jail sentenced, which was suspended to 1 month.

Father Beats Son to Death
An Emirati man who police "suspected" to be an alcoholic had beaten his 12-year-old son to death. He said because he performed poorly in school exams. The father who has 5 other sons is believed to have beaten him across his entire body with an "electrical cable" until the boy collapsed.

He went to the hospital and later died. The police received information about the boy's death from the hospital. They arrested the dad at the home. He showed no feelings over the attack. The police department says: "Such incidents of family violence are rare in our civilized society which is characterized with love and leniency among members of the family. Such people as the suspect don't deserve to live in the U.A.E. society." No formal charges are made against the father. Investigations are ongoing.

Child Killer Deserved to Die
A 30-year-old Emirati man who is a captain of a fishing boat is executed by facing a firing squad. The court convicted him of raping and murdering a little boy in the bathroom of a mosque. His neighborhood welcomed the execution, and the little boy's parents, and three other family members witnessed the shooting.

The killer is known in his community as a drunk and has a criminal record stretching back to 1996. He has "ten" earlier convictions for rape, assault, robbery and theft. He is released from prison in 2008.

A shop owner said: "As a kid, the Emirati would come in and buy cigarettes and food. He never seemed normal, like he was a drunk or on drugs. He even came by the shop with blood oozing out of cuts on his hands. He hung around with a bad crowd and unsavory people, always seemed to be looking for a fight."

Husband and Daughters Found Dead in a Villa
A Pakistani woman returned home from a concert to find her entire family dead. She found her daughters, age 2 and 7-years-old in a bathtub. She called the police, and they searched the home. While searching, they found her husband floating face down in the community pool.

Police think he choked the two girls and then placed them in the bathtub before committing suicide. They believed he was having financial problems and mental health problems. The mother was quickly taken to the hospital in shock.

Friends are disputing the allegations that the father killed his children and himself. They said there was no reason. A former colleague said: "He was a very well established and combined person with amazing decision skills [sic]. There is no way he could do such an act. Not even once I have seen him losing his mind [sic]." He went on to say: "There was no financial problem. He was completely OK, healthy, well settled. The family was living happily."

A family friend also denied the Pakistani man committed the crime. He says: "He was a great father, friend, neighbor and a God fearing practicing Muslim. The man was a great swimmer." No further information.

Father Blamed for Running over Son

A 37-year-old expat is backing out of a driveway when his 18-month-old son slipped out of the villa and ran behind the car. Unaware he was there, the father ran over him. The boy is rushed to the hospital where he later died.

The father will have to stand trial over his son's death, but the office at the "Dubai Traffic Prosecution" has asked the court to be lenient if found guilty. They are asking for a lighter sentence because they are considering the human side and circumstances of the case.

The court said: "In some traffic accidents where the driver causes the death of a member of his family, because of serious mistakes such as not paying attention or negligence, then we have the right to prosecute him."

The judge could order up to 1 year in prison, he could suspend the jail term or just make him pay a fine. The expat will still have to pay $54,451 in blood money to the surviving members of "his" family. Police allowed the man to fly back to his home country to bury his son, but he has returned to Dubai. No further information.

Uncle Runs over Nephew

An Emirati man noticed his 18-month-old nephew playing by his parked car in the driveway. He picked him up and brought him in the house, and the little boy played with other siblings. The boy slipped back outside and behind the vehicle when the uncle was busy in the house.

The man left, got into his car and backed up without looking. He felt as if he hit something so he got out of the car. He couldn't believe it when he saw he ran over his nephew. The uncle and family rushed the little boy to the hospital, but he is dead on arrival.

This is the second incident of family members running over children in a short time.

Teen Accused of Trying to Stab a Man to Death with Fingernail Clippers

A fight broke out between a 24-year-old and a gang of youths including, a 19-year-old Emirati. The teen pulled out fingernail clippers and stabbed the 24-year-old in the chest, stomach and shoulder.

The fight started in front of the home of the victim's grandfather. Medical reports showed the victim suffered major blood loss and would have died without medical help. The case is adjourned.

CHAPTER 5

THE BABIES

Any foreign baby born in the U.A.E. is not a citizen. These babies will have the nationality of their parents. There is no way for foreigners to become citizens unless the foreign woman is wed to a U.A.E. national. But, foreign men who marry local women may not become a citizen.

You can however become a U.A.E. resident as long as you work in Dubai, and your employer is your sponsor. The other alternative is if you are the owner of property in Dubai and are sponsored by the real estate company.

Having a baby out of wedlock will repeatedly have repercussions, but here is a case with a twist. A couple is convicted of having sex outside of wedlock and face a prison sentence up to 2 years. If the woman is pregnant, the court will look at the welfare of the child and allow the couple a chance to get married. But, this doesn't happen in every case and it depends on the judge.

If a mother abandons their illegitimate children, which happens often out of fear of being caught without a husband, they face charges on having sex. She is also charged with endangering the safety and life of a child and for abandoning a child.

The problem couples face is if they do not marry, the child then becomes "fatherless." The child has no records or residency without the father's signature. As stated earlier, documents and paperwork is always filed under the male. What many women don't know and should realize is that the mother can file a lawsuit against the father. This will then prove the paternity of the child which enables her to get records for the child.

It is shocking just how many babies are abandoned, and in appalling numbers. In one month alone, 4 babies are found. Some infants are placed in areas where the mothers are hoping they will be found, while others are murdered, with the moms hoping they will not be found.

While you read the stories in this chapter, you'll see that the public will not intervene while a person in the street is hurt. This holds true even if a woman is pregnant. The reason is to avoid legal complications. The Good Samaritan law is not implemented in the U.A.E. Most of the time a phone call is made by the public to 999 [911], but nothing more is done.

In medical situations, the government said they "entrust qualified medical personnel" to help the victim. They have also come out to say: "There is no law forbidding you to help someone in need as long as the situation requires immediate action." The public will still stay away and not come to your rescue. This is because if the victim dies, the Good Samaritan could be responsible for blood money.

My spouse was out one day and noticed an expat man lying on the sidewalk in the hot sun. Doing the right thing, he rushed over to him as the rest of the spectators stayed back at least 20 yards. He spoke with the gentleman who said that he would be fine. During this time someone in the crowd had called for an ambulance. My spouse then shaded the man from the sun, and stayed with him until the ambulance arrived.

Blood money is common on the other side of the world. If a person is killed, the family of the deceased will then opt to accept blood money from the family of the killer. This means that the person convicted will have a lesser sentence. If the family rejects the blood money, a harsher sentence is given. Often to the accused, this could mean life or death.

The word for blood money in Arabic is Diya. The idea of blood money comes out of the Quran and Sharia law. The amount of money varies between men and women, Muslim believers and non-believers. There are various interpretations of blood money in different Muslim countries.

According to what I know, in the U.A.E. blood money is paid out at the same rate regardless of religion or nationality. If one causes the death or injury of another person accidentally or intentionally, he or she must pay the victim's family. This is especially true if the defendant is found guilty under the criminal code. It is a means of compensation for losing a family member. There is a different rate for men and women. $54,450 is paid out for the death of a male and $27,225 is paid out for the death of a female. If the victim is killed in self-defense, then blood money will not be paid.

There is a case, that you just read where a father accidentally killed his son [by running him over] and ordered by the court to pay blood money to his "own" family. Paying money to your own family isn't unusual.

When driving in Dubai, it is always a good idea to stay away from remote areas at night. Migrant workers who are desperate to end their life will sometimes attempt suicide. They jump out in front of your car to purposely be hit. This is so their family can collect blood money, due to their death.

Blood money was written into our personal car insurance policy. The migrant workers know many people have it on their insurance, and they know their families will benefit. An American colleague of my spouse had a person run out in front of his car at 2:00am with no witnesses. He was kept in jail until his family posted the blood money.

Driving in Dubai is dangerous. You have many nationalities coming together to drive in a way that they see fit. So often you will witness children not wearing a seatbelt, and no car seat for the babies. Many young ones are jumping around on the seats, sticking their heads out of the windows and sun roofs. The adults in these cars are safely wearing their seatbelts. This irresponsible and frightening action just shows the disregard of human life for their own children.

Abused Wife Loses Baby

A 30-year-old Moroccan expat filed for a divorce from her wicked husband after she says he abused her so badly that she miscarried. She explained that just six days after they married he beat her, disfigured her face, and she required surgery.

After the first attack, they worked things out. Though he attacked her again after arguing over why he didn't pay rent and disallowed her money. This time he dragged her into the street, and beat her up for all to see. She told a court that she was pregnant at the time of the attack. Due to the beating, she had internal bleeding causing her to miscarry. She ultimately suffered a mental breakdown.

The woman is asking the court to make her husband pay her $10,890 in rent besides, other costs. Under Islam Law, a woman does not have to live with a husband who abuses her. No other information available.

Robbery

A 20-year-old Emirati man broke into a room where a 24-year-old Filipina woman slept with her newborn baby. She pleaded with him to not harm her baby and she will do as he says. He then raped her at knifepoint, and took her money.

The Emirati man received a 10 year sentence for "sexual assault in front of a newborn."

Chemical Firm Boss Kills 2 Babies

A family is not at all ready to forgive the owners of a pesticide control company. They killed two of their 5-month-old triplets, and left the third severely ill. The owner of the firm says he took precautionary measures when spraying the apartment building, but the fumes from the chemicals entered through a ventilation system.

He said he told the security guard at the building to inform all the residents that chemicals will be sprayed. He apologized to the family for the "unfortunate accident" and is very sad. The father of the babies is not willing to accept any apology and has said that his life is ruined. He lost two children, is now separated from his wife and his career is affected.

The owner of the pest control company received a 4 year jail sentence along with two other employees. The 3 convicted men are required to pay the family a total of $108,902 in blood money. The owner's portion falls to his brother to pay the money. He said that he is in no position to pay since he is in great financial difficulty. He tells how he is struggling to support his own wife and 2 children. The 3 men are planning to file an appeal to have the sentence reduced. No further information.

Illegal pest control performed in buildings happen often. The profit over concern for others appear to take precedence. The owners of these companies don't seem to care about the health of their customers, public or employees.

These workers are spraying highly toxic and poisonous chemicals wearing no protective gear. They often use industrial chemicals intended for farm use out in the open air. There also appears to be no governmental control or oversight of these companies. You can often see them walking around the grounds spraying near children.

Sometimes there is no prior notice given out to residents that spraying for bugs and pests will be performed. The residents are left with burning eyes, severe headaches and nausea. Experienced and certified people need to do the fumigation.

Husband Demands Abortion

A 20-year-old Iranian man held a knife to his 23-year-old wife's stomach. He threatened to kill the fetus if she did not abort the child. The incident happened in the home of the wife's 54-year-old mother who saw him take a knife from a table and threaten her daughter. He told his wife to take his threat seriously.

The couple ended up divorcing, and the ex-wife asked for money in the settlement. Agreeing to this, the man arranged for a friend to deliver $9,801 to his ex-wife. The woman then complained to the police, telling them her ex-husband's friend had also threatened her. The man's friend said that he was surprised when he received a call from the police with the allegations.

No charge is filed against the husband's friend, and the husband pleaded not guilty to threatening his wife. The case is adjourned.

A Man Threw his Wife and Baby out of the House

An Arab woman gave birth to a baby. Her husband who did not want the child, divorced her and ordered them both out of the house. The man who had many children with his first wife said that he did not want children with his second wife. He said: "I married that woman only to please me. I never asked her to produce children."

He started the proceedings to divorce her when she became pregnant.

He mistreated her, and demanded her to leave the home. The Family Court advised him not to throw her out until after she delivered the baby. When she returned to the home after giving birth, she realized she was locked out. Her husband said he had divorced her in court while she was in the hospital. He ordered her to get out of the house, she could no longer stay.

In court, the woman is told that under Sharia law, a father does not have to provide housing for an infant. The baby is required to stay with the divorced mother until grown. The Arab woman then took the case to the Appeal Court. They ruled that it is wrong to deny housing to a "foreign divorcee" who has a baby, and no family in the U.A.E. They ordered him to give housing for the woman and her baby.

Hospital Staff Calls Police

A new mom claims her baby is legitimate, and she became pregnant before arriving in the U.A.E. An Asian woman said she entered the U.A.E. after she had sex with her husband in her home country. She explained to the court that her marriage certificate is in her country, and she did not have a copy of it.

She arrived at the hospital having labor pains, but is not asked for a marriage certificate by the hospital staff. The staff who is required to report to the police anyone suspected of not being married, had turned her in to the authorities.

She said she did not know she needed the documents to prove she is married, to give birth at the hospital. The Asian woman is arrested after giving delivering a baby girl. She is charged with sex outside of wedlock and getting pregnant from an illegal relationship. No further information is available.

A 16-Month-Old Left alone

A Syrian mother left her 16-month-old toddler unattended. The boy fell out of their living room window of the 2nd-floor apartment leaving him in critical condition. The police are notified by a person passing by who saw the child on the ground.

The mom told police that she changed the toddler's clothes, and went into the kitchen for three minutes as the child played in the living room of their apartment. When she went to check on the toddler, he wasn't there. She looked out of the window and saw her child lying on the ground with his toy car next to him. She doesn't understand how it happened since the toddler couldn't walk well. The boy suffered broken ribs and a fractured skull. No further information.

A 4-Year-Old Plays on Window Ledge

A Pakistani couple faces criminal charges. Their 4-year-old toddler girl fell from a window of their apartment on the 8th-floor. The mother claims she left the child playing in the bedroom, and the window was closed. She is preparing food when after sometime she did not hear the child anymore.

After going to look in on the toddler, she saw the girl wasn't there, and the window open.

Looking out of the window, she saw her daughter on the ground in a pool of blood. The girl died at the scene. Police think she climbed onto a table next to the window, opened it to look out and lost her balance. The mother is charged with child neglect.

Police said that no matter how much they campaign to not leave your children unsupervised, people still don't care. They strongly stressed not to put tables, chairs and objects near open windows and balconies.

A 3-Year-Old Falls off 5th-Floor Balcony

An Egyptian family lived on the 5th-floor of an apartment together with their 3-year-old toddler girl. The girl is often seen walking with her father. She is described by neighbors as being very nice and a beautiful little girl. One day the couple left the toddler's aunt in charge of babysitting while the parents went out.

Instead of watching the toddler, the aunt went to sleep, and the child is left unsupervised. It is unclear whether the sliding doors to the balcony are left open or if the child opened them. The toddler ran to the balcony and played on the railing before she fell and died. Neighbors had said the parents were hysterical after they arrived home. The father fainted and is taken away in an ambulance. Also crying and screaming is the aunt.

Just weeks before this dreadful accident, the police burst into the same apartment after they spotted the toddler's legs dangling off the balcony. They learned the parents left the toddler home alone while they were both at work. The parents are charged with neglect, but the mom is the only person convicted, and sentenced to prison for 1 month.

Infant Left Home Alone

A Jordanian father is at home with his 7-month-old baby girl while the rest of the family went shopping. He stepped out to attend prayers at a nearby mosque leaving the 7-month-old baby girl sleeping alone in an upstairs bedroom. While the dad is attending prayer service, a fire broke out at their home.

An Emirati man who also attended the service is driving home when he spotted smoke billowing out of the windows of a house. He stopped and tried to get into the front door, but it was locked, and no one answered to his banging. Climbing through a window on the ground floor, he called out to determine if anyone was there and in need of help, but no one responded.

After passing through the smoky rooms making certain no one was inside, he heard the baby screaming. So he dashed into the room filled with smoke, snatched the baby and rushed out where he met the baby's dad. The girl went to the hospital for smoke inhalation and is doing well. Their entire kitchen is destroyed, and the cause of the fire is yet to be determined.

Hailed a hero, the Emirati is extremely happy no one is hurt. There are no charges in the case.

Baby Girl Left Home Alone

A 24-year-old Indonesian maid had stolen money and endangered the life of a 6-month-old baby girl. She left the baby alone in the home where she worked. Three hours after the Egyptian couple left for the office, the mother called the apartment to check in and make sure everything is OK. The maid reassured the mom that things are fine, and she is busy finishing up cleaning the home.

The mother than tried to call the maid several times throughout the day, but she didn't receive an answer. When the father returned home from work, he found a hat covering their baby girl's face and she was crying. He found the baby alone, and the housemaid was nowhere to be found. The mother then came home from work, and the couple discovered that an envelope containing $4,628 which they kept on their dresser was missing.

The parents thought the housemaid would never pull a stunt like this. The mom said: "She was such a polite and religious woman. My baby is still terrified at night after what happened and wakes at night crying." Police found the maid and arrested her. She is then charged with robbery and endangering the life of a child but denied the charges.

The housemaid received 1 year in jail and then will be deported.

A Newborn Left Alone for Days

An Ethiopian maid gave birth to a baby then left the infant alone for 4 days. The baby is born out of wedlock in an abandoned villa near the home where the maid worked. When the brother of her boss heard crying as he walked passed the villa, he was surprised to find a baby.

He called the police, and the baby is taken to a hospital. The hospital later reported the child is in poor condition due to starvation and exposure. When questioned by the police, the maid became nervous and confessed to delivering and abandoning the baby. She said: "The elder female Emirati boss never even knew that I was pregnant." They then arrested her.

She told the police she had considered an abortion, but she feared for her own life. The outcome of the court case is unknown.

Woman Tries to Sell her Baby

A 22-year-old Indonesian woman said she is not of sound mind. She had made a mistake when she tried to sell her baby for $1,089. The woman came to the U.A.E. in 2011 to work as a maid, but ran away because of terrible working conditions. She then got caught up in the sex trade. She said she had worked in ten different brothels, charging $8 for sex, and she had many customers.

The woman fell in love with a Pakistani customer who promised to take care of her. After she became pregnant and refused to get an abortion, he dumped her. She continued as a sex worker while being pregnant and gave birth to a baby girl in her home. The police received a tip that the woman wanted to sell her baby.

A female and male officer posed as a married couple and met with her. They told her they could not have children of their own so they want to buy her child. The woman said she wanted $1,633 for the baby, but the police officers negotiated with her and she lowered the price to $1,089. They arrested her after she accepted the money and handed over the baby.

The woman claimed she needed the money to return to her home country. The woman is charged with human trafficking and prostitution. She said she wants to see her baby since it has been 4 months since they took the baby away. The infant is being cared for by the Dubai Women and Children's Foundation.

Assaulted by In-Laws Makes Woman Lose her Baby
An Arab woman from the Middle East is assaulted by her husband's mother, three of his brothers and a sister. This resulted in her suffering a miscarriage. The couple was married for 3 years and had two children together. They lived with the husband's family. The wife was ordered by the husband and his family to do all the housework including, looking after her husband's two young brothers who had special needs.

The woman is 3-months pregnant with the couple's third child when a brother-in-law grabbed her by the hair and threw her to the ground. All the family members joined in "beating her with sticks" and kicking her in the back which caused her to have a miscarriage.

She told a court she has physical injuries, but she also suffers from psychological damage as well. The mother-in-law and her 3 sons are ordered to pay a fine of $54 each. Her sister-in-law is given a 3 year "suspended jail sentence" and fined $136. The woman was not happy with the verdict so she sued the whole family and demanded $27,224. The court then ordered the family to pay $13,612.

I don't know the reason for the abuse, but it sounds like a Cinderella treatment from the rest of the family without a happy ending.

Fake Baby Claim
A 52-year-old Emirati woman tried to claim someone else's newborn as her own to get her hands on her dead husband's inheritance. By saying the child is her deceased husbands, she would receive more of his money. The woman walked into a hospital alongside an "unknown" pregnant woman. After the pregnant woman gave birth, the Emirati gave her own ID to hospital staff to get the birth certificate of the child. The woman is unsuccessful in getting the certificate with her name listed as the mother.

Four years later, she went back to the hospital and tried again to claim the same child as her own. This time around, the hospital staff became suspicious and reported it to the doctor in charge. The doctor contacted the police who order a DNA test to be done. The DNA test showed that the

Emirati woman is not the mother of the baby.

After court proceedings, the Emirati woman is finally given a 1 year jail sentence.

Baby Left in Hot Car for 9 Hours

A 16-month-old baby miraculously survived being left in a hot car for 9 hours. The baby is in critical condition and taken to a hospital and admitted. The Emirati parents said they had returned home around 3pm and forgot the child in the car. They said: "We did not notice the baby was missing until midnight." No further information.

Maid Charged with Throwing Away her Baby

A 26-year-old Ethiopian maid is arrested after she threw her newborn baby girl down a trash chute. The maid said she became pregnant out of wedlock from a man back in her home country. She hid the pregnancy from her employers. The maid delivered the baby by herself in her bedroom at the employer's home. She claims the baby was not breathing and is dead after giving birth.

When pressed by the police, she admitted to wrapping the baby in a piece of cloth and placing it in a plastic bag. The maid disposed of the child down the trash chute then cleaned her room and returned to work. The maid is arrested, and an investigation is ongoing into whether the baby was alive or dead when the maid threw her in the trash chute.

Baby Boy Found Strangled

A 1-month-old baby is found by a stranger strangled and buried on a beach. An Asian man walking along the water, called the police when he noticed a piece of fabric buried in the sand with hair sticking out. He said that he thought it could be a baby since he could see the hair.

Police believed the baby was buried for 2 days before being discovered. They think the infant boy is Asian, 30 to 40 days old. They assume, the murder is due to an illegal affair and are checking clinics and hospitals for babies born within the last month. DNA tests are being carried out to find the parents.

Newborn Baby Found in Toilet

A 2-day-old baby boy is found in a public toilet wrapped in a blanket. People using the public facilities found the baby early one morning. The infant is in good health. He will stay in the hospital until either the parents are found, or he is deemed fit to move to a "child care center."

The police believe the baby is born out of wedlock and they are investigating the case.

Baby Found on a Street

A newborn baby girl is found in a "plastic carrier bag" on an upscale street by a resident. The baby is doing fine at a hospital, and authorities are hunting for the mother. The police believe the baby is born out of wedlock and are investigating the case.

DUBAI, 1 CITY 2 DIFFERENT TALES

Abandon Baby Taken Illegally

An Arab woman is found guilty for not following proper adoption procedures. The widowed woman had no children of her own and wanted to adopt a newborn baby 3 years ago, but did not follow the adoption rules. She illegally paid $2,722 to adopt a baby boy. When the child reached 3-years-old, she tried to register him for "kindergarten", but she couldn't produce the proper documents. She was unable to register him.

The school administrators reported her to the police who launched an investigation. The woman admitted in court she did not follow the legal procedures, and the court told her if she follows the procedures, she may keep the child.

This woman did something wrong and just got away with buying a child. Now they are calling it a legal adoption.

Looking for Lost Spouse to Free a Mom and Baby

A 25-year-old Filipina woman and her newborn baby are in a Dubai prison for 1 year. After giving birth, the woman could not produce her marriage certificate so she is reported to the police by the hospital staff. The woman claims she married back in 2007 before she and her husband came to Dubai, but the husband went back to their home country prior to her giving birth.

The woman has 15 days after sentencing to prove she is married before she can no longer appeal her conviction of sex outside of marriage. A human rights group is trying to help find her husband and said: "She is from the southern region of the Philippines that has a population of 4 million." They are searching this area for the husband, but no sign of him.

The human rights group believe her story and are trying to get the Philippine Consulate involved in the case. This will reduce the charges on "humanitarian grounds." Though the consulate stated that they could not launch an appeal on the woman's behalf. They need evidence proving she is married.

There have been many cases of women serving jail time with their newborn babies after giving birth outside of marriage in the U.A.E.

New Breastfeeding Proposal

A new proposal on breastfeeding is being discussed. This law encourages mothers and gives the babies the right to be breastfed for 2 years. The chairman of the committee said: "It is very important for the development of a child and mothers should take it as a duty. Orphans or abandoned babies should have the right to be breastfed as well, and centers at major hospitals should be set up to accommodate this."

Defiant Father said he can't be the Dad, he was in Jail

An Emirati dad insists he is not the father of his wife's baby. The husband said his wife had become pregnant while he served a 1 year jail sentence. In court, he said that he did not have sex with her and he did not share a bed with her after being released. He claims his sister gave a passport copy and his ID card to his wife without his consent.

The wife could then use these documents to get a birth certificate for the baby boy. The court rejected his claims since he couldn't prove them. He is ordered to accept the baby boy as his son. He is told he must register the baby under his name and get a U.A.E. passport and health card for him.

Because he divorced his wife two days after the baby was born, the court then ordered him to pay her $272 a month in child support.

HIV Custody Battle

A husband claims his ex-wife's sister has HIV, and he should therefore have custody of their child. The couple lived with the woman's sister. After they divorced he claimed it was unsafe for his son to stay there with his mother. He also stressed that the mother is always frequenting nightclubs and is not providing adequate care for the child.

The judge rejected his claim and said: "HIV is not transmitted through normal contact among people living together." the child remains with his mother.

223 Infants Stolen and Sold

This story happened in China where a woman had stolen and sold hundreds of infants in less than 1 year. A 51-year-old woman was a leader of a horrific trafficking ring that abducted and sold 223 infants between 2009 and 2010. Baby boys were sold for $4,800 and the baby girls sold for $3,200.

The woman is sentenced to death, 35 others are sentenced from 3 years to life in prison.

The abduction of all these babies was devastating for China when they had the one child law. The traditional preference in China is a male.

CHAPTER 6
RELATIONSHIPS, SEX & RAPE

A senior police officer is insisting that any woman who is raped has nothing to fear by coming forward to report it. When asked if the women will be convicted of having an illegal affair, he replied: "No, not at all. They will not face prosecution." But, many cases of women who have reported rape after his statement are charged with having an illegal affair.

Here, A Norwegian woman is jailed for sex outside of marriage when a colleague in Dubai raped her. She is later pardoned. An Australian woman spent 8 months in prison after she had reported rape. She is gang raped by 3 of her colleagues in a hotel, yet she is the one convicted.

Another issue for anyone living in Dubai could encounter is, how fast a wife and family can be kicked out of the U.A.E. if their spouse passes away. This is due to the husband usually being the visa sponsor of the family. Since no one can become a true citizen, you are given 30 days to leave the country. Regardless of how many years you have lived there, you need to leave.

An Indian lady and her husband, along with their children, were living in Dubai. The woman's husband had a good job, and his employer is his visa sponsor. The woman did not work. When the husband died unexpectedly of a heart attack, she found herself with no sponsor for her visa. She had 30 days to get a new sponsor or find a job otherwise, she would have to leave.

Their bank account was immediately frozen and their assets in Dubai seized and used to pay off debt that the husband had owed. The rest of the money is paid out as inheritance according to U.A.E. law. This can take a long time, and in the meantime, the woman had no money to buy airline tickets to go home.

We personally saw an example of this when our neighbor's husband unexpectedly passed away. The couple had been living in Dubai for 30 years and they were getting ready to retire. We spoke to the woman who told us she had been given 30 days to leave. Through help from friends and family who live in Dubai, she is granted a special 90 day extension. This was to take care of business and tie up loose ends. She ended up being forced to leave the U.A.E.

Peeping Tom Video Backfires

A 35-year-old Kenyan man placed a video camera in the men's bathroom to watch other men. The Kenyan said he wanted to watch "the men's manhood," but he accidentally filmed himself. A cleaner is working in the public bathroom when he had noticed the equipment. He called the police, and after reviewing the footage, the Kenyan is captured on film.

He was filmed when he put up the device in the cubicle to check to see if it worked properly. The man is arrested on "sexual molestation" and will face sentencing.

Friend Asked to be Killed

A 28-year-old Asian janitor had a homosexual affair with a 26-year-old Asian friend. The janitor said that the friend asked him to take his life. The victim was ashamed and wanted to end the affair with the janitor that lasted for 1½ years. He convinced his friend to murder him.

The victim bought a cable and asked to be tied up so the janitor tied his hands and legs. He then stripped off his shirt and strangled him with the cable until he died. An Emirati found the half buried body in the sand. The police found the victim's wallet and cell phone in the janitor's "room." The case is referred to public prosecution.

Firefighter Offended by a Greeting

A 39-year-old Emirati firefighter is on trial for insulting his 30-year-old colleague with a handshake. He said he stroked his palm with his middle finger when they shook hands. He told his boss it was done in a perverted way. The colleague also complained to his boss that the defendant is openly saying in front of others he is gay.

An investigation is carried out and the defendant is warned not to do it again.

Jailed for Love Revenge

A group of cleaners found a severed head in a dumpster. A man had been accused of killing his gay lover with the help of an accomplice. It is not clear how much consensual sex there was between the two men.

A third man is accused of withholding information from police. All 3 men and the victim are from Pakistan.

The suspect told police he had been sexually assaulted by the victim, and he defended himself. But, investigations suggested that there had been an affair between the two men, and the suspect wanted to end it. He told a friend he wants revenge on the man for sexually pursuing him. The police found tools at work used to beat the man and then they hid his body in a remote location.

The suspect along with his accomplice is jailed for 3 years after the victim's family accepted $54,449 in blood money. The third man who withheld information from the police is not jailed, but fined $272.

Laborer gets Execution

An Asian man will be sentenced to death in Abu Dhabi after he killed a colleague for allegedly trying to rape him. A witness said: "I saw the man entered the room of the victim at their accommodations." The police thought he waited there quietly until the colleague entered his room. He then cut the victim's throat with a knife, laid him on the bed and covered him up with a blanket. Police think this was to make it look like he passed away by taking his own life.

The victim's roommate returned from work and found him dead. The suspect claimed the victim tried to rape him, but there was no sign of a scuffle. A medical report showed that he had not been subjected to a sexual assault. The laborer will be sentenced to death.

Life Sentence for Killing Lover

A 23-year-old Pakistani man got into a fight and stabbed his Pakistani lover to death at a labor camp. He went into a jealous rage when he found out that his lover agreed to have sex with another man for $136. His naked body was found at the labor camp. The suspect fled the country but is arrested when he returned. He has been given a life sentence.

2 Homosexual Men in Jail

Two Muslim men have been found guilty of committing homosexual acts. The men claim the police had coerced them into confessing, but they are proven guilty by forensic evidence. They will each serve a 6 month jail sentence and then be deported back to their home countries.

Guilty of Molesting a Disabled Woman

A 26-year-old disabled woman from Yemen went to a tailor shop with her mother, along with her sister-in-law. The woman had accused a 24-year-old Bangladeshi man who worked as a tailor in the shop of molesting her. She said the man touched her bottom, but she thought it was by mistake until he did it again. She became furious, and yelled. He claimed it to be an accident. The Bangladeshi man is sentenced to 3 months in jail and will be deported after serving.

No Sentence for Molesting

A 33-year-old Filipino salesman is charged with molesting a Filipina woman in an elevator. The man is accused of holding a razor blade to the woman's neck. He said if she did not kiss him, he would slash her throat. When the elevator doors opened, she pushed the man off her, and ran out yelling for help.

A 3 month jail sentence has been given to the man but is overturned in an Appeal Court due to lack of evidence. The Filipino man is free.

A Groper Stays in Jail

A 40-year-old Egyptian hotel manager remains in jail after inappropriately touching a 28-year-old Emirati employee. The woman said the man touched her right shoulder, then hugged her to where she nearly lost her balance. She continued to say he then pulled on her bra. She became mad and pushed him away.

The man is found guilty of molesting her and is sentenced to 3 months in prison. The Egyptian appealed the decision, but the Appeals Court sided with the Emirati employee so his sentence is not reduced.

Granddad Attacks

A 20-year-old female Iranian student is molested by a 61-year-old Afghani man. The man is a friend of the girl's grandfather. He gave her a gift to give to her grandfather and then asked to go inside her house. Once inside, he kissed her and handed her $54 to keep it quiet. The man pleaded not guilty and the trial was adjourned.

Jogger Molested

A woman out jogging became aware that someone was following close behind her, so she quickly picked up her pace and ran faster. A 25-year-old Pakistani picked up his speed too and caught up with her. He grabbed her shoulders from behind, and pushed his body into hers. She screamed, and a person passing by came to her rescue, and restrained him until the police arrived.

The Pakistani man is sentenced to 6 months behind bars.

Mr. Fix is a Fake

A 21-year-old Indonesian woman heard a loud knock on her front door. When she answered, there stood a Sri Lankan man. He explained that her roommate called and asked him to come and "fix a closet." She told him she is very tired and to come back later. She tells the police he did not leave and said: "He pushed me down on a bed and touched and hugged my body."

The defendant denies the charge. No further information available.

Restaurant Worker Kisses a Woman

A 42-year-old Lebanese woman became lost when she missed her stop on the train. She asked a Pakistani restaurant worker for directions, and he offered to hail a cab for her. When she opened the back door of the cab to get in, he tried to kiss her, and she yelled for help.

The defendant pleaded not guilty, and the case is adjourned.

Window Cleaner Cleared of Molestation

A 38-year-old Filipina woman noticed her window open so she closed it. She took her clothes off and proceeded to take a shower. Coming out of the shower she noticed the window opened again and a Bangladeshi man watching her. Closing the window once more, she then covered her body. Seeing him open the window one more time, she yelled at him and called the police.

He said that he was "only cleaning the window." The charges brought against the man are for "sexually molesting by looking through a window," but he has been cleared by the court.

Elevator Assault

A woman who was working at a 5-star resort in Dubai stepped inside an elevator. A 45-year-old Indian man who is a guest, got inside with her. As the door closed, and they are alone, he tried to hug her, but she pushed him away and yelled for security. The man is held by guards until police arrive. He insisted that he had not touched her and merely inquired about his room number.

When police reviewed the CCTV footage, it showed that he tried to hug her. The defendant pleaded not guilty, and the case was adjourned.

Assault Captured on CCTV

A Jordanian woman entered an elevator at a 5-star resort in Dubai when a 27-year-old man from Afghanistan also walked into the elevator. She explained in court that the man said: "You are such a white person and then he pinched my arm and touched my breast." CCTV captured the incident, but the man denied molestation. The court was adjourned.

Woman Stab's out of Fear

A 28-year-old woman from Uganda said she was so afraid of being sexually assaulted by a security guard, she stabbed him with a knife. She says she blindly stabbed at him then ran. A colleague of the victim, a 27-year-old security guard from Uganda said he went over to the building to visit with his friend.

He entered the building, he saw the accused woman frantically running down the stairs with blood dripping from her hands. The woman is charged with premeditated murder and is awaiting trial.

Motorist Touches Woman's Bottom

A 39-year-old Emirati leaned out of his car window and pinched the bottom of a 28-year-old British woman. She was walking through a mall parking garage and arrived at her car. The woman stood by her vehicle when the Emirati came by, stuck his hand out of the window, and pinched her bottom. She quickly turned and watched him drive away with his hand still out of the window.

The man is ordered by a court to see a "shrink."

Burglar Touches Woman's Bottom

A 33-year-old Indian woman is sleeping in her home when a 28-year-old Indian man broke in. He took $449 and three cell phones. The man entered the woman's bedroom and touched her bottom. She woke up terrified and screaming, and the burglar fled through a kitchen window.

The "next morning", the woman's daughter said she saw a man going through her purse and that's when the woman noticed her money and phones were missing. The man admitted to the police he broke in but denied touching the woman. Police said they will charge him with burglary, but there is not enough evidence to charge him with molestation.

Woman Wakes to Find Intruder Lying next to her

A 31-year-old Uzbek businesswoman woke up at 4am to find a man lying next to her in her villa. A 28-year-old Sri Lankan man is responsible for several sex attacks against women in their own homes, including a British couple where he molested the wife. The businesswoman woke up and sensed someone was in her room and is shocked to see the man in her bed.

He covered her mouth and then climbed on top of her. The woman fought off the attacker and knocked him to the floor. He then got up and escaped out of the kitchen window, but left behind a shoe. The man is arrested near the villa where the incident occurred.

During the investigation, police found that he previously had been convicted of a similar crime. The man confessed and said, "I did it for sexual kicks." He is given 6 months behind bars. Police are investigating an attack on an Asian woman and are looking for links to the Sri Lankan man.

Man Enters Couple's Home

A 27-year-old Bangladeshi man jumped the wall to a Jordanian family's villa. He entered the home to rob them while they slept. He molested the woman, and her husband woke up to her screams. The husband fought the man, but he got away. The man was later caught and arrested and brought before the court. The case was adjourned. No further information.

Man Touches Woman in her Villa

A Russian woman woke up to a 26-year-old Bangladeshi man who had snuck into her bedroom when she slept. The woman's husband had been sleeping in another room since he was ill. The woman felt a hand go up her leg but thought it was her son until the man touched her intimately on the thigh. She turned to look and saw the Bangladeshi on his knees next to her bed, and she screamed.

Her husband came running and ended up calling the police. The police said they had many reports of a man sneaking into villas in the area. The Bangladeshi man is arrested, and police found that he previously had been charged with trespassing.

When he appeared in court he denied the charges but said: "I have been accused of molestation and trespassing in five separate cases your honor." Later on he confessed to entering 14 different villas because he said, "I love touching women's bodies." The man is sentenced to 3 months in jail and will be deported to his home country after serving.

Self Defense

A man broke into a home of a Ugandan woman while she slept. She said she had met the man once. He woke her up and asked her to have sex with him. She refused and went into the kitchen to get a knife and stabbed him to death. She told the judge she did not intend to kill him, but did so in self-defense.

The woman is given a lighter sentence as the court accepted her self-defense plea, and she is jailed for 3 years.

Breaking into homes like the stories you have just read happen pretty frequently. A man broke into the home of our friend and was caught in their bedroom.

Bus Driver Attacks Passenger

A 35-year-old Egyptian city bus driver molested a 32-year-old Filipina telephone operator. There are no other passengers on the bus when she boarded. Once they arrived at her stop, she is still the only passenger on the bus. She tried to get off to go to work asking the driver to open the door and let her out. He said he will in return for a kiss. She refused and began banging on the door.

The driver got out of his seat and touched her rear-end and chest. He insisted that she kiss him. She responded by screaming and threatened to call the police. The driver got scared and opened the door. The man received 1 year behind bars and will be deported back to his home country when the sentence is served.

School Bus Driver Rapes Teacher Assistant

A Pakistani bus driver dropped off the children and teachers after school as usual. A Filipina teacher's assistant is the last person left on the bus. The assistant became suspicious when the driver didn't take her to the building where she lived. Instead, the man took her to a remote area and raped her, and then dropped her off at home.

The woman went to the Filipino Embassy who helped her lodge a complaint with the police department. The bus driver is in custody and will stay there until the hearing. No further information.

Man Grabbed a Woman from the Street to be his Girlfriend

A 27-year-old Pakistani man grabbed a 26-year-old Filipina working as a cashier, from the street. He threw her into the car. The woman was walking back to her apartment just after midnight when the car pulled up, a man got out and dragged her into the backseat. He drove off with the woman screaming for help.

While in the car, he offered her a cup of water that calmed her. He told her he kidnapped her because he liked her. She begged for him to let her go, but he drove for 40 minutes then stopped. He kissed her on the head and then drove her home. A 31-year-old Indian woman saw the man dragging the woman into his car so she quickly wrote down the license plate number and called the police.

The police found him and he was abruptly arrested. The Pakistani man denied the charges, and the court was adjourned. No further information.

Stalker gets Personal Information from a Road Transportation Authority Worker

An Australian man is infatuated with a 36-year-old married Egyptian woman. He retrieved her personal information from a friend who worked for the Road Transportation Authority. The woman was getting a tire fixed at a shop when she received a message on Yahoo Messenger through her BlackBerry phone. It came from someone who said they wanted to get to know her.

She ignored it, but he kept chatting and said: "I hope you get your tires fixed." The woman now became afraid. She left the shop and went straight home, and found a friend request on Facebook from the man. He lied and said he had gotten her information from her license plate. He wanted to know if she was married, and wanted to meet her.

She replied to him and said, "That would cause problems." Messages continued for a week before she finally called the police. Authorities found that a Lebanese Road Transportation Authority employee had gotten the woman's confidential information from a "toll system" and passed it along to his Australian friend.

Both men are out on bail until a verdict is reached.

Unequal Rape Sentences

A Pakistani man had his rape sentence increased to 15 years. While a police officer, who raped a Moroccan girl telling her she is his "fifth victim" and admitting the rapes to the court, is only sentenced to 1 year.

Woman is Stabbed

A 32-year-old Filipino shop assistant is attacked in a busy mall by a 40-year-old Syrian man. The man befriended the woman on Facebook. He followed her around for weeks and threatened to kill her if she didn't have a relationship with him. When he found out where she worked, he repeatedly came to her work place at the mall.

One day he waited outside the mall for her to arrive, and when she did, he attacked her and stabbed her under the chin. She tried to defend herself as he cut up her arms. An Arab man witnessing the attack intervened and restrained the man until security came.

The woman went to seek help from the Philippine Embassy who accompanied her to the hospital and helped her file charges. The Syrian man is in police custody. No further information available.

Kisses at a Play Area

A 29-year-old Pakistani man conned his way into a children's play area at a mall so he could kiss the children. The man lied to security at the door of the play area by saying his family is inside and he wanted to join them.

The guard asked where his ticket was, the man lied, and verbally gave a random number. Security did not check for a wristband since there were too many people waiting in line so he allowed him to enter.

After being inside the play area for 15 minutes, he saw a 9-year-old boy. He grabbed the boy by the neck and tried to kiss him but is unsuccessful. He then spotted a 13-year-old boy and kissed him on the cheek, but the boy pushed him away. One of the boys complained to the guard, and the man was arrested.

In court the man admitted he went to the play area to "kiss children." He denies molestation and the case was adjourned.

Molested by a Salesman

A Pakistani salesman molested a 31-year-old Filipina as he helped her to try on clothes. A security guard at an entertainment attraction told the woman she had to cover up since she is wearing short shorts. He suggested a shop where she could buy something to cover her body. She entered the shop, and the salesman came with a piece of fabric and told her he can show her how to wear it. He then touches her inappropriately.

The man denied the charges, and the case was adjourned.

Birthday Kiss, a No-No

A Jordanian man gave a Russian woman a birthday kiss and now both of them are accused of "public indecency." The two accused are colleagues and work at a hair salon. The man gave the woman a birthday kiss on the cheek that is caught on CCTV. He said: "She is my friend, I didn't hug her, and it was the first time I kissed her on the cheek."

It is their manager who reported them to the police. He is disgruntled at the pair for having lodged a complaint against him with the Ministry of Labor. The duo is acquitted by the court of the "public indecency" charge.

Kissers Claim CPR

A 25-year-old Filipina woman and a 28-year-old Indian man are caught hugging and kissing in a lifeguard tower on the beach. An Emirati woman watched the couple for "50 minutes" before calling the police.

She said: "I saw a man and woman in there. The woman was sitting on the man's lap, and they were hugging and kissing in a sexual position, and she was making sounds like she was having sexual intercourse." The Indian man said: "I was giving her CPR because she was cold."

They both are accused of having an illegal relationship, consuming alcohol and indecency. They have denied charges, but were given 1 year behind bars.

Kissing Couple

A "married" couple had been caught kissing on a beach. The woman said: "A security guard turned us in because of a grudge he had against us." The couple's lawyer said: "They would never have done such a thing in public." A 6 month sentence behind bars is handed to them.

A lower court then ordered the case to be returned to the Appeal Court to be reheard, so they can reconsider the verdict. No further information available.

Jail Sentence Cut for Rape

An Emirati man is convicted of raping a "psychologically disturbed" Iraqi woman, after DNA proved that he sexually abused the woman. The Emirati is given a sentence of 5 years, but the Appeal Court reduced it to 2 years.

Female Shoppers Molested

An Egyptian man is caught by the police at a mall for inappropriately touching women. Police received a call from mall security guards informing them that so many women are "complaining" they are being touched in a sick way by the man. Assaults are caught on CCTV.

The man confessed and said he took advantage of how busy the mall was so he can "bump into them." He has been referred to public prosecution. No further information available.

A Man Rapes Women he Wants to Marry

A 29-year-old Emirati man is on trial for raping women who he wanted to marry. The man drove one woman out to the desert, and tried to rape her. She scratched him as she fought back. He then drove her to her car but is stopped before he got there by the police. They were looking for him in connection to a rape of a different woman.

The Prosecutors told the court that while he had been released on bail, he raped yet another woman. The Emirati denies the charges and said, "I wanted to marry these women." No further information available.

Egyptian Man Assaults Woman

A 33-year-old Egyptian man met with a 26-year-old German event planner. As they talk about his upcoming party, he hugged her and tried to kiss her. She is shocked and pushed him away. He then sent her messages apologizing and said he "could not control himself."

The messages continued as he kept telling her he "loved her." She finally contacted the police to make him stop. The case was adjourned.

A Kiss That Lead to Assault

A woman who is sexually assaulted is on trial for kissing and having an illegal affair. A 36-year-old Emirati policeman met a 25-year-old Indian woman when she asked him for directions to the U.S. Embassy. They chatted for a while, and he asked what her name was. After a week, he called and asked her out.

They went to dinner and a movie. The Emirati had asked the woman to come to his house, since he said, he's tired and needed to rest for an hour before driving her home. Both were in his bedroom and they kissed. He wanted sex, but the woman refused, and he said he will take her home.

Instead, the Emirati drove her out to the desert and asked for sex again.

She refused and tried to get away from him, but the car doors were locked. She cried and begged him to stop, but he threatened to kill her. After raping her he apologized and drove her home. The woman called the police and filed charges.

The policeman was arrested and charged with kidnapping and rape. They "also" arrested the woman and charged her with having an illegal affair, since she kissed him in his bedroom. It is discovered that he had an earlier conviction of kidnapping another woman and having sex with her. He is given a 6 month sentence for an illegal affair, but is acquitted for kidnapping charges. The rape victim didn't appear in court.

This case came just 3 weeks "after" a senior police officer said: "Any woman that is raped in the emirate has to come forward to report it as they have nothing to fear and will not face prosecution."

Facebook Fighting Ends in a Fine

A U.K. woman victimized by a cyber-stalker on Facebook is fined for swearing, in retaliation to his explicit sexual messages toward her. A 35-year-old American software engineer became attracted to the married mother from the U.K. when he saw her profile picture on the site.

He bombarded her inbox on Facebook, asking her to become his "sex slave." His messages became increasingly explicit. She told him to leave her alone and swore at him. She reported him to the police, and they set up a meeting point at a hotel for both of them to meet so the police can arrest him.

In court the woman is found guilty of "insulting behavior" and is fined $544. She left Dubai and said: "I will not return for a very long time after the unfair treatment at the hands of the Dubai courts. I will have a friend pay the fine, and I will make sure I receive all the paperwork saying the case is closed." The American who lodged a complaint accusing the mother of insulting him is given a fine, the amount unknown.

Taxi Sex

A U.K. woman and an Irishman are found guilty of having sex in the backseat of a taxi. They drank at a Friday brunch that continued on until 10:30pm. The driver picked up the couple and saw that the man was still drinking. He told him he can't have alcohol inside the taxi but he drank it anyway, and threw the glass out of the window.

The next thing the driver knew, the woman is on top of the man naked. He said: "She was moving up and down making noises." Pulling over, the taxi driver alerted a parked police officer of what was going on in the backseat of his cab. In court, the officer said: "The woman was sitting naked on top of the man for 4 minutes before I knocked on the window."

The lawyer for the couple said the taxi driver made up the whole story as he tried to blackmail the couple. Both are given 2 months behind bars. The woman sold her story to a British newspaper, and the man was quiet

throughout the case.
Raid on a "Mixed Sex" Home
Six Filipino people sharing an apartment are arrested since four of them are women, and two are men. One man explained that someone turned them in for sharing the apartment [under Sharia law, it is illegal for unmarried people of the opposite sex to live together]. The man said there was no inappropriate behavior between anyone.

All the accused ended up in court and can face up to 1 year in jail and deportation. When they arrived in court, the defendants had their legs chained together, but the chains were removed during the hearing. The women took turns holding a baby [in an unrelated case], which belonged to a Filipina maid who stood before the same judge for unlawful sex. No further information available.

Sorcerer Wanted Sex
A 48-year-old Iraqi man claimed to be a sorcerer and have magical powers. These powers could solve all the problems that women had, but only if they sleep with him. A woman placed an ad in the newspaper saying she is looking for work. The man answered her and said he has a job position open at a department within the government.

She met the man but couldn't believe it when he told her that; he lied about the job. He told her about his magical powers and said he can make any man marry her or control her husband if she is married. When he learned she was married, he told her to bring back materials to him. He wanted 16 pieces of paper, a piece of her husband's clothing, incense and expensive perfume.

He asked her to "have an affair" with him and claimed that sexual relations are very important to make his magic work. The woman turned the man into the police, and he is arrested. The man admitted to the scam and is referred to public prosecution.

Sex Offered from the Trunk of a Car
A man is hiding his female pal who is a prostitute in the trunk of his car. He rode around Dubai trying to "advertise" her. The couple worked as a team, and he said that he brought her to the customers as she rode in the trunk. This is because they didn't want to get caught and no one would suspect them. Unbeknownst to them, someone did see them and called the police.

The officers said they thought that maybe they would find a dead woman in the trunk, but instead she was fully awake with no signs of abuse on her body. The outcome of the court case is unknown.

Raped, but Locked up for Drinking
A British woman is raped, but received a jail sentence for drinking. An Emirati man and a British woman met at a nightclub. The two kissed inside the venue and then got a hotel room together. The man claimed that the

woman initiated the sex, but he changed his mind since he wasn't attracted to her. He took a shower instead while she ended up falling asleep.

The woman told the court she had been so drunk the night before that she couldn't remember anything, but she "knew what she felt." She woke up naked lying next to the Emirati. Neither one showed up for the verdict in court. He is sentenced to 3 months in jail for having sex with the woman who was unconscious, and she is given 1 month in jail because of drinking.

The Emirati is now in custody, and the British woman will have to go to the police station and surrender otherwise, there will be a warrant out for her arrest.

Gang Goes to Prison

Three women and 1 man have been sentenced to jail for human trafficking. The gang told a 27-year-old Uzbek woman they can get her a job at a clothing store in Dubai. When the 27-year-old woman arrived, the gang took her passport away. They told her that her job is not in a clothing store, but she is to become a prostitute.

The clan has been found guilty of luring the woman to Dubai and will each serve 3 years behind bars.

Trafficking

A 33-year-old Filipina woman is pulled to Dubai by a 30-year-old woman when she told her she can work in a hotel. After arriving at the Dubai airport, she is taken to an apartment and told she will have to sleep with men until she paid off her $7,079 debt. This is money spent in getting her to Dubai. The victim escaped and ran to her embassy for help.

The 30-year-old woman ended up getting 5 years behind bars.

Man Saves Trafficking Victim

A man who is pretending to be a customer, is alone in a bedroom with a victim of forced prostitution. He helps her to escape. An 18-year-old Bangladeshi woman is lured to the U.A.E. She had been told she will work as a housemaid in a private home. Instead, when she arrived in Dubai, she found herself locked up in an apartment with another female. Both women are forced to have sex with 20 men a day.

A 27-year-old Nepalese man is walking by when he is approached by a man. The man claimed he had Nepalese prostitutes at a nearby brothel if he wanted to have sex. The man is shocked, but curious and said he wanted to see them. He is taken to the apartment.

After selecting one of the girls, he went into a room with her. When they were alone, she cried, and collapsed in his arms. He calmed her down and promised to help her. He told her she needed to write a letter to the police, and he would deliver it. When he left, he paid the pimp even though he did not have sex with her.

The next day, he returned and picked up the letter from the girl. After receiving it, he went to the local police station and told them what is happening. Armed with this information, the police raided the brothel and arrested the man and woman. The couple is charged with trafficking and running a brothel. The couple denies the charges. No further information available.

Rescued Sex Slave

A 20-year-old Pakistani woman is lured to Dubai and promised a job as a housemaid, but instead is forced into the sex trade. Three days after arriving in the U.A.E. the woman is told by a 38-year-old Pakistani woman she will work as a prostitute. She told her if she did not comply she will be hurt, along with her family, in Pakistan.

The woman often took her to the customers. Occasionally, she is taken to Abu Dhabi [1 hour away], where a man keeps her for 3 days in exchange for $1,088. Afterwards, he drops her off at a bus stop so she can take the bus back to the Pakistani woman's place.

A man found her at the bus stop crying and asked her if she needed help. She told him her whole story. The man then accompanied her to the police station. The court case was adjourned.

Killers Executed

A Bangladeshi man is murdered by 3 Bangladeshi pimps for helping a prostitute escape. The man also helped several runaway maids break free from bad situations. He is brutally beaten and strangled in his home by the Bangladeshi pimps furious at him for helping the prostitute getaway. Two of them grabbed him from behind, tied his feet and legs together, and the third man beat him with a steel pipe. They finished him off by strangling him with a rope.

The court said the case fell under Sharia law and rejected a claim that said the men did not have "adequate Arabic translation." But, a signed statement from their translator showed the men did receive adequate help in translation. The 3 Bangladeshi men received the death penalty.

Victim Arrested After Making a Complaint

A 20-year-old Moroccan woman is arrested for prostitution when she went to the police for help. She claimed she is a victim of human trafficking, and forced into prostitution. The woman said she was lured into the U.A.E. by a Syrian man and his wife who promised her a good job. When she arrived, she is taken to several apartments, islands and farms where she is forced to sleep with men.

She explained to the court that often, she is forced to do sexual acts with the Syrian's wife while men watched. She said she is forced to sleep in the same room with the man's wife, because they are afraid she will run away. Sometimes they allowed her to call her family back home, but they monitored her conversations so she doesn't tell them anything.

Once she escaped from the apartment and went straight to the local police station, but they sent her away saying she had no evidence to prove her claims. The woman went back to the police station a second time pleading for help. Police detained her, and "charged her with prostitution."

In court the Moroccan woman repeated her claim about the Syrian couple. She said they forced her into having sex with men against her will, and she had not been paid any money. The judge became confused when he looked into the records of the Syrian couple. He found they were charged and convicted back in 2009 for human trafficking and are supposed to be in jail. He is to serve a 7 year prison term, and the woman should be serving a 5 year prison term.

The judge cannot understand why they are free. The case was adjourned to figure out why the couple are not in prison.

A Maid Kidnapped and Forced into the Sex Trade

A 25-year-old Bangladeshi housemaid and her colleague are kidnapped from the street when they went to take out the trash. The maid said the two of them were dragged into a car by two Bangladeshi men and taken to an apartment where they were held for 2 weeks. A Bangladeshi woman who is in charge at the apartment told them they had to work as prostitutes.

They were always locked up in their rooms, but given food and something to drink. The Bangladeshi "madam" assaults them when they refuse to sell themselves.

One maid thought about escaping but said it is difficult since the apartment is on the 12th-floor. She said she stood by an open window crying, she began arguing with the "madam." Suddenly the woman pushed her out of the window, but the maid grabbed on to a cable from a cradle used for cleaning windows. She was able to lower herself down. A security guard at the building found her on the ground bleeding, and he called the police.

She was taken to a hospital where they gave her medical treatment. She suffered from a broken leg, and injuries to her hands and face. A 41-year-old Bangladeshi man is accused of locking her in the apartment, and he did not appear in court. The Bangladeshi woman is accused of pushing her out of a window. No further information.

A Female Gang Lures Job Seekers

A group of 4 women from the Philippians are promising women jobs via Facebook. When the women answer, they find themselves forced into the sex trade when arriving in Dubai. A 25-year-old Filipina became friends with a 24-year-old "madam" on Facebook. The Filipina woman is told it is not a problem to arrange a job for her at a cleaning company in Dubai. She is provided a telephone number of a representative in the Philippines and instructed to call the guy, and he will make the arrangements.

The woman met the representative and paid him cash for a passport, visa and her travel to Dubai. She added that in the beginning they were nice to her, but suddenly they took her to an apartment, and said she will now be a "sex worker." She was frightened and refused, but they assaulted her.

They forced her into becoming a prostitute. The 4 women are on trial. No further information available.

10 Years for Human Trafficking

A 17-year-old girl is lured into the U.A.E. on a promise she will work as a maid. The girl's father told her he had made arrangements, and she is going to Dubai to work. When she arrived in Dubai, she is taken to a 1 bedroom apartment and locked up for several days. One day she is escorted to another apartment where a 42-year-old Bangladeshi man in a wheelchair raped her to prepare her for prostitution. During the taxi ride back, she jumped out and ran screaming toward a crowd of people.

The police raided the apartment and found another Bangladeshi woman, who was forced into prostitution. They found a 28-year-old Bangladeshi man, who is a partner of the man in the wheelchair.

Both Bangladeshi men are sentenced to 10 years in jail and then will be deported after serving their sentence.

Female Pimps

Two Chinese women lured 3 women from their home country to work in a message parlor. The women believed they were working for a legitimate company, but after 1 month they are forced into the sex trade. One woman refused to have sex with the men that her captors brought to her. She is threatened with physical violence. The women are forced to work 16 hours a day performing messages and sex acts for their clients.

A customer helped one victim escape and took her to the police station. She then took the police back to the message parlor where they found the other two women. The victims told police they did not pay them and said, "We worked for food."

Both women will stand trial, along with the son of one defendant, who cannot be found. No further information available.

Lifeguard Ripped off by Prostitute

A Sri Lankan lifeguard had $1,361 stolen from him, and now he is jobless. The lifeguard was drinking in a hotel bar with a woman who he believes was a prostitute. She followed the lifeguard to an ATM, talking to him while he is taking money out. She could see his pin number, then stole his money and card from him and used it several times that night.

He claimed it happened so fast she had to be a professional. The man is fired from his job the next day from a 5-star resort when they caught him sleeping in the changing room by the pool. He says he was up the entire night trying to find the woman to get his money back. He said: "That is still no excuse for falling asleep on the job."

The man went to the bank to ask if he can look at the ATM CCTV footage but is told the order has to come from the police. The outcome is unknown.

DUBAI, 1 CITY 2 DIFFERENT TALES

Women Sold

Two Bangladeshi women living in Abu Dhabi, are sold by 5 Indonesian men to their colleagues. They are sold for $680 and will work as prostitutes in Dubai. The victims ran away and sought refuge with other women they knew in Dubai. The men then went to the house where they stayed and forced them into the car. One victim called the Dubai police, and the men are arrested but deny human trafficking. No further information available.

Sex Ring Smashed

A gang of pimps are forcing housemaids they find walking down the street to become prostitutes. Five Emirati men are posing as police officers and stopping women. They tell them they have to go to the police station, but instead drive them to a brothel. If the girls did not do as they are told, the men threatened them with knives and swords.

The police raided an apartment after a witness reported seeing a kidnapping. When they arrived, 3 men tried to escape from a window, but are arrested. They found 2 girls from India, and 2 girls from Bangladesh in the apartment. The police also found drugs and alcohol. No other information available.

The incident came just weeks after the police warned the public not to fall victim to people posing as police officers.

Home used as a Brothel

A Chinese woman was running a brothel inside her apartment. She is given a 3 year sentence and a $272 fine. Police seized money and alcohol from the woman. Two other women are jailed for prostitution.

Brothel Worker Runs

Seventeen people are arrested in a raid on a brothel. One prostitute climbed out of a window and is on the run. But, it is believed that she does not have her passport. The group arrested are from China, Turkmenistan and Uzbekistan. A man who worked in "administration" within the brothel and 2 clients are also arrested. They all appeared in court where the women wept, asking for "mercy." No further information available.

Man Accused of Rape, but lawyer Says it was Made-up

A man is accused of raping a Russian woman. His defense lawyer said: "It is very common for Russian women to come to the U.A.E. and make claims of rape to get money in exchange for dropping the claim."

The 28-year-old Russian woman met the Egyptian man online. She had invited him to her apartment to talk business. Instead, the defense lawyer claims she locked him inside her apartment when he refused to have sex with her. He called the police before breaking down her door trying to escape. CCTV shows footage of the man being chased by the naked woman outside of her apartment. She was trying to pull him out of the elevator.

A verdict has not yet been reached.

Rape in the Desert

A 23-year-old Arab man and an 18-year-old Arab boy have both been sentenced to prison. They are caught beating up an Asian woman, and sexually assaulting her in the desert. The two saw the woman on the street when she waited for a taxi one evening after work. She said: "The man sprayed something in my eyes and they dragged me into their car." They drove her to the desert, and beat her until she was unconscious. They each raped her, and took her money and cell phone.

The 2 men are arrested when their semen is found on the woman's body. They are convicted of kidnap, assault, rape, robbery and endangering the woman's life. The 23-year-old Arab man received 28 years in prison and the 18-year-old Arab boy received 10 years.

Massage Turned into Sex Attack

A 40-year-old Egyptian man who worked at a business that supplies massage equipment, is accused of raping a 29-year-old Filipina woman. The employee invited the woman to his office for a "demonstration" of new equipment. The woman worked near his office so she went to see the machines. When he explained how to use them, he started to massage her shoulders. The man then ripped off her clothes and raped her. She told the guard in the building who then called the police. The case was adjourned.

Serial Rapist

A 29-year-old Emirati man using WhatsApp lured women to him, so he can rape them. The man enticed a 24-year-old Emirati woman by saying he sent her a message by mistake, and then called her. He told her he is divorced, and used a fake name. Their relationship developed into love and he said that he wants to marry her, they decided to meet.

He wanted to show her his family farm, so they drove out to the desert. The Emirati suddenly stopped the car, and touched the woman. He took her clothes off and raped her. She felt dizzy and in pain. Afterwards he dropped her off at the original meeting place. She was so afraid to tell her family or anyone about the rape that, she kept it a secret for 3 months.

He is accused of raping two other women in two separate cases that "same" night. The Emirati denied the charges, but was convicted. He contacted the woman's mother while behind bars and asked for forgiveness, saying he will marry her daughter. No further information available.

Gang Rape

Two men are given 10 years in jail for raping a 28-year-old British woman when they lured her from a taxi cab while she was drunk. The woman had been drinking at a club when she caught a taxi home. She fell asleep in the backseat, but suddenly woke up and told the 37-year-old Pakistani driver to change the destination. She said she needed to stop at an ATM. The driver took her to the nearest ATM, but she returned with no money. A car pulled up with 3 Iranian men in it, and they told the driver they know who she is, and they will take her home. The men then paid the driver, and brought the woman to their car, and drove her to an apartment where they raped her. The next morning the woman was in severe pain and bleeding. She couldn't remember what happened the previous night.

Two of the defendants showed up in court with the third still being on the run. They denied the charges, and said she made up the story. Their attorney said, "She watches a lot of action stories." The court did not believe the defendants and sentenced them to 10 years in jail.

Bus Driver Jailed

A 26-year-old Pakistani bus driver raped a mentally disabled passenger in her 20s on his bus as she traveled home from a special needs club. The sexual assault took place in front of a female supervisor on the bus. She was there to look after the passengers. The driver was given 5 years in prison, and it is not known if charges were filed against the supervisor.

Rape Case Sentence Cut

A 27-year-old Indonesian male flight attendant raped his 28-year-old Filipina female friend. The two had been friends for a very long time. She even knew the man's girlfriend. The flight attendant asked his friend to come to his apartment for a drink, and he took off her clothes and raped her.

The man is given a sentence of 2 years behind bars, but the Appeal Court slashed it to 6 months.

Man Dubbed the "Woman Hunter"

A 30-year-old Egyptian man that attacked 5 women in an elevator has been called the "Woman Hunter." The man waited by elevators for Asian women between the ages of 26 and 30-years-old. He then force them into the stairways with a knife. One woman said: "He beat me up and tried to strangle me before raping me." DNA found traces of semen on her body.

Residents of an apartment complex woke up at 4am to screams and knocking sounds. They alerted the building security guard, and he found a woman lying on a bathroom floor with a cut on her forehead, and her underwear torn. Police believe this may have been the same man.

The Egyptian received a 10 year sentence, but a higher court has imprisoned him to 25 years.

Duo in Rape Case

An Emirati man, and a Yemeni man pulled a woman from the street and tried to rape her. The woman admitted to being a prostitute, and agreed to have sex with the two men. When she asked to be paid, they sprayed perfume in her eyes, threw her in their vehicle and drove to a remote location. They beat her up and then tried to rape her. The case was adjourned.

4 Men Attacked Victim

Four Arab men broke into a home of an Arab woman while she slept, and raped her. The woman was alone in the house, and the men over powered her as she tried to fight back. They beat her up, stripped off her clothes and raped her one after another until she fell unconscious. Then they took off running.

She identified the men from a police lineup. All of the men denied the charges and said that the woman is making it up. DNA confirmed that the woman had been raped. The case was adjourned.

Fake Cop

A 60-year-old Emirati man posed as a policeman in Abu Dhabi. He grabbed a 33-year-old Ethiopian housemaid from the street while she shopped. The man was driving along the road when he saw her. He stopped his car, and asked to see her passport and then dragged her into his vehicle. He took her to a remote area, ripped off her clothes and raped her inside of his car.

The man "claimed" she had agreed to have sex with him, and the court sided with him. The Emirati is jailed for having illegal sex with the housemaid. Her punishment is not made known. Just the day before, the court "dropped" other charges against the Emirati for "raping" his 2 housemaids. They had said there is not enough evidence that his Indonesian maid, and Filipino maid had been raped, or sexually abused.

Not Guilty of Rape

A 24-year-old Emirati man asked a 29-year-old Emirati woman to marry him. She rejected the proposal and married someone else. The man became angry and kidnapped the woman. He drove her to a hotel and raped her. The Emirati is charged with kidnapping and rape, but did not show up in court. He is given a 15 year jail sentence.

The Appeal Court squashed the sentence, and said it is only an illegal affair. They said, "The woman consented to sex." The sentence for the illegal affair is unknown.

Tourist Rapes

A 25-year-old Syrian visitor raped a 30-year-old Maldivian woman at the apartment where he was staying. The two met at a nightclub, and she danced with the man. She then left the club, and got into a cab when he chased after her and jumped in. He told her the apartment he is staying at is near where she lived and asked if she wanted to come over. She told him yes.

When she walked in, she saw men playing cards. He then dragged her to his bedroom and raped her. The man pleaded not guilty and claims the woman agreed to have sex with him. No further information available.

Lawyer Removes Himself from Rape Case

A father is accused of raping his own daughter and his Arab lawyer has stepped away from the case. The lawyer said: "I will not defend a person who commits such a horrific crime." A 48-year-old Asian man raped his 16-year-old daughter twice. First was in their home country, and the second time in the U.A.E.

The Asian man confessed to the rape, but said he is "unaware" of his actions. His lawyer was shocked at his confession and was adamant about not representing him. He said, "This is alien to the Muslim society." The Asian is given 25 years in jail. The man plans to appeal when he can find another lawyer.

2 Men Rape a Housemaid

An Asian maid is assigned by her supervisor to clean the house of two Arab men. She is raped by both of them. The maid said: "They beat me up and then tore my clothes off, raping me one after another, and then threw me out of the house." The men said they knew the woman, and they paid her for consensual sex. A medical exam was done which confirmed intercourse. The case was adjourned. No further information available.

In many of these rape cases, the men are continually saying that sex was consensual. If that were the case, would they be in court?

Woman Accused of Adultery

A Russian woman claims 4 Emirati men kidnapped her, and raped her in the desert. The woman met with her friend [one of the accused] at a hotel. She is then forced into a car where the three other men are waiting. They beat her up, took her cell phone and tied her hands as she tried to fight them. They raped her one after the other until she fell unconscious in the backseat of the car.

The friend said he met her at the hotel, and she agreed to have sex with him. She did not ask for money, but he gave her $190. A medical exam had showed no signs of rape and no bruises on her body. There was no evidence that showed she was tied up either. The court was adjourned.

Husband's Secret Life

An Arab man in his 50s, married a second wife in secrecy and had a child without the first wife knowing. His first Arab wife is married to the man for 30 years, and they had 3 children now over the age of 25-years-old. She said he had not slept with her for a long time and said he can no longer father anymore children. She was shocked when she learned of his second wife [of a different nationality] and son.

The first wife, and her three children are in court trying to deny the "love child's" rights to the Arab man's inheritance when he dies. He admitted to having a son now over 5-years-old. He said he was afraid to tell his first family because he thought they would be angry at him. The court counseled the couple and settled their issues. No legal action is taken. By law, a local Emirati may have up to 4 wives.

Man Blows $2,177,987 on Luxury Goods for Fiancée

An Emirati man in his late 20s borrowed $2,177,987. Wanting to "impress" his bride-to-be, he tried giving her a lavish lifestyle. He bought her jewelry, a luxurious car and gave her large amounts of cash. He even as much as sent wads of money to her family who are overseas.

The man is engaged to the Arab woman who has very expensive taste. Realizing that his salary is not enough to keep up with what she wanted, he borrowed money from friends and gave them post-dated checks. He told them that the money is for different startup businesses, and they will get a part of the profits. He also took out bank loans.

It finally caught up with him when he couldn't pay any of it back so complaints were filed against him.

The Emirati is serving time behind bars. No further information.

Secret Wife gets $272,245

A man married his second wife in secrecy, but it only lasted a few days. She wanted a divorce and demanded he gives her what he promised before they married. The man is bored in his first marriage and fell in love with a younger woman. She demanded to get married or she would stop seeing him. The man did not want to lose the woman and married her overseas so his first wife wouldn't find out.

The second wife is upset because he is living with his first wife and children, so she demanded financial security. He agreed to buy her a brand new car, an apartment and gave her a check for $272,245 to be cashed if they are ever to divorce. She ultimately decided to call the first wife to tell her all about their marriage.

Her husband was furious at her over the phone call she made, and refused to give her what he had promised. She took him to court where he said he only wanted her as a "girlfriend." The judge said there is a clear agreement between the man and second wife. He is forced to buy her a new car, an apartment and give her a check worth $272,245.

Jealous Lover

An Arab man sent photos of his ex-girlfriend to her husband. In the letter he claimed he is in love with her. This led to the couple getting a divorce. The woman met the man on the internet before she married, and they had a relationship. She ended it simply because they are from different nationalities, and her family would never approve of a marriage between them. The angry man decided he was going to destroy her marriage. The court fined the Arab man $1,361.

Traits that U.A.E. Men Look for in a Wife:

Today	15 Years Ago
Physical Appearance:	
60%	19%
Desirable Features:	
slim, tall	high morals, wise, good family
Employment:	
preferably employed	must not be employed

Police get Love Child

A 35-year-old Sri Lankan man is raising his 5-year-old daughter on his own. The child's mother was deported back to the Philippines after she is caught being in the U.A.E. illegally. He asked his 35-year-old Sri Lankan neighbor who is a friend, to take care of the child since he's going to jail for check fraud. He wants her to go to the Sri Lankan Consulate to get an ID for his daughter. The intent is to send the child back to her mother in the Philippines.

The friend is unable to do anything since the girl is not registered, and has no birth certificate. She cared for the girl for 20 days, but can't afford to feed and keep her anymore so she took her to the police station. The Sri Lankan man claimed he is married, but the mother took the marriage certificate with her when she was deported. He said he is in the country illegally so he can't get an ID for his child.

Since the man can't produce marriage documents, he pleaded guilty to the affair. He is given 1 more year in jail for an illegal affair on top of his check fraud sentence [unknown], and a fine of $816. When his jail sentence is served, he will be deported back to Sri Lanka. Even though the mother is not present, she is given a 1 year jail sentence.

The child is staying at the Women and Children's Center next to the jail where her father is serving time. The public prosecutor's office is helping in trying to get the girl a passport.

Trial Interrupted for a Marriage Proposal

A 37-year-old Emirati man proposed to his 29-year-old pregnant Filipina girlfriend in court. This happened before being charged with having an illegal affair. Police went to the Emirati's apartment when they thought he had been involved in a robbery and kidnapping case. They found the Emirati man with a Filipina housemaid who ran away from her boss, and is now in the country illegally.

She told a court that when she met the man, their relationship grew. She told how they had sex inside his car many times, and for several months before she became pregnant. They were referred to prosecution for an illegal affair when the Emirati asked the judge if he can make a marriage proposal. The judge "smiled," and allowed him to propose to her, and she accepted. People in the court room "beamed."

He asked the judge if he can give her $54 for expenses while he is in custody, and the judge granted it. No further information is available.

Contraception Delivery Stopped

A company launched an online service called "SOS Condom." It is claimed that the U.A.E. is the only place in the world where you can click on the mobile app, place an order and have a condom delivered to your home. They pride themselves on being very discreet and professional. Also claiming the delivery men will come dressed as a pizza delivery boy, a lost tourist or a policeman.

The advertisement on YouTube featured unmarried couples in intimate positions and had attracted 705,200 hits. The company that delivered condoms to your door is stopped after being in business for just one week. A U.A.E. cultural expert said: "The company encouraged promiscuity. The service was totally inappropriate, and to promote such a sin is more sinful than the sinner. It is damaging to a younger generation." Before being shut down, one resident said: "Ironic that it's available in one of the places in the world where one can go to jail for premarital sex."

Forced to Wed

An Emirati man, and a Moroccan woman are charged with having an illegal affair. The couple is given a choice to get married or face punishment. Eventually the judge himself decided and "ordered" them to marry. The woman went to the police, even though she was 8-months pregnant to complain about her boyfriend refusing to marry her.

The couple ended up in court, and the Emirati is shown documents that linked him to the affair, such as love letters he sent the woman. After the judge ordered them to marry, the couple agreed. He asked to be released from jail, so he can go to the marriage department, and sign the "marriage contract."

The judge agreed and told the prosecutors and police to quickly speed things up, so the couple can be married. His family present in the court room, are delighted with their decision. A verdict was issued banning the Moroccan woman from leaving the country until they are married.

Ex-Wife Demands Money

A woman filed a lawsuit against her ex-husband after they divorced, claiming she is mistreated by him. The ex-husband is ordered to pay her $24,504 towards furniture and jewelry she bought him during their marriage.

She asked to be paid an additional $54,454 to cover the expenses for their wedding, other furnishings for their home and money she gave him. That claim has been rejected.

Wife Abuse

A 55-year-old Emirati woman filed for divorce against her 60-year-old husband. She claims he beat her up and has assaulted and insulted her in front of her family for many years. She said: "He stopped supporting the family and no longer pays the rent." The woman is demanding $2,722 a month in alimony. No further information is available.

Wife Sends Husband too Many Text Messages

A 29-year-old Egyptian man met a 33-year-old Filipina woman on Facebook, and they got married in the Philippians. When the husband complained to the Dubai police that his wife is sending him too many text messages after midnight, they didn't believe him. The police arrested the couple and accused them of having an illegal affair.

The duo ended up in court where they are charged with having sex out of wedlock, which resulted in the couple having a young child together. But, they presented a marriage certificate from the Philippians while in court.

The man explained that they settled in Dubai. When his wife became pregnant, she went back to the Philippians without telling him she is pregnant. She gave birth to a baby boy. She then returned to Dubai informing him she had given birth, and the baby is his. He wasn't entirely sure that it was, until he saw the baby and said, "He looks like me."

The baby is then registered under his name at the Philippian Consulate in Dubai. The woman told the court that there had been financial problems in their marriage. She told how her husband used her bank card to withdraw $1,361 and he used her car while she was away in the Philippians. He had racked up $1,306 in traffic fines. She is now left to pay the fines since the car is registered in her name.

The court acquitted the couple of having an illicit affair. No further information is available.

Nude Photos

A married Arab woman is accused of posting nude photos of herself on a pornographic site. She is arrested after her husband turned her into the police. She claimed that her husband who took the photos of her, posted them to frame her. The woman is sentenced to 3 months in jail.

Uncle Tries to stop his Niece's wedding

An Arab family is split over the family fortune. An uncle who is the legal guardian over his niece tries to stop her from getting married. After her father died, the woman lived with her grandfather. Her grandfather had shares in his son's property, and access to his son's money. When he passed away the grandfather willed the fortune to his granddaughter.

The uncle then became the legal guardian over his niece [per Sharia law]. He refused to give permission for his niece to marry because he is furious that her grandfather left the fortune to her and not him. He said she took advantage of his age and mental status, by making him sign documents handing everything over to her.

He stood his ground, but the niece took him to court over the marriage. The court ruled in favor of the woman and said she can marry the man of her choice.

Divorced by Phone

A 20-year-old Emirati woman's marriage ended in just 3 days. Her Emirati husband slept at a relative's home on their wedding night. He returned to his new bride three days later and apologized. Later in the day, he called her and said that he divorced her. He didn't give a reason, other than he didn't want to be unfair to her.

She is suing her ex-husband for a monthly allowance, and a "divorce dowry" of $8,167. She wants to know the real reason he divorced her. The case was adjourned. No further information available.

Teacher Forges Documents

A couple from Yemen married when she was just 14-years-old. They wed in their home country of Yemen back in 1999. Her husband, who doesn't have a job, said: "The next thing I knew, she was divorcing me." She presented to the court documents saying he had to pay $2,349 if they are ever to be divorced. Her husband told the court the document is fake.

Police sent the papers to a forensic lab that showed they were forged. The teacher denied the charges of forgery and said: "I was 14-years-old when my father forced me to marry him, and I didn't know what to do." The court found that she had changed the divorce payment from $469 to $2,349. The case was adjourned.

Stalked for a Marriage Proposal

A 29-year-old Filipina is being threatened by her 26-year-old Nepalese friend for not marrying him. The man became upset when the woman refused his marriage proposal so he followed her around. He threatened her twice with a knife, grabbed her by the neck and said he will kill her if she didn't sleep with him. Both times the man had been drinking.

In court the Nepalese denied the charges, but admitted to drinking. The court will give a verdict at a later date.

Who Cares if you are Married or not?

A woman says she doesn't understand the obsession on whether a person is married or not. She says that people in Dubai try to set her up all the time with a future husband. Everyone is asking about her marital status, from the lady at the spa, bartenders, taxi drivers to waitresses.

She said: "People want to know within 2 minutes of meeting them what my marital status is. When I tell them I'm not married, they want to know why not, and is there a problem? People in Dubai assume that there is something wrong with you if you are not married. You must be miserable without a man in your life, as if it's their place to tell you." She also said: "As much as people complain about their children's problems and spouses, do I really need to sign up for the same suffering? Is this a case of misery loves company?"

Another woman has said that she too gets asked if she is married. She said: "It's normal in Dubai for people to be nosey. They have no problem telling a perfect stranger what's on their mind. I have even been asked in job interviews why I'm not married at my age. It is also incomprehensible to people in the country that a woman can go out by herself alone and not have a male accompany her, or be with a male friend and not be married."

Husband Threatens to Kill Wife via Facebook

A 29-year-old Egyptian wife found death threats from her 33-year-old Egyptian husband on her Facebook page. The two had been married for 5 years and have a daughter together. They were having problems in their marriage. She wanted to divorce him as he often beat her. She left Dubai to have a surgical procedure done. When she returned 3 months later, she didn't tell her husband she was back.

She went onto Facebook and is surprised to see all the threats on her timeline. He said: "I will kill you and my last resolution with you is putting an end to your life. I swear by my father that I will put an end for your life [sic]. This is it…..nothing will calm me down just killing you." The court prosecutor arranged a meeting between the two, but she said she will never forgive him and wanted the case to go to court.

The husband denied the death threat, and the case was adjourned.

Divorce over Disability

A woman went to court to get a divorce when she said her husband, who is physically disabled, can no longer have sex with her. She said: "He suffers from an illness that affected his sexual organs, and he can no longer please me." The court granted the divorce. The judge ordered the man to pay legal expenses. He appealed, but the Appeals Court upheld the original verdict.

The Appeal Court ruled that the woman needed to pay back the man's dowry of $46,283. She appealed the dowry ruling through the court that had originally granted her the divorce, and they dismissed the payback of the dowry.

A Bride gets Cold Feet

An Arab woman is ordered to pay back gifts, and a dowry that is given by her fiancé when she backed out of the marriage. The guy's father handed over $12,251 to the woman's family [per Islamic law], along with jewelry worth $1,203 to the bride-to-be. She then backed out and decided not to marry the man, but refused to give the dowry back.

A court ordered her and her family to give everything back to the ex-fiancé. The woman's father is appealing the verdict. No further information available.

Wife Attacked

A 37-year-old Tajikistani businessman tried to kill his 18-year-old wife over a "potential rumor." The woman arrived home with their newborn baby and asked her husband how his day at work went. He said: "It is not your business" and punched her while she held the baby.

She couldn't understand why he had done this, but he continued to beat her. He then called his friend to tell him what he did. She heard the friend talking to her husband. He said, "She has relationships with strangers." The husband then threw her off a 2nd-floor balcony and tried to kill her.

The businessman is jailed for 3 years for trying to kill his wife.

Accused of Kidnapping

An Arab man in his early 20s kidnapped his girlfriend after her parents told him he can't marry their daughter. The couple knew each other since childhood and the man is friends with her brothers. A few years ago, he proposed marriage to her. The family was pleased. But, he is told by her parents he needed to get a job before he can marry her.

The young man could not find work so the family of his fiancée said no marriage. One day the mother and daughter drove to a shop together. The daughter stayed in the car and waited for her mother to come out. When the jilted ex-fiancé saw her sitting there in the car alone, he became enraged and snapped.

He jumped into the car and took off driving with her in it. She yelled at him and tried to jump out, but he grabbed her arm. He pulled her back into the car leaving bruises on her. The woman's brother saw what happened and told his mother, who then called the police. Her mother phoned the ex-fiancé and tried to talk to him. He refused to let her go unless they marry at once. She was able to escape 2 hours later.

He denied the assault, and kidnapping charges. The Emirati is cleared of kidnapping and assault charges since the court said that there isn't enough evidence.

Husband Watched and Smiled at Wife's Abuse

A Yemeni man watched his Pakistani friend rape his wife. The husband, and his friend had been drinking one night. The woman's husband asked her to have sex with his friend. He threatened to kill her if she didn't. She is then attacked by the Pakistani friend, while her husband sat in a chair, smoking and smiling as she is being raped.

Afterwards, both men had sex with each other. The husband and his friend are given 3 years behind bars for the rape, 80 lashes each for drinking alcohol, and 1 more year for sodomy.

Blackmail

A 24-year-old Emirati man promised to marry a 25-year-old woman. The man asked the woman to send him a photo of herself so he can show his mother. When she sent him photos, he backed out of the marriage. A week went by, and he told the woman that his mother will not allow him to marry her. She then asked him to delete the photos she sent him. He told her if she paid him $408, and she agreed to it. After she paid him, he asked for more money.

She took him to court, but he denied the blackmail charges. The case is adjourned.

Kissing Cousins

Emirati cousins are accused of having an illicit relationship after one of them is reported hosting sex parties at her villa. The police went to the villa, and the man admitted having a 5 year sexual relationship with his cousin. But, the two denied the illegal affair in court and are cleared.

Wife Abuses Husband

An Arab husband took his wife to court for abuse. He begged the court to stop her from attacking him, abusing the children and to make her obey him. The man has been married to her for 10 years after separating from his first wife. He has 3 children with her, and 2 children with his ex-wife.

In court, he said his wife mistreats the stepchildren and swears at them. She even has the nerve to come to where he works, and insults him in front of his co-workers. She also accuses him of being an adulterer. He said: "She is always beating me up at home too."

The man doesn't want to divorce the woman because he wants his children to grow up with their mom. He said: "My big fear is that if I separate from her, and marry another woman, the 3 children I have with my current wife might go through the same situation with my new wife, as my 2 daughters did with my current wife [sic]."

The man said he quickly got married after divorcing his first wife because he urgently needed a woman to help him take care of his two daughters. He wants to go back to his home country, but his wife refuses to go.

The woman denied the abuse. The judge had marriage officials counsel the couple and advised them to settle their differences. The husband withdrew the complaint.

Wife Beat for Cash

A Bangladeshi woman refused to give her Pakistani husband $5,445 to get a divorce, so he beat her. The woman said: "The first year of our marriage was good, but then he became increasingly hostile." She wants him arrested for beating her. The woman told the court that her husband waited until she left her work at a cleaning company and then jumped on top of her and severely pummeled her. She said the beating is not the first time, in the past he has done it several times. The man travels in and out of the country for work and she thinks he is in another relationship.

He will not give her a divorce until she gives him the money to pay for it. She doesn't have any money since her salary is not good. The woman said her friends are telling her she doesn't have to pay him money to get a divorce. They told her she can get the divorce for free.

No verdict is announced.

Wife Killed

A 47-year-old Iraqi man killed his 30-year-old Iraqi wife because he said their marriage is in a world of trouble. The man turned himself in for murder and admitted to killing his wife. He said they had a heated argument which is nothing new for them. They never saw eye to eye throughout their marriage. The couple has 3 children. Two daughters age 13 and 16-years-old, and a 21-year-old son.

The son walked into the home and found his mother lying on the bedroom floor in a pool of blood. She was dead from several stab wounds and multiple bruises. The case is adjourned.

Lovers Jailed

A 34-year-old Emirati woman, and her 27-year-old "stateless" relative both have the AIDS virus. They are behind bars for an illegal affair. The woman, and her estranged husband were having marriage problems. They separated for a year. He had a hard time dealing with her, so he hung himself at his parent's house.

One day the woman called the police to report a burglary in her home. Police took fingerprints around the house. They found that the prints belonged to her male relative. When confronted by police, the relative confessed to having an "illegal affair" with her. He said the last time he had sex with her was 5 months before her husband committed suicide. A medical exam showed traces of semen on the woman.

The 2 relatives will each serve 1 year in jail for having an illegal affair with a relative.

Interesting how a medical examination is done on the woman since police are called for a burglary, and not a rape case.

Honor Killings

A journalist, feminist and human rights activist named Rana Husseini broke the silence against honor killings, and crime. This was done in her home country of Jordan. She has become one of the major voices on this issue in the Middle East. When she first spoke out, she said she received death threats and claims she is anti-Islamic. She has advocated that violence against women has no foundation in any religion. Rana said:

> Honor killings usually happen when the family wants to save their family name, or they don't want to be disgraced when a family member has been raped or involved in illicit sexual activity. The family will sacrifice the female. In most cases, the killer is usually a male member, but some of the mothers have been found to be the perpetrators. A case that happened in the 90's was of a 16-year-old girl who became pregnant by her brother. The family married her off to a much older man who ended up divorcing her. The day the divorce became final, a different brother killed her. A daughter was in a relationship and was killed with an axe in her sleep by her mother. The mother received only 1 year in jail. A Pakistani girl had asked for a divorce from her abusive husband. The mother planned a trip with her and had conspired with the driver to kill her. An estimated 5,000 women around the world are affected by honor killings.

Emirati Buys an Indian Girl

A 47-year-old Emirati man traveled to India to buy an 18-year-old Indian bride. She was to serve as his housemaid in Dubai. The man quickly wanted to marry the girl in India. He told the Indian officers when they became suspicious, that she is 21-years-old. She was only 18-years-old at the time. Police questioned her and she told them the Emirati said: "It is normal for women to marry their employers."

She said she had a sister living in Dubai and was told she has to get married. The sister said the large sum of money the Emirati man will pay helps them since they are very poor. The Emirati already had given the girl's family a car and a house. Both are in custody for illegal marriage and fraud. If convicted, he will get deported, and face a lifetime travel ban to India. The girl will face months in jail.

A strict law is in effect in India making the age 21-years-old to marry. Marriage is forbidden based on cash and influence.

Mannequins need to Cover up

In Mumbai, India the Municipal Council is trying to get a handle on rape. The council thinks store mannequins have a lot to do with assaults. They said: "The mannequins displaying lingerie, and skimpy clothes could provoke men to attack, as they are a replica of a woman's body. Mannequins are also degrading to women, and it is not in the Indian culture."

The shop owners are banned from putting the scantily clad mannequins outside of their shops or windows. But, they can still display them how they want to inside their stores. Business owners in Mumbai are opposed to removing the mannequins. They say it will have no impact on violence against women.

CHAPTER 7
OH DEAR!

Many people in the U.A.E. truly believe in witchcraft, sorcery and special powers. There are con artists lurking around every corner trying to swindle and deceive people. These hustlers are trying to get their victims to hand over huge amounts of cash as they prey on their emotions. The innocent are hoping to receive a better life, or perhaps a solution to a problem they may be experiencing. These barracudas often are looking for sex too as they prey on the innocent..

Some of the stories in this chapter revolve around bizarre crimes, and assaults by different individuals of various nationalities. As you read them, you immediately discover that friends are not always friends, since they constantly appear to battle it out and murder each other. Often, the gruesome violence towards one another is over financial disputes. As the saying goes, with friends like these, who needs enemies?

Here, a businessman was at his office typing when an Iranian man arrived. He struck him over the head with a screwdriver then tried to stab him with a knife. This followed a financial dispute. Once again, the sentencing by the court will vary drastically, and you'll see that there is no rhyme or reason to the punishments that are given out.

Special Powers and Sorcery

A con man who goes by the name of Tarzan is accused of scamming people by saying he is a sorcerer. The man who visited the U.A.E. many times had a history of conning people. He befriended worshippers near mosques and told them he had special powers and he will help them with their problems through sorcery.

Tarzan told a victim to obtain gold and bring it back to the victim's house. He then read to him from the Quran, referencing fighting off the bad spirits. After he was finished, he ordered him to go and donate money to local charity. While the man was gone, he took off with $37,025 worth of gold left behind by the victim and he tried to sell it to a jewelry store.

Many reports started coming into the police station about him. The man was caught and detained at the airport while he tried to leave the country. He was identified by the jewelry store owner as the person who tried to sell him the stolen gold. Tarzan was charged with robbery. No further information is available.

Money Made with the Help of Genies

A trickster told an undercover policeman he can make $6,806,148 fall from the sky with the help of genies. The 30-year-old man from Chad claimed he had a relationship with a spirit, and if customers tip the genies, then he can create money. No further information is available.

Home Raided and Sorcerer Held

A 52-year-old Asian man told people he had special powers. He said he can heal psychological problems, solve family issues and bring happiness to married couples. The man wrote "mysterious" words on a piece of paper for money, and he did this at his home. Officers raided his house while he was with a customer and found sorcery material such as sketches, and pieces of paper with "mysterious" words written on them.

The outcome of the court case is unknown.

Witchcraft used in Solving Marital Problems

Two women from Africa claimed they can help put a rocky marriage back on track for $13,612. One woman was a 36-year-old hairdresser, and the other was a 50-year-old visitor. It is alleged that they practiced their magic out of the hair salon and apartment. A female undercover police officer met with the two woman saying she needed help in her marriage. The officer was trying to set them up.

One woman told the officer to cut off a piece of her husband's hair when he was sleeping and bring it back to them. They also gave her other witchcraft materials to take home. The women were arrested and confessed to practicing witchcraft. Police found a variety of items in the apartment such as pieces of hair, rolls of cotton, wool, herbs, coins and riddles forming a pyramid. No further information available.

Wife Killed over Witchcraft

A wife was killed by her husband and son when the man believed she was bewitching his nephew. The Emirati beat up his wife when he thought she was practicing witchcraft. This left her with severe head injuries. He then ordered her son and a Pakistani man to stab her with knives he had given them. She arrived at the hospital in critical condition and later died of the stab wounds and beating.

The woman's brother testified in court. He said the couple had gotten in an argument when the husband accused her of practicing witchcraft and bewitching his nephew. He said that none of it was true. The three denied the charges, and the case was waiting to hear from more witnesses.

Witchcraft Suspects Held

Three Arab suspects were arrested for conning people by saying they can solve problems and heal people using witchcraft and the Quran. A woman had contacted the men when she was having marital problems with her husband. She gave them $4,083 for the sorcery but contacted the police when the problems were never fixed.

The police arrested two of the men who were just visiting the U.A.E. A third man who acted as a broker was also arrested. They found herbs, talismans and other items used in witchcraft in their hotel room. No further information is available.

Black Magic

A 57-year-old African man who worked at a laundry service, targeted women. He promised that his special powers will cure diseases and solve marital problems. Along with physical, psychological problems and other social issues. All of this for a fee.

Police received several complaints from women when none of the things he promised came true. He charged each woman $19,059. An undercover cop arrested him. They found in his possession items commonly used in witchcraft. He denied the charges and said: "I was only giving out herbal medicine that cure heart diseases." No further information is available.

Victim Possessed by Spirits

A man who claimed he was a Djinn healer [a spiritual person known in Islamic tradition], killed a woman. He tried to "beat out the evil spirits" that he believed was trapped inside of her. The Emirati woman was taken to a witch doctor by her brother and a female friend. She was severely beaten all over her body with a "special" stick used for the treatment.

She returned home, but succumbed to her injuries later dying in a hospital. The medical report confirmed she died of internal bleeding and a failed respiratory system, due to the beating. All three have denied the charges.

The healer was charged with assault leading to death. Also for breaching public morals of Muslims, claiming that he cures people suffering by using the Quran. The brother's attorney said the sister suffered from an illness and was taking many prescription drugs. He said that is what might have caused her death.

He also said: "The medicines affect the white blood count, and cause bruising and internal bleeding and affect a person's liver and digestive system." He claimed her brother was not involved in taking his sister to the man for treatment. The Arab brother and Arab healer both received a 2 year jail sentenced. But, was reduced to 6 months.

This sentence was given after the victim's family waived their rights and pardoned the defendants. The sentence of the female friend is unknown.

Scarred by Cooking Oil

Two Asian laborers got into a squabble. One roommate refused to turn on the air-conditioner, so the other one threw hot cooking oil in his face. The two shared a room at a labor camp near the construction site where they worked. They could never see eye to eye. They continually argued until the supervisor moved one of them to another room. He said this way they wouldn't have to be together.

The defendant became angry since he had to move out, and the other one got to stay. When the victim left a bathroom near the accommodations, the defendant chased him with a pan of hot oil. He threw it in his face. He said: "If you like the heat, you can have it." The victim received severe burns, and scarring on the left side of his face, neck and shoulders. He has damage to his left eye.

The defendant admitted to the attack saying he was angry at being forced out of their room. The case was adjourned.

Pasta Death

Three employees worked for a Dubai based food processing company. They are accused of wrongly causing the death of a co-worker. He was sucked into a pasta making machine. The 3 employees charged were a 54-year-old British security and safety officer, a 30-year-old Filipino electrician and a 40-year-old Indonesian machine operator.

Charges were failure to provide proper training and education on the dangers of working with machinery. Also, for not providing supervision. The company claims they use the best technology and is always creating more awareness and enforcing safety precautions. All 3 men will be due in court soon.

Killer Cook

A Bangladeshi cook has been found guilty of dismembering a Pakistani laborer and spreading his body parts around a city near Dubai. The cook worked for a private family. He invited the victim to his room at the family's home to discuss money. The court believes they became involved in a dispute over $544.

He stabbed the laborer several times then cut him up with his kitchen knives. He placed the body parts in plastic bags, spreading them throughout the city. The cook was arrested, and the court believes his plan was to leave the country. Under Islamic law, he can face the death penalty. This is only if the family of the victim travels from Pakistan and demands it. He could also receive a reduced sentence if the family takes the standard $54,449 in blood money. The outcome of the court case is unknown.

Attack with a Frying Pan

An Emirati woman and her Emirati male neighbor, a former policeman, beat the woman's Ethiopian housemaid to death with a frying pan. The woman confessed to beating the maid and said: "It was only to discipline her and I did not intend to kill her." When she went to trial, the woman claimed her neighbor beat her, she said: "The maid threatened to expose his homosexuality."

In court, an Ethiopian woman who briefly worked as the woman's maid said: "The victim was beaten daily. The day of her death, I could hear screaming and found the housemaid lying on the floor naked." The two were convicted, but it wasn't clear which one struck the lethal blow. Both were given a sentenced of 13 years behind bars, but the sentenced was cut to 7 years. No explanation had been given. They were each ordered to pay $54,449 in blood money.

Potato Peeler Murder

A Filipino nurse murdered his friend with a potato peeler after getting into an argument. They both had been at a dinner party with two other friends when they began to argued after drinking. The nurse was arrested at the airport when he tried to leave the country, the day after he killed his friend. He was given a 5 year sentence.

Released from Court after 50 Denials

A man charged with killing 2 Arab men was set free. The judge asked the man to "swear 50 times" that he was not involved in the murders. Under Sharia law if you swear 50 times that you are innocent of any charge, and nobody from the victim's family will swear that you are guilty, this is enough to be found not guilty. Here, no blood relative of the victims showed up in court, so they had to let him go after he swore 50 times he was not guilty. They also did not have enough physical evidence.

Killed over Insults

A Bangladeshi man attacked his Emirati boss and continually hit him over the head with an iron bar until he died. The man said he bought an iron bar at a nearby store, close to where he worked. He hit the Emirati with it when the boss continued to insult him. The Bangladeshi man said: "I never intended to kill my boss. He was alive when I fled the scene."

The Bangladeshi man was convicted of murder. The family of the Emirati man said they will not take blood money for a lesser sentence. They want the man to pay with his life. The case was adjourned.

9 Lives for a Cabbie who tries to Commit Suicide

A 25-year-old Indian cab driver wrote a note on his final try to commit suicide. He was so unhappy over having to leave Dubai that he tried to kill himself 3 times. The driver loved living in Dubai before he had to go back to India for financial reasons. While back home, he became very depressed turning to alcohol, and drinking daily.

First, the man slit his wrists with a razor blade, leaving one cut so deep and severe that it could have killed him, but it didn't. He then tried again, and went into the bathroom. The man pulled out electrical wires to electrocute himself, but that didn't work either as it only shocked him. On the last try he wrote a suicide note in blood on the floor. He explained his financial crisis and how he longed for Dubai.

His third attempt at death was successful when he climbed into a "water barrel" and drowned himself. Doctors at an Indian institute said: "This bizarre method of attempted suicide [3 unusual attempts] is not common. It is unusual and not found in available forensic literature."

Woman who Watched her Television at Full Volume is Fined

Neighbors at an apartment building were fed up with a noisy 27-year-old Algerian woman. She not only watched her tv at full volume, but listened to her music loudly too. At first tenants thought she was having a party until she continued to do it every day. The Algerian left the tv and music blasting even when she left her apartment.

A woman complained to the building management after not being able to sleep, but nothing was done. She then called the police who knocked on her door, but no one answered. Police ordered security to switch off her electricity, and still no one came out of the apartment.

The Algerian woman complained in court that her electricity was always being turned on and off by the building management. She said: "I would always turn off my tv, but maybe when it came back on, the tv worked automatically." Explaining this was why she left the tv on. The woman was found guilty and fined $27 for disturbing the peace.

Inmate Endangers Lives by trying to Spread HIV

A 20-year-old Emirati inmate with HIV allegedly cut his wrists and tried putting his blood in the tea and food of 40 prisoners. In jail a 28-year-old Bangladeshi man was distributing food to the solitary confinement section of the prison. The Emirati asked him to leave behind the food cart and go get a warden.

The guard said: "If I didn't get a warden, all the inmates would assault me." He was terrified as the Emirati yelled at him, so he ran to find a warden. When the 21-year-old warden from the Comoros Islands arrived, he noticed the food cart next to the jailbird. He listened to the Emirati threaten to either mix his blood with the food, or commit suicide.

The warden told a court that the inmate mixed blood into the food when he slit his wrists. He also dropped blood into the tea, and a bottle of water. The defendant denies the charges and said: "How in the world would I be able to threaten anyone while I am inside a solitary cell?" No further information.

Assaulted over an Early Break

A laborer who was an electrician, asked his supervisor if he can take his midday break at 11:30am. The temperature outside was scorching hot, so he wanted to go early. He is informed that he couldn't, and he will have to wait until 12:30pm. The laborer became irate and struck the supervisor with a metal bar.

Both argued over the break until a manager appeared. He dealt with the matter by telling the laborer he will be moved to a different job location. The supervisor went to rest during the scheduled break time and was fast asleep when he felt something on his leg.

He opened his eyes and found the laborer standing over him with a metal bar. He smashed the supervisor's leg. When the supervisor tried to fight back and defend himself, he is whacked in the head and the arm. The defendant denied the charges. No further information available.

I will Kill you if you don't Marry me

A 43-year-old Afghan man threatened a 30-year-old Canadian singer over the phone. He told her if she didn't marry him, he would throw acid in her face.

The man said he was a rich man and promised the woman a happy life if they married. When the woman refused, he said he will send a man from Afghanistan to kill her, making it look like a car accident. He told her he will burn down her house, and the restaurant she owned in Dubai. In court, the singer's mother said the Afghan called her. He told her he will disfigure her daughter's face with acid, if she didn't marry him. He said if she married anyone else, he will kill her and himself.

In court, the Afghan said: "She made the whole story up after I loaned her $920,000 for her restaurant and she had no intentions of paying back the money." The outcome is unknown.

Man Comes after Women with Swords

An Omani man and his mother sat in front of his house in a taxi and argued for reasons unknown. The man ordered his mother to go into the house and get his swords. When she refused, he beat her up. He ran into the house himself to get the weapons. Three women stood outside and watched the scene unfold. He then insulted the women and chased after them with the swords. They retreated into their houses.

The man is given a 6 month sentence for brandishing swords.

Assault Leads to Extra Jail Time

An Afghani man was sleeping in jail when 2 inmates who were playing cards stopped and came up to him. One man insulted him and his mother. The Afghani became angry and broke the victim's teeth. In court, his attorney said he will now have problems chewing. The initial sentence is not known, but an additional 6 month sentence is given to the Afghani man.

Friends Kidnap their Friend

Seven Pakistani men all between the ages of 22-years-old and 32-years-old blindfolded their friend, tied him up and beat him. They drove him in a bus to Abu Dhabi and kept him imprisoned in a room for 2 whole days. The reasons are unknown.

A court sentenced them for kidnapping and beating up their friend. The Pakistani gang leader received life in prison. The rest received 6 months. An eighth person received a fine of $1,361 for driving the bus.

Ax Murderer Hired

A 29-year-old Afghani man hired his friend to kill his stepbrother because he didn't like him. The 29-year-old constantly fought with his sibling and often thought about killing him. He hired his friend who was desperate for money to do the job. He paid him $1,361 to commit the murder. The two friends bought an ax, and "sharpened it well." They hid the weapon in a vehicle.

One evening after midnight, the victim was in a "warehouse washing his clothes." The hitman entered and struck him twice on the head while the victim's stepbrother watched. The body was later found in a tire warehouse located in an industrial area. The victim's head was entirely smashed in, and his body covered in tires.

In court the stepbrother showed no remorse. The 2 men are referred to public prosecution. No further information.

Coke Can Attack

An Emirati man passing by an expat woman in the street solicited her for sex. She responded by throwing a coke can at him. This landed her in jail. The woman from Uganda explained in court that an argument broke out on the street.

The Emirati man approached her assuming she was selling herself because she was African. She yelled and was angry that he disrespected her. The man shouted back and said, "This is my country!" He slapped her, she then threw the coke can at him. The Emirati called the police and "claimed" he was assaulted. He told police he only approached her because she was disrespectful in her manner and dress. The woman is arrested when the Emirati showed police the "coke can."

She went from the police station to a woman's prison. They locked her up for 5 days before appearing in court, showing up in a prison uniform. She told the court she merely went to meet friends when the incident happened. They are still holding her while the prosecutors decide on whether they will pursue assault charges against her. No further information is available.

Air Hose Backfires

A 29-year-old Bangladeshi janitor injured his 26-year-old Indian friend when he put an air hose into his rear-end and turned it on. The janitor said that he did not assault him, but just tried to clean off his clothes. This incident happened at a plastics company. Some of the other laborers had gathered around to watch. After a while a supervisor is informed, and an ambulance is called.

The friend ended up in the hospital for 6 days and had to have surgery. The victim said: "Even though my clothes were on, it still hurt really bad. I felt a horrible pain. My stomach and face inflated like a balloon, and I fell to the ground."

A medical report said he is left with disabilities from the attack. He still goes to the hospital for medicine due to the incident. The janitor claimed it was only a joke, but he is being detained and remains in custody. No further information is available.

Boss Assaults Cook

A Bangladeshi cook is hit over the head with a blunt object by his elderly Emirati boss, which left him with hearing problems. The cook claims he has had problems since that day in 2009 when the incident happened. He was taken to the hospital. Since the incident, he cannot hear well.

The 25-year-old daughter of the Emirati told the court that her father did not hurt the cook as he was too weak. The man is now in his seventies. She said she was in the house the day of the incident, and it just didn't happen. The Emirati man is charged with assault causing permanent injury, which he denies. The case is adjourned. No information as to why it took so long for this case to go to court.

A Battle over the Bathroom ends up in Court

A Filipino man was washing his clothes in the bathroom of his apartment. His Filipino roommate came barreling in wanting to use the facilities. The man refused to stop washing clothes. He said there are 3 bathrooms to use. The two argued then it escalated. One threw a plastic water bottle hitting the other in the forehead. Punches flew, both men are left bloodied.

The man washing clothes tried to file an assault charge but is told he was the aggressor in the case. He is worried they will send him back to his home country as he holds a good job. A verdict in the case is reached. But, the decision is sent to the court clerk for processing. The outcome of the case is not known.

Finger Biting over Money

A 28-year-old Bangladeshi man defended his younger brother when he got into an argument with another man. Both brothers worked at a fruit market when a customer argued with the younger brother, over money. The man threatened to beat the younger brother with his shoes. The older brother pushed the man away. He left, but after 15 minutes the thug returned with a friend.

The two beat up the 28-year-old and bit his middle finger. Both men denied the assault. The case is adjourned.

TV Fight ended in Murder

A 48-year-old carpenter killed his roommate after arguing over the volume of the tv. Both are roommates at a labor camp and were drinking.

The victim was singing using an annoying voice and turned up the volume on the tv. The defendant asked him to turn it off. He refused, so the defendant turned it off himself. This resulted in a fight between them.

The carpenter is accused of knocking the roommate to the ground, slitting his throat and stabbing him repeatedly. The laborers in neighboring rooms called their supervisor to come and intervene. When the 33-year-old Indian supervisor arrived, he could not open the door to the room since it was locked.

Looking in the window, he saw blood covering the floor. He witnessed the defendant looking drunk and distraught. He sat next to the body on the ground. If a guilty verdict comes back, the death penalty will be sought since the crime was so violent. No further information available.

Killer Smashes in Friend's Head

A 52-year-old Egyptian man sits on death row. He is waiting to face the firing squad after smashing in his friend's head. The man beat his friend repeatedly over the head with a baseball bat until he died. Then, took his cell phone, car and credit cards. He went shopping and bought jewelry worth $1,905. He even took his girlfriend out to dinner and a movie.

CCTV is reviewed, and the man is clearly identified and given the death sentence.

Death Row for 2 Bangladeshi Men

The death sentenced is confirmed for 2 Bangladeshi men who killed a 23-year-old Bangladeshi man. A dispute broke out among one of the men and a Bangladeshi fruit salesman. The man borrowed $952 from the salesman and now, refused to pay it back.

The two Bangladeshi men lured their countryman out into the desert where they killed him with a metal bar. They took his cell phone, wallet and cigarettes. No date is set for their execution.

Flight Attendant Falls from an Airplane

A catering truck collided with an airplane at the gate. This caused a Russian Flight Attendant to fall out of the plane. The flight is scheduled to go from Dubai to Russia. A catering truck rammed into the back of the airplane. Impact caused the jet-bridge to move, leaving a gap between the jet-bridge and the airplane door. This is where she fell from. She is treated for broken bones, a concussion and is in intensive care. No other information.

Lifeguard Jailed

A 31-year-old Filipino lifeguard is jailed for 1 month since he caused the drowning of an Indian man. The court said he did not watch him while he was swimming. The lifeguard said he did watch the man very carefully and noticed that he could swim well, so he left the pool to get more towels. He said the man visited the pool four other times.

The lifeguard is gone for 15 minutes when two children came running to get him. They told him the Indian man drowned. He rushed back to the pool and tried to save the man. Eventually he had to call for an ambulance. The man died 2 days later in a hospital.

In court the man's 34-year-old Indian wife said her husband had been very depressed. This started when he was fired from his job on the day he went to the pool. She said he went for a swim to feel better. He had just learned how to swim 1 month before the incident. She said: "He was exhausted, or maybe suffered problems from diabetes and wasn't taking his medicine when he should have." The lifeguard is given 1 month in jail.

Gang Forgot to take Phone from the Person they Kidnapped

Four Pakistani men kidnapped a man over a financial dispute. They locked him in a "container." He called the police when the brilliant group forgot to take his cell phone away. The financial deal started a few years ago when one Pakistani loaned the man $108,896. They agreed it will be paid back in a year. After 2 years he kept delaying the payment.

The man is kidnapped in front of his home by the Pakistani gang and taken to an industrial area. There they locked him in a "container," and threatened to kill him. When the man is left alone, he used his cell phone to call the police. He told them he is kidnapped.

The victim is freed by the police. The 4 kidnappers are caught and arrested. No further information. The investigation is ongoing.

A Kidnapped Victim Calls Police

A man is locked in a room for 2 days by 4 Bangladeshi migrant workers. They wanted him to raise money to pay off his $4,900 debt so they let him keep his phone to make calls to family and friends.

Because the victim was having a problem paying off the debt he owed, they all agreed to meet and discuss it. When he arrived at the meeting place, all four men suggested they go to an apartment building. The victim agreed, and they all walked a half hour to get to the apartment. Once there, they locked him in a room and slid food to him under the door. He was told to call whoever he needed, to get the money. After "three days," he finally called the police.

The 4 men are arrested on kidnapping charges, but their attorney said: "It wasn't kidnapping. He had his phone, so it wasn't kidnapping as he could call anyone he wanted to, including the police. He could have cried out to someone on the street as they walked for a half hour." The outcome is unknown.

CHAPTER 8
BEVERAGES

Alcohol is forbidden to Muslims and highly restricted to other individuals. Dubai does have liquor stores, but they are disguised well from the outside. Buying liquor at the store isn't straightforward because you need to apply for an alcohol license. Additionally, you must have this license to keep it in your home. When applying, and on the application form, you are required to specify your religion. The process can take up to 3 months to be approved, as it did for us, and the cost is $50.00 for 1 year.

Once that process is over, you receive a card with an amount that you are allowed to spend each month. The liquor stores keep track of all your spending on their computers. You are not to go over the allotted amount. Liquor is extremely expensive in Dubai, and if you have a drink in the hotels or the resorts, you will pay a stiff price. For many individuals, to avoid buying a liquor license they drive to another emirate, not regulated.

The liquor store is located out in the desert not far away from Dubai. Customers will load up their cars with liquor and beer, then carefully drive back to Dubai so as not to get caught by the police. The shoppers are particularly attentive at the liquor store since devious people hang out there to observe you loading your car.

When driving back to Dubai through the regulated emirate, these shady people will purposely cause you to be in an accident. The police then arrive and arrest you for possession of alcohol. They could also blackmail you into giving them money. If you don't pay on the spot, they call the police and you go to jail.

Aside from alcohol being restricted in the U.A.E., the city still receives their fair share of drunk drivers on the road. The worst part is the punishment doesn't consistently fit the crime, and justice isn't always served. A drunk driver who killed a triathlete and injured two people only received 1 month in prison. But, a couple caught kissing on the beach received 1 year in prison. Even though Muslims may not consume alcohol, many still do, and specifically on airplanes. They will ask the flight attendants to discretely pour the alcohol in a plastic cup and supposedly no one will be the wiser.

When determining a sentence, there is no jury. Whatever the judge feels like doing on that day goes since it is up to him. He is the individual who ultimately decides.

80 Lashes for Drinking Alcohol

An Arab man had his sentenced slashed from 1 year to 3 months in jail for stealing. The same Appeals Court had included a new punishment of 80 lashes for consuming alcohol. The guy stepped into a phone store with a friend. He asked the staff if they wanted to buy a used phone from him. When the pair left the store, the employees noticed a phone was missing. After reviewing the CCTV, they saw him stealing the phone.

The man argued in court he was not aware of his actions. He said he was "drunk" when he committed the crime. Since he admitted to drinking alcohol, the court ordered that he be whipped. The friend is given a fine of $272 for not reporting the crime to the police.

Driver Spreads Corruption on the Earth

A young Emirati man was driving recklessly at 75mph hitting vehicles on his right and then on his left. Eventually crashing into 6 cars injuring all the other drivers. He had been drinking and using drugs.

In court a Chief Justice spoke to the young man. He said: "The court has three hearts, and it is more merciful with you than your own mother. What you have done is not easy. You were spreading corruption on the earth."

The driver admitted to hitting the vehicles and drinking, but denied the drug charge, he realized he made a mistake. His lawyer argued that if he is found guilty, the punishment should be rehabilitation since he is so young. The verdict was still out.

Spiked Orange Juice

A 30-year-old salesman is passed out, thanks to a group of 5 Pakistani men, when they came to buy tires at his store. The men spiked a jug of orange juice with alcohol then gave it to the salesman. When he drank it, he passed out, and the men stole $2,450. They took his credit card and ID. All 5 men are arrested and received a prison sentence of 3 years.

Store Worker Attacked Because he Couldn't Understand an Accent

A Bangladeshi salesman said he was attacked because he struggled to understand his customer's accent. The man is busy helping patrons when a Vietnamese guy walked in and asked for a product. The salesman did not understand him so he asked him to repeat what he said. He still couldn't understand so he asked him again to repeat it.

Eventually he told the Vietnamese man he didn't have what he was asking for. The customer became livid and yelled. He then went out of the store to tell his friends that the shopkeeper refused to help Vietnamese customers. The man grabbed a metal bar and went back in the store with his 3 cronies. He hit the shopkeepers arm and broke it while his pals kicked and punched him. Another Bangladeshi salesman working in the store tried to intervene.

The men fled back to their labor camp. The shopkeeper suspected the Vietnamese men had been drinking heavily. Police nabbed the 4 suspects at the camp where they were living. They are expected to appear in court at a later date.

Expat Fled to the Airport after Killing a Motorist While Drunk

A 31-year-old Brazilian man tried to skip the country, after he mowed down a 29-year-old tourist and killed him. The tourist was in town visiting a friend on a 4 day break. He was crossing the street in an undesignated area. When he reached the second lane he was hit by the car.

A witness to the accident said the Brazilian didn't try to stop when he ran over the tourist. He immediately left the scene of the accident. The witness described the car, and the license plate number to the police.

Afterwards, the Brazilian drove straight to his office to retrieve his passport, and headed to the Dubai airport. Police caught him in the duty free store just before boarding a flight to Beirut. The court handed him a 2 month jail sentence. He is ordered to pay $40,838 in blood money to the victim's family.

The friend of the victim said they had been friends since grade school. He said: "The 2 month jail sentence is disgraceful and for those reasons, I will be leaving Dubai."

Cabin Crew Restrains a Drunk Passenger

An Asian man is in jail after he disrupted a flight by asking the cabin crew for the "keys" to the emergency exit. The drunk man was traveling to Abu Dhabi from Europe when he got out of his seat. He shouted at the flight attendant for the keys to the door as he walked through the aisle. When the other passengers told him to be quiet so they could sleep, he became angry with them too.

A female flight attendant asked him to take his seat, he did, but later got up again. As she walked down the aisle, the man grabbed her blouse and pushed her. The cabin crew, along with passengers, restrained the man. He is arrested at the Abu Dhabi airport when they arrived.

A 3 month sentence is given for assault, abusive behavior, causing a disturbance and endangering an aircraft. He had both alcohol, and hashish in his system. He'll be deported after serving.

Three Jailed for Shoe Attack

Three Indian men had been drinking just before they attacked their 39-year-old friend. The man simply asked the guys to take off their shoes before entering his home. One defendant took off his shoes, and hit his friend with them, and then they beat him with a metal bar. The incident happened at a labor camp. The 3 men are jailed for 1 year.

Death Sentence over a Fatal Scuffle

An Asian man will be executed after murdering his colleague. He is found guilty of stabbing another Asian man in the stomach several times with a kitchen knife. He fled afterwards. The murder took place at their accommodation.

When the murderer heard other workers talk about the crime, he pretended he knew nothing. A worker saw the pair in the room together and told police. They arrested him. The man admitted to killing his friend, but said they were both drunk. He said: "I did it in self-defense because he tried to strangle me. I then ran to the kitchen to grab the knife when he came after me again and that prompted me to stab him many times in the stomach." He says he did not intend to kill him.

The court cannot reach any of the relatives to seek pardon for blood money. He is therefore handed the death sentence.

Jilted Lover tried to Kill Ex-Girlfriend

A 33-year-old Nepalese man attacked and stabbed his ex-girlfriend at a hair salon where she worked, inside a mall. The man is upset with her for ending their relationship. He also went after her co-worker and stabbed her before turning the knife on himself to try and commit suicide. He denies the charges of attempted murder and assault, claiming he did not attempt suicide either. No further information.

Boozed up Worker try to Con Cops

An Asian man tried to get deported when he handed himself over to the police. He claimed he was in the country illegally. The man allegedly had gotten in a booze fueled argument with his roommate. This was after the roommate insulted him. He repeatedly hit the man on the head with a bottle until he killed him. Afterwards, he turned himself in. Police investigated and found the dead man.

Prosecutors are saying it is premeditated murder. The Asian man's lawyer said: "My client was drunk when the incident happened and was not aware of what he was doing." The outcome of the court case is unknown.

Busted for 80 Crates of Booze in a Trunk

A Pakistani man and his accomplice are jailed. They tried to smuggle 80 crates of booze in the trunk of a Lexus. Both men were returning from a wholesaler and making their way to Abu Dhabi. The Pakistani man hoped he and his friend could sell the beer, whisky and vodka worth $6,806 to party planners. He thought maybe individuals and entertainment venues would buy it too. Neither men had a liquor license.

The police became suspicious when they noticed the back of the car weighed down. They pulled him over and found 80 crates in the trunk. The owner of the car is given 6 months for bootlegging, and his vehicle is seized. His accomplice is given a 1 year sentence but had it reduced to 2 months.

The Pakistani man said: "The police said they were amazed that we fitted so much alcohol in the back of the car [sic]. Now the alcohol and the car which was less than a year old are both gone."

Charged in Bootlegging

An Asian man is being charged with having 169 bottles of beer, wine and spirits in his possession. He hid the booze in his room at a farm where he worked. Police are tipped off by another employee. He allegedly had been illegally selling the booze to other Asians in the area. The man is arrested. He is referred to public prosecution on charges of bootlegging. No further information available.

More Bootleggers Arrested

Seven Indians, and a Bangladeshi man are caught selling booze to workers in an industrial area. The men had large quantities of liquor they hid in deserted areas, vehicles and trucks. The guys admitted to the illegal activity and are referred to public prosecution. No further information available.

CHAPTER 9

COPS

In Dubai, emergency calls pass through a 999 system, like dialing 911 in the United States. When an individual gets into an accident, even as minor as scraping your car, they still need to dial 999. A police report is also mandatory to be able to file a claim with the insurance company. Legally, a repair shop is not supposed to fix your car without looking at a police report first.

The police are complaining the emergency lines are being clogged, and all the stress it leaves on the operators. But, there is no non-emergency line to call so these calls are being filtered to 999. Some of the calls they get are motor vehicle emergency and non-emergency, life threatening calls, prank calls from children and ridiculously nonsense calls. Without designating specific lines, the 999 line is choked.

Dubai cops are proud of their high end fleet of fabulous cars and are adding to the collection. A Bugatti Veyron Grand Sport was next in line to be included to the already $4,083,849 police fleet. The department has Ferraris, Aston Martins and a handful of other top of the line cars, explained further in a later chapter.

A police officer, in charge of the traffic division, has a vision of a high-speed "gold class" highway. This highway will allow motorists to zoom at speeds of 125mph. A safety road campaigner who created "Buckle in the Back U.A.E.," replied she is "gob smacked" at gaining a super highway.

The department head "dismissed" the notion that speed is to blame for accidents. He said: "Studies show that high speeds can't make accidents unless there are other factors." A 24-year-old salesman who owns an Audi

R8 has commented on the new highway proposal. He said: "I speed anyway, this is a great idea, because I can do it in a safer way."

The highway is being compared to the Autobahn in Germany. But, individuals claim the driving standard in Germany is much higher than the U.A.E. People are expressing money and time invested in the new highway should be poured into improving driver education, and stronger enforcement of existing traffic laws. The top officer sees a target of "zero deaths" on the highways by 2020. I think that is nothing more than a pipe dream.

Policing in Dubai is done to a large extent by use of surveillance cameras. Police chases are rare. When the need for chasing someone arises, the pursuing police officers will make a call into their command center. They describe the car and location, and then the center will take over the chase by watching surveillance cameras. When the suspect stops, the command center will direct police cars in to make an arrest.

Every year on December 2nd the U.A.E. celebrates National Day. This is when the U.A.E. formed as a country, splitting away from the British in 1971. It is a celebration like the Fourth of July in the U.S. Leading up to the festivities, the police maintain that they will not tolerate reckless drivers or anti-social actions. The motorists are being warned that they better behave, or they will have their cars taken away, and their license confiscated.

The do's and don'ts were posted on social media. They said that you may not stand on your vehicle, drive in an outrageous manner, and block the route for others. You cannot overload the vehicle by exceeding the number of passengers, sit on the roof or stick your head out of the sunroof.

Drivers are banned from "spraying strangers" with foam and silly string which has become a popular practice. Police say it is too distracting and causes accidents. Spraying your car with U.A.E. and royal colors is now banned too unless, you get permission, before changing the color of your car.

The police said: "We want the drivers to express their joy in a civilized manner." If anyone is caught in violation, their car is impounded for one month, and they will receive a fine between $54 and $5,445. They will also receive 12 "black points" against their record. A few years ago more than 90 vehicles were seized, and in Abu Dhabi 600 motorists are fined.

Some of the things police say you can do is write phrases that "do not insult" others. You can place a flag on vehicles that doesn't pose a risk to safety.

Don't Call 999 for a Headache

With nearly two thirds of the emergency lines being backed up by nonsense questions and requests, police felt the need to launch a campaign. They told people to stop wasting their valuable time. A caller phoned in complaining about a headache and asked if he should take Panadol [like

Aleve] or another painkiller. While someone else called after midnight and wanted to know which pharmacies were open.

Yet someone else said they took a cab from point A to point B and wanted to know if they were cheated on the fare. The police say they receive hundreds of prank calls from kids who hang up when the operator answers, and when they call back the parents pick up and apologize. The head of the operations department said they still respond to 99.9% of all calls within 10 seconds.

Um Police, I can't Find my House

More strange calls keep crippling the 999 emergency control room. A woman who just moved to a new part of town had phoned in asking for help when she couldn't find her house. The police eventually helped the woman find her home as she was standing right behind it.

An old man called the emergency line requesting help in "stopping" the strong winds that led to a dust storm, since he wanted to go out. He followed the advice of the emergency staff who told him to stay home for the rest of the day for his own safety.

A Pest Calls 999 More than 100 Times

A 53-year-old Pakistani man wanted to be deported, so he called 999 more than 100 times in one day. He begged to be sent back home to his country. Police warned the man to stop calling, but he refused so they arrested him. The Pakistani lived in the U.A.E. for 30 years. He worked for the police in their technical department. He was fired and had his residency visa canceled when he didn't show up for 2 days.

The man told police he wanted to go home, because he didn't have a job and couldn't find one, he had no money. He said he couldn't afford to go home, so he called 999 knowing he will be in trouble and hoping he will get deported. He will be sentenced at a later date.

A 999 Call over Traffic Noise

A man called the emergency line 52 times complaining about traffic noise. But, instead of getting rid of traffic noise he found himself in court. The man was at a beach when he complained about the traffic and loud sirens. He called the hotline day and night. He is told by the operator to stop calling, but ignored the request.

The beach guy ended up in court and pleaded not guilty to the charge of "annoying the police." He said: "I was surprised when they didn't come and respond to my calls, so I kept calling." The man is given a 1 month suspended jail sentence for the abuse of the line.

Police Officer Steals 79 Cars

A 25-year-old Emirati police officer who worked in the traffic department scoured the city to look for abandon cars. He also forged warrants on seized cars. The officer took the documents to a locksmith and had a new set of keys made for the cars. He then gave the keys to his two buddies, who stole the cars.

The vehicles were then sold, or stripped for parts, handled by a fourth pal. In 1 year the thieves had stolen 79 cars of various makes and models. The policeman confessed in court and said: "I felt pain and guilt as I was supposed to serve and protect the law, but I was stealing cars. I was not able to sleep at night because of the guilt and nightmares." He told of how his friends came up with the idea when they brought him to work one day and saw dusty cars parked all over the place. The cop explained to them they are left behind by people who fled the country. The money the police officer profited from his illegal activity paid off a credit card debt of $43,561 and a $54,451 loan. No further information available.

You can still find parked cars abandoned around the entire city and airport, left by people who skipped the country for various reasons.

New Driver Gets Fined

A female driver just received her license. She was driving down a road when a car quickly came up behind her and tailgated her. The car flashed their lights to get her to move out of the way [a common practice in Dubai]. She became nervous and desperately tried to move over to avoid being hit by the driver.

Police notice the incident and stopped her. She explained to them what happened, but they gave her a fine. They said that she was in the fast lane slowing down traffic, but she was going 50mph in a 44mph zone!

Cop Forges a Sick Note

A 24-year-old Emirati police officer forged a doctor's sick note to give him two days off instead of one. The cop has gone on trial and admitted to changing the number with a pen. No further information available.

Policeman Agrees to have Sex with a Woman

A 21-year-old policeman was spotted going into a building wearing his uniform. He had sex behind the emergency door with a woman from Uzbekistan. He allegedly agreed to have sex with her, in exchange for not arresting her for being in the country illegally.

The woman claims she had consensual sex because she was afraid of him since he was a policeman. The woman received 3 years in jail, and so did the policeman, but he had his jail term cut to 1 year.

Policeman Jailed for Porn

A policeman took hundreds of pornographic photos, and videos of people he had arrested besides, taking $816 in bribes. The policeman stopped a Pakistani man and told him that his car is leaking fuel, and he took his license away. He told him he is facing a fine of $2,722 but if he gave him $816 he will give him back his license and forget about it.

The driver called his boss and told him what had happened. His boss, then contacted the Traffic Department and is told no such fine exists for a fuel leak. Police told the driver to pay the $816 to the officer so they can arrest him. After being caught, they found 266 pornographic photos and videos in the officer's car, that he had taken of men he arrested. He then released the men and didn't take them to the police station.

In court the officer admitted to making up bogus fines to more than 80 motorists, and 70 people paid him between $54 and $816. The officer received 1 year in jail for porn and 6 months for taking bribes.

Officers Involved in Prostitution Ring

Major corruption was uncovered at the police department. Three police officers are involved in a prostitution ring. An officer stopped women on the street and ask them for their identification papers. If they can't produce them, he takes them to the police station for questioning. While at the station, he doesn't fill out the paperwork on them. Instead, the officer tells the women who overstayed their visa he had a way out for them. They can become prostitutes. He then sold them to a Bangladeshi pimp.

The cop received $6,806 for trafficking a woman who had been arrested on a visa violation. A female officer and another male officer are involved in forging paperwork to hide evidence of police involvement.

Three Bangladeshi men and an Indonesian woman are also charged in the case. The woman is charged with prostitution, uncertain if the woman volunteered herself, or if she is a victim. One of the Bangladeshi men is charged with bribing a police officer to supply him with women. The other 2 Bangladeshi men are charged with running the brothel where the visa violators were taken. A fourth man will appear in court at a later date.

The defendants claimed they were assaulted by "anti-corrupt officers." One police officer, in court that day for a different case and is identified by the defendants, is accused of yanking a Pakistani man's arm behind his back. He pulled his hair and grabbed him by the neck. The officer denied any involvement with the accused men.

All 3 police officers will go on trial for selling women detainees to pimps. The Department of Justice said: "The police are keen to show that it is tough on corruption. We want to deal with it in a fair, honest and open way." No further information available.

Police Chief Denies Assault

A 23-year-old Emirati man left his home to visit a friend at his house, when according to his mother, a group of 15 men attacked him. They hit him with stones, stabbed him and slashed him with swords. The police chief said: "It is impossible that someone who is walking peacefully would get beaten up for no reason."

The man claims he did not know who the men were, but said they harassed him on another occasion, while walking to his friend's house. But, the police chief said what happened was, the man and his friend were trying to get the attention of a young girl. This is what started the trouble.

They yelled out of the car window at the girl who was standing outside of her house. One of the girl's brothers got mad and yelled at the men, and in response to that, one man jumped out of the vehicle. The commotion attracted the girl's four other brothers who came out and became involved in the fight. The brothers eventually went back into the house. Both friends drove off to get another friend for backup.

They came back to the girl's house bringing sharp weapons with them and entered the home. All of them fought, and the 23-year-old Emirati sustained severe injuries. The 5 brothers and 2 friends are detained, while the 23-year-old, is recovering in a hospital and under the watch of a guard. No further information available.

Cops Beat up Bounced Check Suspect

A 27-year-old Emirati policeman and his 47-year-old partner beat up a 45-year-old Egyptian man. They did this over a check that had bounced for $5,445. The Egyptian man explained to a court he had been at a grocery store paying for his groceries. All of a sudden two cops approached him and showed him their badges and demanded he goes with them.

He asked the officers to wait until he finished paying for his items. The cops took him out of the store and pushed him on the ground, and his nose bled. He asked them why they are arresting him, but they both kept beating him until one policeman saw that a crowd was gathering.

Then they took him into a civilian car where he is punched 20 times in the left eye. When they stopped at a traffic light, they "spit" on him. They also stopped at a gas station where one officer "bit his chest." When they arrived at the police station, he found out it was because of a bounced check.

The man's wife arrived and saw the bad condition her husband was in. She said his clothes were ripped and covered in blood. He was assaulted with injuries all over his body. The defendants deny the assault, and the case is adjourned. No further information.

American Jailed over Swearing

A 35-year-old American mother lost her temper at a traffic cop and "supposedly" swore during a road incident. A 24-year-old Emirati policeman told a court he blocked a service road due to an accident. He was waiting for paramedics to come and help the motorists that were injured.

The mom came along and asked if she could pass through since the building she lived in was right there. The officer said he told her to wait five minutes and directed her where to go, but she refused to move. He told her she will have to move her car, and then she yelled and swore at him.

He told her to calm down, but she drove away and repeated the "swear words." The housewife denied swearing at the officer and said she had been waiting for 40 minutes. She says she was with her baby who was sick, and she just wanted to get home.

Admitting to only yelling to clear the way, the mom is found guilty. She

received 1 month in jail for swearing at a police officer in a "road rage."
Policeman Steals Co-Workers Cash
A policeman is on trial for taking money from 2 policewomen at the Dubai airport. The policewomen left their purses unattended in a private bathroom when the Yemeni officer snuck in and stole $735 from their bags. A 35-year-old airport janitor from Nepal saw the officer going into the bathroom.

A CCTV showed the officer entering the bathroom twice putting the money in his pocket. The defendant pleaded not guilty to theft, and the trial is adjourned.
Motorist Produces Someone Else's License to Cops
A 29-year-old Dubai born Egyptian woman is pulled over by the police. The incident happened early one morning when the officer did a routine check on her plate, and he saw she had 30 outstanding driving offences. Stopping her, he asked for her license.

She refused and said she had done nothing wrong. He then told her it was for a "security check." She handed over the license, and the picture was clearly a different person. She said she had plastic surgery and insisted that it was her. The license really belonged to an Emirati woman. The Egyptian was also trying to hide the previous trouble she was in with her driving offences.

She told the officer she will teach him a lesson then drove off, but the officer followed her home. At the woman's house she became angry and said if he didn't go away she will report the officer to the police chief and have him fired. She "kicked his car" and wanted to "back into it," but a relative stopped her. The officer called for backup, and they arrested her.

The woman didn't attend the hearing, and the case is adjourned. She faces up to 3 years in jail and deportation if found guilty on all charges.
Cop Runs over 10-Year-Old Boy with a Jet Ski
A 10-year-old boy is severely injured, because a 23-year-old off duty Emirati police officer on a jet ski ran over him and left. The young boy was playing in the water at a beach when a jet ski crashed into him ripping one side of his face wide open. The cop left the boy in the water to drown when he started his jet ski back up and vanished. Luckily, the boy's friend was there to save him.

The child is due to have his third facial surgery that will cost $26,000 and is facing multiple reconstruction procedures. The doctors also said they need to remove the hardware they put into his skull during the second surgery. That surgery cost $62,000. After the third surgery is completed, he will then undergo multiple cosmetic procedures to fix the scars. The 10-year-old has a long road ahead of him.

He endured intensive surgeries to save his right eye and to repair the damage. There is a hole on the right side of his belly from a skin graft they performed to fix the side of his face. Doctors said skin grafting will have to be done two, or three more times.

The boy and his mother are now living in the U.S., and his father plans on joining them when the legal proceedings wrap up. As for the Emirati policeman, he is sentenced to only 1 year in prison. The father of the boy did not have high expectations of a lengthy prison sentence and said: "I actually expected something like 2 months."

Tinted Windshield Crack Down

A HUGE problem that Dubai has is most of the windows on the vehicles are tinted so dark that they are practically blacked out. Motorists have to roll their windows down to see. It is not uncommon for vehicles to also have the "front windshield" heavily tinted.

The traffic police are cracking down. They said: "30% [of sunlight blockage] is the legal limit, but motorists have up to 70%, leaving them unable to see objects in front of them." Violators will face a fine of $136 and have their car seized for 30 days.

CHAPTER 10

PHYSICIANS

There has been "56" physicians and nurses caught working "illegally" in hospitals, and many other medical facilities without a license. The Health Authority is struggling to develop a solution to crack down on unlicensed medical staff. They want to raise awareness to let everyone know, just how many individuals try to practice without a license.

Additionally, the Ministry of Health's Alternative Medicine Committee is warning anyone who is considering beauty treatments, or cosmetic work to check for the beauty therapists' license. Recently the committee reported that laser technicians must have a certificate when they perform treatments such as hair removal, and any person consulting someone on weight loss.

There is also an enormous concern as to why physicians are generously giving out medicine as if it were candy. If a doctor doesn't have a definite diagnosis of what your illness might be, and frequently if they do, they consistently give out antibiotics. In addition, you are provided a whole slew of other types of pills.

A patient went into a clinic with chest pain and breathing problems and stepped out with a "heavy duty" antibiotic. They were told it could be an infection. As time went by, the patient eventually found out it was bronchitis. The antibiotic that was originally given, resulted in the patient having horrible side effects, in which they still continue to suffer from.

While we lived in Dubai, there wasn't a designated cancer treatment center, or no bone marrow transplant provision. The Sheik [Ruler of Dubai and pronounced shake] has now ordered a cancer facility to be built. The director of Dubai Health Authority is launching a study on the center. He said: "They will recruit world class oncology experts to lead research into the most effective forms of treatment for the killer disease."

All expatriate people who are diagnosed with diseases are held at a deportation center. This could happen to anyone. They stay in two tiny cells and live in squalor. One is for the men, and the other is for the women. They can be held in these cells for over 2 weeks awaiting deportation back to their home countries. Guards are placed at the doors of these rooms making sure that no one escapes.

The rooms are filthy, and trash is spread across the floor. They are badly ventilated and mattresses people lie on are dirty. The reality of how this deportation center operates is ghastly, sometimes 9 men are sprawled over limited bunk beds, and others on the floor on top of mattresses. While on the other side of the wall, women are kept in the same condition with guards standing watch. They are treated as if they were criminals. There is a door leading into the room that has a small window used to pass food and for communication.

A man who was diagnosed with HIV was not even aware he had it since no one told him. He said: "After I went to renew my residence visa, I was told to go to the hospital. They asked me to go into an x-ray room and once inside they locked me up."

The Ministry of Health said: "We have instructions from the police to lock up expatriate patients and not to inform them about their illness." There are laws and regulations in place that are "supposed" to protect the public. There is no reason to treat people in such an inhumane way just because they are sick.

Many laborers refuse to visit a doctor for things such as diabetes, high blood pressure and other medical problems. They fear their disease will be reported to their employer, and their job will be terminated. Since these people do not see doctors in their home country, they are not going to see one in the U.A.E. either.

A doctor who is very concerned over the laborers health said: "They make up a huge percentage of the population in the U.A.E. They tend to come from Asia where there is a lot of people with tuberculosis, which is a time bomb. Even though people who do suffer from tuberculosis are banned in the U.A.E., the workers go back home to visit. They come in contact with a person who has it."

A rule has been implemented saying that if you are sick, you need a doctor's note to go back to work. You will be charged $16 for the physician to write it out. The money that is collected goes to the government.

The doctors are prohibited to write sick notes for longer than 3 days at a time, regardless of your illness or injury. You are required to go back to the doctor every 3 days and pay each time. By having to pay to get a doctors excuse for not being at work, only gives the laborers more reason not to visit a doctor. Sometimes they don't even make $16 in a day. Since no one needs a prescription to buy most kinds of medicine, the migrant workers feel they don't have to see a doctor. If they think they know what ails them, they can just go to a pharmacy and ask for medication that fits their self-diagnosis.

Rules for Emirati Doctor's License are Waived

The health authorities in Abu Dhabi said there is no need for "work experience" and "exams" for Emirati doctors. They are trying to fill the shortage of physicians in the country. They believe that by scrapping some of these rules, this will encourage local Emirati grads into the health field.

The physicians already practicing are worried about the patients' safety. Experts in the field say that educators must do more as the sector booms and the students lack the skills for healthcare.

But, the health authorities are still waiving the 2 year work experience for Emirati graduates. They said: "Previously, work experience was required yet there was none to be offered." Emiratis also do not have to take the medical exam still required for expats. New found grads who leave the U.A.E. programs with a 4 year degree will still have credentialing, and verification procedures done before they can receive their license.

The Ministry of Health in Dubai is using some of the same practices as Abu Dhabi. They said they will not give a license to a doctor unless that doctor works at a private healthcare facility. Expats in Dubai are still the only ones who need to take the medical exam. They too waived the 2 year work experience, not only for locals, but expats.

The grads in Dubai are immediately employed at a government hospital where they have to work for 1 year then are evaluated and given the status of a General Practitioner. After they work 2 years at a public healthcare facility, they can work anywhere and open their own clinic if they wish. Almost 26% of doctors in the ministry's facilities are U.A.E. Nationals.

Doctor Loses Lawsuit after Bad Diagnose

An Arab man went to the hospital when his eyes and mouth turned red, and he developed a body rash. After being examined, he was told that he had a disease like smallpox and because it was highly contagious, he needed to keep away from his wife and child. He then was given medicine and told to go home and rest.

A week later his condition worsened, he was in pain so he returned to the hospital, but this time a different doctor was assigned to him. Again, the same diagnosis was given, and he was prescribed medicine. Nothing was helping the man and his condition only intensified.

For the third time he returned to the hospital. He was told once more it was a disease resembling smallpox. He then tried a different hospital to seek opinions of other doctors as by now he was losing consciousness. The new doctor found that he was suffering from an allergic reaction that has now affected his kidneys, and blood sugar level. It took 3 weeks to recover fully with the proper care and treatment.

The man sued the first set of doctors for an improper diagnose, and he was rewarded $35,394 by the court.

Botched Birth and Doctor Pays

A 50-year-old German doctor delivered a baby vaginally to a 39-year-old Swiss woman at a local hospital. It resulted in her baby becoming paralyzed down one arm. The woman was giving birth when according to the doctor, she stopped pushing when the baby's head was out. The doctor said: "It was dangerous to stop pushing since it could cause the baby brain damage, especially with the umbilical cord wrapped around the baby's neck."

The child's shoulder became stuck as the doctor forced the mother to give birth naturally. This resulted in the doctor trying to pull the baby out which caused 35% to 50% of the baby becoming paralyzed down one arm. The baby girl weighed 10 lbs. 5 ozs.

The court said the baby should have been delivered by C-section. The doctor was fined $2,722 for negligence.

Doctor Causes Death after Woman gives Birth

An Indian doctor and 4 Bangladeshi women are tried over the death of a housemaid when she had complications after giving birth. Four Bangladeshi women took a housemaid and her newborn infant to a clinic when she began bleeding heavily after she gave birth.

At the clinic, an Indian doctor treated her then released her. But, the housemaid died in the car on the way back home. The Bangladeshi women dumped the body and the newborn infant, outside of a hospital. The Indian doctor claimed she never treated the woman. She said she only advised the Bangladeshi women to get her to a hospital since she was in critical condition.

During the trial, the doctor was absent since she was visiting her sick husband in India. In court they found the 5 defendants guilty. The doctor was sentenced to 1 year in prison. She had since returned to the U.A.E. No further information on the Bangladeshi women.

Doctor, Nurse and Private Hospital Charged with Endangering a Baby

The parents of a baby are given out-of-date milk, making the baby sick. Parents of a 3-month-old infant took her to a hospital for a routine checkup. The doctor gave them a prescription for a fortified milk to help with the girl's development. The wife picked up the formula from the head nurse of the children's wing.

After returning home, the mother gave the baby the formula and then noticed that the 16 cartons were 6 months out-of-date. The mother went back to the hospital to inform the doctor who told her to go home and dump the formula. She soon returned to the hospital, but this time with the baby girl as she was vomiting, and suffering from diarrhea.

The father was so angry that he reported the hospital to the police. The doctor, nurse and private hospital have been charged with endangering a baby's life. No further information is available.

Doctor Charged in Botched Operation

An Asian doctor has been charged for leaving a man infertile after a medical operation. An Arab man went in for what appeared to be a common medical procedure. The doctor cut into the patient's scrotum using an incision not common, nor recommended for this surgery. He was left infertile.

The court ordered a Medical Review Committee to look into the case, and they found that the infertility was a result of a medical error. The doctor was ordered to pay the man $27,225 and was given a fine of $2,722.

Medical Professionals Flocking to Dubai

A CEO from a medical firm is speaking out by saying the world's top talent from the most prestigious medical institutions are heading to Dubai. He said: "This is due to our massive increase in investments which in turn has been attracted by Dubai's impressively high quality of services. This chain reaction will create a continuous cycle because the best professionals want to work at the best hospitals which in turn attracts the best investments and so on [sic]." Really?

Negligent Docs Cause Death of Premature Baby

A 35-year-old Filipina mother went into premature labor and had twins. She delivered 2 baby girls 13 days early. Twenty-two hours after giving birth, one of the baby girls died. The twin had complications, she did not cry and her lips were turning blue. She was transferred to the intensive care unit where she passed away.

During the autopsy, it was discovered that the baby died due to bleeding in her lungs. There was an infection that neither the Canadian doctor, nor the Indian doctor realized.

The Canadian testified that he had done his job perfectly and took proper steps in caring for the baby. The court handed each doctor a 6 month suspended sentence. The mother said she was doing well.

Patient Finds Lump after Doctor says no need for Breast Exam

A 52-year-old Jordanian woman requested a breast exam from her gynecologist. She was told it wasn't necessary. She then asked the doctor to show her the right way to do a self-exam. Again the doctor refused, and she was told she need not worry because she carried none of the risk factors.

The woman stopped seeing the doctor since the doctor complained she did not have time to talk. She said she was so busy seeing 70 patients, in an 8 or 9 hour period every day. The problem was that the woman had a family history of breast cancer.

A few years later while taking a shower, she felt a hard lump. She didn't want to tell her family since a special lunch was planned that day, but her daughter saw her tears and knew something was wrong. The next day she had a mammogram and a biopsy done. She discussed the results with her daughters. The decision was made to travel to the United States for treatment.

The physicians in the U.S. diagnosed her with stage three breast cancer, but they could treat her. The woman is now cancer free.

A hospital director in the U.A.E. said: "The patient load on the doctor is at times too much. They see 24 to 30 people each day depending on the specialty and the shortage of doctors."

Hospital Found Negligent over Death

A patient suffering from a disease [unknown] hadn't been given enough medicine, which weakened his immune system. This resulted in his death. The family filed a lawsuit against the doctor and hospital. They demanded $68,064. The doctor and hospital insisted they had no part in the patient's death.

In court the judge ordered a report by a Medical Review Committee that confirmed there had been negligence. The doctor and hospital were ordered to pay the family $68,064.

Fake Prescriptions

A 25-year-old Emirati man is accused of writing fake prescriptions for painkillers after buying a prescription pad. The man bought the prescription pad for $544 from an unknown person. He forged "official stamps" on it, to make it look legal and used it at various pharmacies. He successfully got away with writing 12 prescriptions before getting caught at a hospital.

The Emirati entered a hospital emergency room claiming he had "anemia," and he needed painkillers. He flashed the prescription at the hospital pharmacy and said it came from a doctor. The pharmacy thought it was suspicious when he showed them the pink copy of the prescription since that piece is usually kept in the patients file. Another giveaway was that the prescription was written out wrong, along with the dosage.

The pharmacy called the police. The man had been referred to the "psychiatric" ward for drug addiction.

Man Bites Nurse's Face

A Jordanian woman was attacked by a Pakistani man who stole her cell phone. The attack happened near her home in Dubai. The nurse was getting out of a taxi when a masked man grabbed her from the back. She tried to pull his mask off, and this made him furious so he bit her face. He then grabbed her cell phone and took off running.

Due to the injuries on her face, the woman had to undergo 3 cosmetic surgeries. She went back to her home country of Jordan to recover. The police asked the victim's sister if she would help catch the thief. She agreed, so the police had her call her sister's cell phone and talk to the bandit. To make him more relaxed, she told him she was in the country illegally.

She started a general conversation with the robber to arrange a date. The thief agreed to meet with the sister after talking a few times. They met in the same spot where the girl's sister was attacked. The man showed up wearing the same mask. When the police tried to arrest him, he resisted and bit off one officer's finger. The thief denies theft, assault and resisting arrest. He claimed that it was the police who assaulted him. No further information available.

Lab worker takes Cash in Exchange for Clean Bill of Health

A 40-year-old Indian tech at a medical testing center exchanged bad blood samples, with good blood from himself. The employee took cash from individuals affected with disease, such as hepatitis and those with heart problems. This helped them obtain visas to remain in the U.A.E. In a 3 month period, he falsified documents of more than 20 men who would otherwise not pass their medical for their work visa.

It is suspected he raked in $245 for each clean bill of health he had given out. A staff member of the facility, approached his Emirati manager to voice his suspicions of the Indian guy. They agreed 3 men will be ordered to redo the tests. However, none of the men came back.

The Indian tech informed his company he was leaving the country to care for his sick father. He never came back either. The testing center called the police. All 3 men are subsequently arrested, two of them from Pakistan and one from India.

The guys showed up in court. One man with hepatitis said he worked for a fishing company weighing and handling fish. He added: "I did not want anyone to find out about my disease because I knew I would lose my job and be deemed unfit to work with food."

All 3 men are charged with falsely getting a medical certificate for their visa, and all three denied the charge. The main suspect is still being hunted by police but believed to still be in India. No further information available.

Hospital, Doctor and Health Service Guilty for Burning Toddler

A 3-year-old Arab girl suffered severe burns on her legs during an ear operation. An Anesthesiologist placed a hot thermal bag on the little girl's legs, while a cochlear implant was performed. The hospital, doctor and health service firm are ordered to pay the parents $54,452.

Nurse Accused of Dropping Baby

A nurse holding a newborn baby tripped over electrical cables, but said she never dropped the baby. The nurse is convicted in a lower court of causing an injury "by mistake," and endangering a child's life. She is fined $816.

The case went to the Appeals Court. Her lawyer said: "The baby was released that same day and that would not have been possible if the baby was injured. Complications during birth resulted in temporary blood clots in the baby's head and that had nothing to do with the incident." No verdict was announced at the Appeals Court.

Hospital Pays for Burns during Laser Hair Removal

A woman received second-degree burns during a hair laser procedure at a hospital. She paid $6,806 for the treatment. The woman sued the hospital when her burn marks turned black. She claimed she suffered physical and psychological damage and demanded $170,165 plus the $6,806 for the procedure.

The hospital claimed no medical error had occurred. They said it was normal for people with sensitive skin to suffer from burns. The hospital said she was warned of possible side effects. They want the claim rejected by the court and said: "She could still recover fully from the burns."

The court ruled in favor of the patient. They said one reason for the burns [sensitive skin] wasn't enough and wanted a second reason. The hospital couldn't give another reason. They only said it was normal for people with sensitive skin. The court also said the hospital offered no proof of warning her of the side effects. Previously, the woman was awarded $27,226 by a lower court. After complaining that the amount was too small, the Appeal Court awarded her $40,839.

Doctor Accused of Killing a Toddler

A 3-year-old girl from Yemen was being treated by a 78-year-old South African doctor for leukemia. The doctor is accused of causing her death by not giving her a blood transfusion, which she needed. The doctor is claiming he gave her the blood transfusion. But, the doctor can't prove it because his lawyer said the paperwork is "missing" from her file.

The doctor went back home to South Africa before being charged. He was unaware he was on trial and sentenced for the girl's death. When he traveled back through Dubai airport many years later, they arrested him. He says that the "medical company" that he worked for should have told him he was wanted.

He said: "If I had been informed, I never would have traveled through Dubai." The doctor was held in jail for several weeks while he was fighting his sentence. Ultimately, he is found not guilty in 2 appeals. He said he is considering suing the "medical company" over his detention.

Reusing Nasal Spray

A woman with a sinus problem went to a doctor for an exam. A nurse took out a "used bottle of nasal spray," and insisted it was fine to use on the patient because she cleans it. The woman jokingly said that she is sure her insurance pays for a new bottle. She wonders if they reuse needles too.

Doctor Cleared of Patient Death

A doctor said he was not responsible for the death of a 60-year-old woman who had been battling cancer for years. He is cleared by a court.

The woman came to the United States back in 2002. She was having a liver, pancreas and partial stomach transplant. This was to stop the spread of cancer.

After she returned to U.A.E., she is repeatedly admitted to the hospital for stomach pain. She was referred to a surgeon who recommended that she have another part of her stomach removed. Soon afterwards, the woman died. Her family insisted that the health board take action against the doctor. A 1 year suspension for practicing was imposed.

After the year was up, the doctor fought the blemish that was on his record. He wanted it to be taken off. The case went to Dubai's highest court, the Federal Supreme Court. They looked at his record and saw it had been clean for 7 years in the U.A.E. They saw he graduated from a British surgical college where his record was also clean. The court then found him not guilty.

Plastic Surgeon Busted for Smoking Hashish

A Plastic Surgeon from Canada is arrested outside of a hotel. He got into a fight with a taxi driver and broke the driver's nose. The doctor began to argued with security guards at the hotel. A taxi driver who saw the argument, told the guards he will call the police if they want. The doctor then punched the taxi driver and broke his nose.

The doctor claims his finger got caught in the door of the taxi. He said he was only trying to get the taxi drivers attention when he "accidentally" hit him in the face. Traces of hashish are found in his urine which showed he had smoked it within the last few weeks.

The doctor claimed he may have "accidentally" inhaled the hashish at a nightclub he was just at. He also said: "In my line of work as a surgeon, many painkillers and medicines are used. It's possible they showed up in my blood stream, which was confused with hashish." In an earlier statement given by the doctor, he said he had eaten foods that contained hashish while in Canada.

The doctor is facing 4 years in jail and deportation. No further information available.

Doctor Jailed for Debt

An Indian couple who are both doctors wanted to start up a medical clinic. They borrowed $21,781 from a friend to help them out. They paid back most of it, but were short $5,445. Their friend took only the female doctor, and not her husband to court. She is fined and jailed for 4 months for not paying back the rest of the money.

The case is appealed and found to be too excessive so her sentenced is reduced to a fine of $408.

An Overweight Doctor can't be Trusted

A patient suffering from a mild illness had consulted many doctors. She said she noticed that every physician she met "were actually fat." The patient said: "Even after seeing so many doctors, my medical condition never improved either. If they were good to themselves, they would live a healthy lifestyle and as a result have a healthy physique. How can a doctor actually be allowed to be in control of other people's lives and wellness? Do authorities check out doctors before giving them permission to practice medicine? They should start looking at the FAT issue of the doctors."

Many public opinions followed this comment. Someone said: "The best doctor I have experienced is a genius in diagnostics, extremely talented and thorough. He is a chain smoker, eats snickers for breakfast and never has time to exercise because he spends his life at the hospital. Go judge him if you dare."

Mom Dies Giving Birth

A 34-year-old Emirati died after going into labor. Her uterus ruptured killing her and the baby. She's rushed to the hospital when she went into labor. The doctors delivered the baby, but the child did not survive. They tried to save the woman as she stayed in a coma for 12 hours but died of severe blood loss.

The victim's brother said that his sisters condition had gotten worse causing her to have high blood pressure. He said she asked for a caesarian section to be done. The hospital insisted that she could have a natural birth. They argued that it had worked in three other similar cases. The family requested specialists be brought in from other hospitals to save the woman's life, but the doctors refused. The doctors then performed a hysterectomy. No further information available.

Nurse Gives an Intravenous Injection Wrong

A nurse who gave an intravenous injection wrong caused clogging in a vein, and calcium to leak into a baby's arm tissue. This resulted in the baby's hand being amputated. Parents sued for the amputation of their premature baby's hand. The claim was for more than $136,128. It got reduced to $54,451.

In court attorneys said: "The error of the nurse was only one reason that caused the tragedy. The baby was just a little over 2 lbs. when it was delivered prematurely. It was not the result of the hospital entirely." No other information.

Wife Claims Husband is Bewitched by First Wife, Doctor says he's Fine

A wife is asking a court to issue a temporary order to stop her Emirati husband from traveling. She says this is only for his own protection. Her spouse become sick after visiting his second wife in another country. The first wife is claiming that her husband's new bride "bewitched" him and his oldest son. She says that whenever he visits the second wife in her country, he comes back suffering from witchcraft related illnesses.

The man eventually brought his second wife to Abu Dhabi and set her up in a rented house. During this time, his first wife and children are abandoned for a few months. When he returned to the first wife, his health was just fine.

The second wife then moved back to her home country which left the husband traveling once more. The first wife said he became ill again, and so did his older son. She took her husband to the hospital when he complained of a headache and pains all over his body. The doctor had found nothing wrong and said he was healthy. Then she took him to an Islamic Scholar who read verses from the Quran. He claimed to have exorcised djinns [demons] from the man's body.

She went to the police and told them she believed the djinns will return if he went back to visit his second wife. They advised her to take the case to court and seek help from a judge. The court agreed to enforce a temporary travel ban against the husband because he had fallen ill while abroad. The ban will be lifted when it becomes safe for the husband to travel again.

Illegal Skin Injections

A woman is arrested for performing illegal skin whitening injections. She admitted to ordering $1,633 of the drug online and hired a man to make all the deliveries. The woman imported a well-known anti-oxidant drug which doctors prescribe to patients that have liver and lung problems. The drug should only be taken under medical supervision. If the drug is taken in wrong doses, it could have very dangerous side effects.

The drug blocks the body's production of melanin, which turns the skin darker when it comes in contact with the sun. There is a huge market for this drug in Asia where the women want to lighten the color of their skin. No further information available.

Doctor Warns about Botox Coming to your Door

A surgeon is warning women that people are coming door-to-door offering Botox treatments. She said she is seeing more and more facial disfigurements such as deformed lips, cheeks and eyebrows tailing off in different directions.

The doctor is specifically talking about the Chinese counterfeit Botox. She said: "The concentration is entirely different from the certified Botox. The legitimate substances in the certified Botox has been copied and this can cause many deformities such as deviation of the mouth. The injection technique is also not correct since most of these people are not certified doctors or nurses." She has seen several patients who have used this Botox because the price was cheaper.

One of the worst cases she saw was a TV personality whose cheeks turned to stone after accepting the door-to-door treatment. She said: "Her cheeks were so hard that you could knock on them." The doctor is cautioning people to not have any kind of treatment done outside of a licensed healthcare facility. She says certainly not in your home.

She encourages the public to phone police if any shady people come to your door.

Man says Cancer Stops him from Smoking

A 29-year-old Egyptian man is caught with Hashish in his system. He said he is innocent because doctors told him not to smoke since he has cancer. The man is arrested at an apartment. In court, he said: "I didn't smoke hashish or take drugs. I have cancer and it's dangerous to even smoke a cigarette, doctors have banned me from smoking. I'm using special medicine to fight cancer."

He claims he had been in his home country and his friends were smoking hashish the day he left to go back to Dubai. That's how the drug entered his system.

The man's brother presented a medical report to the court that said: "A person who sits in a smoking area can be affected by the smoke." The outcome of the court case is unknown.

Kissing Cousins

A 14-year-old is taken to a hospital and found to have a low potassium level. They diagnosed the child with a rare kidney defect found in families who marry their cousins. Further tests showed that the child's siblings and cousins appeared to have the gene too. This gene is what causes the rare kidney defect. The child's parents were cousins who married and both sets of grandparents are also married cousins.

CHAPTER 11
LABORERS

Most of the laborers come to Dubai from various countries such as India, Bangladesh, Pakistan, Philippians and Sri Lanka to mention a few. These men work exceedingly long hours with limited time off, and meager pay. Oftentimes companies try to get away with not paying them. It's difficult to understand, but when a business stops paying their employees, they continue to work, hoping to receive pay in the future. They invested time into the company so now they can't just walk away.

There are families to support back in their home countries besides, supporting themselves, so they believe their salary will come. Unfortunately, and more times than not, they work for free.

Construction activity is being carried out all over Dubai, and safety issues do not appear to be a concern. Quite often safety equipment is not supplied, or equipment is inadequate. You will see laborers working on multi-story buildings with no safety harness or hard hats.

They will work in every weather condition. Including, sandstorms with gale-force winds, and the mere precaution given by their employers is to put on a mask because of the swirling sand. The extreme heat presents another set of problems too. More safety measures need to be set and adhered to.

The men live in very miserable conditions within their accommodations [place of residence], or labor camps. Complaints were coming in from laborers who work for a security company stating that their labor camp has joint bathrooms together with their kitchen. The toilet area used by the men is in the same place where they have to wash their dishes. Many men are becoming sick, and they don't understand why they are being treated in this manner. The guys have raised complaints within the labor camp but added that the superiors pay no attention to them.

Camps and accommodation areas are usually not peaceful either as fights and quarrels often break out among the men. Stress, resentment and hostility is so great it doesn't take much for a killing to occur. There isn't a day that passes that you don't discover a story like these two.

A fight broke out at a construction site when a colleague dropped cement on the face of a 23-year-old Pakistani man. The guy told his colleague to stop as he was approaching him, but he continued anyway with a friend. The two colleagues held the Pakistani and struck him with a metal bar then "cut off part of his ear." A witness saw a piece of his ear laying on the ground. The two men deny any wrongdoing. The case was adjourned.

An Asian laborer lost two fingers while operating a piece of machinery at a construction site. The worker sued, but the firm fought back and said that it was his own fault for not wearing protective gloves. His attorney said he lost his source of income because he only has "three fingers remaining." Experts are called into the court, and they agreed that he should be compensated as he has a disability. The Asian man sued for $59,899. The court rewarded him only $13,613.

High suicide is prevalent around the labor camps. Here a 53-year-old Asian laborer committed suicide inside his accommodation. He took a rope, tied it to the ceiling and hung himself. He is found by his roommate.

Often though it doesn't take much to please the men. New uniforms are given to 1,800 park employees which put a smile on their faces, and it boosted their moral. The new uniforms were orange and bright yellow, and are supposed to keep the men cooler, and safer because they can be seen from a distance. They are said to be more comfortable too.

But, security guards are not happy with what they have to wear to work. They said: "We don't mind wearing a uniform, but we do mind wearing a tie around our neck, a beret on top of our head, especially when it is hot. Summer is when relief should be given to avoid unconsciousness, we are not on the catwalk."

Guards told to Sit in the Hot Sun all Day

The security guards that keep watch over the construction sites are forced to sit out in the scorching sun all day. They are not allowed to go into the guard shacks unless there is an emergency. The men are forbidden to turn on the generators in the shacks that supply electricity for the air-conditioning. Often their lunch is ruined due to the heat, and they go hungry until the end of their shift when they can go back to their accommodations for dinner.

There has been a government crackdown on not giving laborers their breaks while making them work during the hottest part of the day. A rule is in place telling employers they must let people working outside rest from

12:30pm to 3:00pm. This rule is in effect for the 3 hottest months of the year. They also have to offer a shaded place to rest and also provide safety equipment.

There have been 87,571 companies investigated to make sure they have been following the rules. They found 312 were in violation, companies were not providing a shaded place to get out of the sun to prevent dehydration and heat stroke. A fine of $4,083 is imposed for each occurrence.

Unsafe Scaffolding

Two Asian laborers were fixing a sign when the scaffolding they were standing on collapsed and left one worker dead, and the other 60% disabled. The 42-year-old Indian engineer was busy at other job sites and had not been there when the scaffolding was built. The scaffolding was put up improperly causing it to fall. In addition, the two workers were not wearing their safety hats.

The court sentenced the safety engineer to 3 months in jail and ordered him to pay $54,450 in blood money to the family of the deceased.

Killed by a Water Tank

A 36-year-old Indian laborer is crushed when a water tank he replaced came crashing through the roof of his dilapidated house. The man's home was ancient and falling apart. Just before going to bed one evening, the laborer replaced his water tank with a larger one, on top of his roof.

As he slept, the water tank along with pieces of the roof fell on him, and killed him instantly.

Laborer Chops off his Own Fingers

A Bangladeshi man cut off four of his fingers while being distraught when his girlfriend broke up with him. A roommate noticed how depressed and withdrawn he became, after he return from his home country. One morning all the men woke up and went to work, except for the Bangladeshi man, and one roommate.

The man walked into the kitchen, grabbed a knife and cut off four fingers on his right hand that was tattooed with his ex-girlfriend's name. He then placed the fingers in a cloth and laid them on his bed. When the roommate walked in and saw the blood, he didn't know what to do so he called the landlord who then called the police. Eventually an ambulance came and took him away. No further information.

2 Die Inside of an Oil Tank

A 34-year-old Egyptian man, and a 27-year-old Pakistani man died while cleaning out a diesel tank. The two men inhaled toxic fumes and are found dead inside. Two other men are found in critical condition outside.

Four men entered the tank taking no safety precautions or used any safety equipment. Toxic fumes quickly overcame the 4 men, leaving two of them trapped. The two surviving men are quickly rushed to the hospital and admitted to the intensive care unit. No further information.

Laborer Guilty of Causing a Heart Attack

A Bangladeshi laborer had gotten into a fight with another laborer over a water pump. After the victim is hit by the Bangladeshi, he suffered a heart attack which resulted in his death.

The Bangladeshi is sentenced to 2 years in jail, but had his sentence increased to 3 years for causing the man to have a heart attack.

Laborer gets 10 Years in Prison

A 29-year-old Bangladeshi carpenter is insulted, so he retaliated by killing the person who insulted him. The Bangladeshi met the victim drunk at a bus stop. The victim was asking for help back to the labor camp where he lived. He ended up urinating on himself when he yelled and insult the carpenter.

The carpenter retaliated by punching and kicking the victim which ultimately killed him. He said, "I could not help myself." The carpenter then took the victim's cell phone, along with $6. The Bangladeshi man is sentenced to 10 years behind bars.

No Wages for 16 Workers

An Emirati man who owns a company performing cleaning and maintenance services, hired 16 Bangladeshi men from a Bangladeshi subcontractor. The men worked for the Emirati for 3 or 4 months when they came to him and said that the Bangladeshi boss has not paid them.

The 16 men filed a complaint with the court. When the Emirati is asked by the court why the men had not been paid, he said he paid the subcontractor every month, and didn't know why he didn't pay them.

The boss pocketed the men's money and left them with empty promises of payment. All the men said how crucial it is to receive their pay since their families back home are waiting for the money. The Bangladeshi boss was not in court. The outcome of the case is unknown.

Employer Imposed Work Ban on Worker who was Injured

An Arab man is injured in a road accident. He had spent more than 6 months in his home country trying to recover. When the man tried to go back to work in the U.A.E., he learned he was terminated. He found a new job, but that's when he found out that his former employer filed a 6 month ban against him. The previous employer said: "The Arab had given unclear reasons for not being at work."

The court sided with the Arab man and said the ban isn't allowed and they canceled it.

CHAPTER 12
PAWS-N-CLAWS

The rise of maimed animals on the street has not gone unnoticed. The public is screaming out to end the torture of animals, and they feel a demand for a discussion on the regions animal welfare laws. People have found animals with plastic bags tied around them, pets that are burnt and some with slash marks done with a knife.

Responsibility of owning a pet means nothing to many in the U.A.E. They buy puppies and kittens because they are adorable and cuddly, but as soon as those animals grow bigger, they are disposed of as if they are rubbish. There is no compassion what-so-ever. Abused animals are treated for being shot, stabbed and poisoned. Many say awareness needs to be carried out teaching people how to live with pets. A vast population in the U.A.E. don't know how, they only know farm animals.

It infuriates people that animal callousness can go virtually unpunished in Dubai. There seems to be an absence of care and concern by the authorities. This on top of small fines when an individual is caught abusing animals is unacceptable. People have claimed if camels or Arabian horses were involved in cruelty, there would be much tougher regulations, fines and possible prison time. The current fine is merely $272. People believe the fine should be least $2,722.

The brutality found towards families pets is also overwhelming. Often these pets are stolen and abused. A 2-year-old female cat found her way home, and was bleeding from either having a thin wire, or a fishing line wrapped around her neck. She was given to a child as a birthday gift, and the youngsters of the household are devastated to see their pet in this condition. The cat devotes most of her life now just staring, and each time she twists her neck the wound opens, and bleeds. The family said: "It's going to take time to heal."

A motorist saw a kitten being flung out of a car, the kitten struggled to fend off being struck by moving vehicles. The motorist was numb, and couldn't stop due to the moving traffic, but eventually turned around. The motorist reached the kitten and said: "It was too late as the kitten's body was mutilated." The body was placed in a plastic bag and set on the side of the road. The motorist said: "This is a game or sport among youngsters."

A dog owner wondered why the shoulder of her dog was injured. The maid informed the owner she had caught 2 Arab boys with a sling-shot, firing objects from across the street into the yard. The owner is now considering putting up a CCTV.

Warning to the Public to Stop Buying Exotic Animals

Believe it or not, many photos of large cats inside vehicles were being snapped. These animals are lions, tigers and cheetahs hanging outside of car windows in Dubai. Some people think it's OK to have these animals as a pet, but the government is warning the public to stop buying these cats.

The animals are being bought illegally for $4,083 to $13,612 overseas and are then importing them into the U.A.E. People are purchasing these cats as a "status symbol," and are thinking purely of themselves and not the wellbeing of the animals. They are not only putting themselves and other residents at risk, but taking part in illegal trade of wildlife.

These creatures belong in the wild and are not suited as pets cruising around in cars. A lion is spotted roaming around freely in a Nissan Armada, and a photo is snapped of a young lioness in a separate vehicle. But, the police said: "There is no law saying you can't transfer a wild animal in your car, but use common sense."

A Monkey Frequents a Nightclub

Patrons are outraged when a person paraded a wild monkey around in a club filled with cigarette smoke, loud music and drunk people. The public is calling for a boycott against the club.

Management at the club is saying that the person snuck the monkey in to the establishment. They said the moment the staff noticed the monkey, they told the manager who then kicked the customer and his monkey out. The customer is now banned.

Caged Monkeys and Chained Falcons Spotted

Two large monkeys and eight falcons are being treated inhumanly, as the monkeys sat in a tiny, filthy cage near a motorcycle rental store. The condition of the monkeys are atrocious, with large painful looking growths on their backsides. The teeth of the larger monkey chatters uncontrollably. They were sitting out in the blazing hot sun with no water, and no food.

The eight falcons are chained to the ground by a short rope tied to their legs. When they tried to fly away, they are jerked back down. The birds too are in the hot sun with no water or food. These people abusing animals desperately need to be stopped.

A Stolen Gazelle

A gazelle is stolen from a farm and is abused so badly that it died. A 29-year-old Emirati man had stolen a gazelle along with 4 sheep from an Emirati farmer. He drove his 4x4 to the farm, walked into the barn and dragged out the gazelle. He tied it up in his vehicle then went back into the barn and dragged out the sheep. The man who had an Emirati friend along with him, both went to the animal market to sell the animals. This was after they badly abused them.

A Bangladeshi market trader watched the man drag the injured gazelle into his store. He then bought it for $952, but it later died due to broken bones in her neck and internal bleeding. When the Emirati farmer realized that his animals were missing, he contacted the police. Police launched an investigation that lead to the Bangladeshi market trader.

Both men are taken to court. The Emirati thief said he really needed the money to pay his ex-wife and children so that's why he stole the animals. He is given 6 months in jail. The Emirati friend and Bangladeshi market trader are each given a fine of $544 for aiding and abetting and possessing stolen property.

Cats Doused in Chemicals

Pet owners are horrified as their cats are being tortured, leaving them burned and traumatized. Families are finding their cats are being soaked in lighter fluid and burnt. The animals are coming home to their owners trembling, panting and shortness of breath, in obvious pain. The cats are taken to veterinarian hospitals with burns all over their bodies.

Police are notified by the families, but could not do much without a name. They said: "Anyone who torches an animal will be fined $272."

Friend Steals Dog

An Asian man steals 2 rare dogs from his friend while he was away and caused the death of one. The Asian man is seen entering the house of his friend and taking the two dogs. The man knew the dogs well and had known his friend paid $2,178 for the dogs because of their rare breed. He intended to sell them, but he kept the dogs in such poor condition that one dog died.

He is taken to court by his friend, but the trial is adjourned to a later date. No further information.

A Clinic for Fat Pets

Dubai sets up their first ever obesity clinic for pets, and 100 dogs have benefited so far. Owners were giving their pets pizza, burgers, ice cream and chips, and one woman even gave her dog spicy burritos. She couldn't figure out why her pooch had diarrhea.

The new establishment didn't run without their own glitches. A Border Collie at the clinic weighed 100 lbs. and was being fed standard dog food by the clinic. The clinic just couldn't understand why the dog was not losing weight. They set up cameras and saw the dog bullying and eating the other dogs' food.

After the clinic resolved the problem, the dog is now in shape weighing in at 42 lbs. The clinic has gotten other dogs' weight under control such as a mixed Bernese Mountain Dog who weighed in at double his size and tipped the scales at 176 lbs. The clinic is pleased to announce all the dogs have slimmed down and are doing great.

Dogs Put Down after Owners Run up Kennel Bill

Authorities put down 4 dogs after the owners ran up a kennel bill of $5,172. The kennel owner said he desperately tried for months to get the owners to pay. He said he reluctantly, and as a last resort, went to the authorities concerning the dogs he was holding. Authorities said: "The dogs are not suitable for adoption and would have to be put down."

The couple who owned the dogs said they were rescue dogs. Both ran into financial difficulties and is forced to downsize their home, which left no room for the dogs. They faced having to board their dogs at the kennel for a discounted rate of $6 per day for each dog. A normal rate at the kennel is $27 per day. The couple said they love their dogs and admit the payments being made were not always consistent, but they were struggling with their bills.

They struck a deal with the kennel owner to pay $2,586. The kennel owner agreed and said he will drop the case he made against them with the authorities. They were due to make the final payment within a month, but the dogs were already put down. The kennel owner said: "I have a staff of 28 people and I pay rent in the amount of $98,012 for the facility, I'm not running a charity."

Dog Killed at a Pet Show

A family was mourning the death of their poodle after it is killed by an American Staffordshire Terrier at a pet show. A witness said they saw the little poodle on a short leash sniff the terrier from behind while he was occupied. The terrier became startled, and his instinct was to turn around and bite. That's when the incident happened, with no further attack.

The terrier's owner said the dog has never been violent. The family said they will demand compensation from the family who owned the dog and the organizers of the show. The family said: "The organizers of the show should have enforced any high risk dogs or aggressive dogs to wear muzzles. They should at least keep the big dogs separated from the little ones."

The terrier was put into a "doggie jail" but eventually let out when the municipality officials deemed him not to be a threat. The owner of the terrier is fined $1,361 for not controlling the pet and failing to prevent him

from harming others.
How to Avoid an Attack by a Camel in Heat
Warnings were circulating on how to avoid a camel in heat. Experts said:

> *The time to be careful is between November and March as this is the time camels can become irritated by humans. The male camels are thinking of the female camels. If you see a pink balloon coming out of the side of the camel's mouth stay away. The camel is trying to attract female camels and are more likely to strike out at humans. If you are attacked expect it on the left side of your body. For some reason, most of the camels tend to bite the thin parts of a person's body such as the neck and upper limbs. We discourage you to make any noise that might sound like a female camel since that can bring a world of trouble.*

Glad we got that straight!
Dubai Loves their Coffee, but Civet Droppings?
Kopi Luwak Coffee is popular in Indonesia, but there is a debate in Dubai whether drinking the upscale and expensive coffee should be boycotted. Small nocturnal animals from Asia named the civet is captured and put into cages. The tiny animals are fed coffee cherries, and after digesting and excreting, the cherries are then collected to make coffee.

I have to admit that the entire process sounds terrible and disgusting, but while I was in Bali, I went to a coffee plantation where I learned the process. The coffee was pretty good. It is advocated that these animals are kept in small cages. I saw only one civet in a rather large cage, and I witnessed no abuse.
Otters Masters of Painting
Six otters at the Dubai Aquarium and Underwater Zoo have learned to paint. Any visitor wanting to watch them are more than welcome. The aquarium said you can buy the finished artwork or have a picture painted and pick the color of paints.
Fish Fans not Amused over Gimmick
A publicity stunt at the Dubai Mall has dropped a replica of a sparkling cherry red Mini Cooper in the Dubai Aquarium. The promotion is a campaign for a car company. This has left a fishy taste to animal lovers. They said it is not fair to the creatures inside the tank since it puts them at risk of pollution and is detrimental to their wellbeing.

The Dubai Mall said: "The suspension of the car in the aquarium was planned and executed very carefully. The car weights 530 lbs. and the frame is treated to prevent any adverse impact on the water or aquatic animals."

Cat Tortured in a Microwave

This story took place in Lebanon. A young man put his cat inside a microwave and turned it on while his friend filmed the torture. In the video, the friend laughs and said: "Here is the criminal H. H. imprisoning a cat in the microwave and warming it." The cat survived, but was badly burned. Lebanon has "no law" that says such an act is a criminal offense. Some people have said Lebanon is raising young criminals.

CHAPTER 13

JOBS

Getting a job in the U.A.E. use to be straight forward. If you had the proper skills and experience, you got the job. Now, it is beauty instead of brains. Candidates are going under the knife to boost their careers. The employers nowadays are seeking "good-looking women." They are focusing on facial features, and overall physical appearance. This is what it comes down to on whether you get the job. Having the proper qualifications does not matter.

Most jobs that are advertised in the U.A.E. want you to send your resume in, but they require a photo of yourself. An applicant said: "Wake up Dubai, good looks may not last forever, but knowledge does."

Many women are perturbed at seeing females as nothing more than a side-line in the U.A.E. You will find young beautiful girls appearing in major corporate announcements and advertisements, they are told to smile and don't talk. But, the Arab world has claimed they are trying to raise the participation rate of women in the workforce. It is being said if they wish this to be a success, they need "more" women in leadership roles, not just standing quietly looking pretty.

A long-time resident of 9 years said they saw a huge racial discrimination in jobs, very blatant. The resident stated: "It is always best to be white or Arab." The resident stressed the strong laws against discrimination in the U.S., Europe and Australia and says they hope one day the region too will follow them in Equal Employment.

Fired for being Pregnant

A woman is fired and given a short notice to leave her company. She is pregnant, and the company didn't want to pay for her medical insurance.

The office the woman works at is closing, the rest of the staff is being transferred, except for her. There are two openings at the new branch, both are in her department. The company filled these positions by promoting other employees and didn't offer a position to her.

She composed a letter to her boss explaining that she received a level A in her evaluations, and there has been no complaints about her. She informed him she could not get a new job while being pregnant since "no one will hire her." At first the boss told her she could work at the new branch until she delivered her baby. She could then use her maternity leave to look for a new job. He later changed his mind and said there were no further positions available, and dismissed her at once.

The company where she worked is voted the "best" in the U.A.E. for women to work for.

Fired for not Cleaning up after a Friend of the Boss

A woman is working in an office as an "office girl." She wasn't trained by anyone or even told what she needed to do, but she figured it out on her own, and was always professional.

The woman's male boss had a friend who visited the office occasionally. He asked her for a favor and wanted her to go to his apartment and clean it after she got off from work. She refused since it wasn't in her contract. From that point on the friend caused trouble for her. He tried to get her boss to fire her.

One day, the friend brought in another woman to do her job at the office, and the girl ended up getting fired. She was upset since the boss's friend doesn't even work for the company. She doesn't understand how he has the power to bring in and remove staff. At this point she is seeking advice and isn't sure what to do.

Waiting 4 Hours for a Walk in Interview

Thousands of people stood in line for hours waiting for a job interview. Most were turned away due to the company being unable to handle the vast amount of people. Many of the job seekers said they preferred to fill out an application online, but the company didn't set it up that way. Applicants believe this would have eased the long lines, and chaos due to the many thousands of people waiting outside to get in.

You must have patience and perseverance to find a job in Dubai that suits you.

Lunchtime Sunbather Spotted on a Bench

People were in shock when they saw a man with no shirt, lying on a bench in public during lunch hour. They couldn't believe what they were seeing, especially since a bunch of students were in the area. Public comments are made, they said: "People do not want to see that sort of thing since it will spread. That behavior is unacceptable, and the bench was also situated right next to office buildings." Other people said: "If only the U.A.E. cared more about the murders and rapists as much as they do about the sunbathers and kissing!"

Salon Workers Fight over Clients

Two men working at a salon got into a fight over clients. One man said the other stole his customers, and the other is accused of hitting his colleague over the head with a hairdryer.

The two men at first got along well, things soured once they found out they were on commission. They both needed the money to send back to their family members. The men are from Arabic countries in political turmoil, and the money is needed to bring their families to the U.A.E.

One stylist was a hairdresser his adult life, and the other just learned the trade in the U.A.E. when taught by his colleague. The experienced hairdresser said his colleague likely didn't understand how the salon operated. It started when one man gave out his business card to the other man's client at the front door.

One day the hairdresser noticed his client sitting in his colleague's chair. He suspected his clients were being stolen from him and that this was going on for several months. After the client left, the fight broke out. One man pushed the other against the wall and hit him in the face with a hairdryer.

He told a court it was in self-defense. No further information available.

Boss Flees Leaving Hundreds Unpaid

An Indian man who was the boss of a construction company fled the country and left the company in a crisis. It is unclear how much of the company assets he took with him. There are 1,500 workers, and 500 support staff left without a paycheck, and they were frantically trying to get their money.

An engineer from Sudan is owed $27,224. Her boss stopped paying her in November, but she stayed with the company until July believing they will pay her. The courts are flooded with claims, and a group of employees even contacted the Indian Embassy to see if they could help with locating their boss.

Documents showed that one month after fleeing the country, the Indian man turned over legal responsibility to a business partner. No further information available.

Sued over a Complaint Made on TV

A 28-Year-old Indian man is sued by his former boss for saying, his employer was unfair, and the labor camp was unorganized and dirty. The man worked for a jewelry store as a salesman. A tv news show that suspected the company was mistreating its staff, had invited him to come on the show to be interviewed.

The man told the news show that his boss docked him 4 days of his salary when he only took 2 days off from work. He said they don't get their weekends off including Friday [like our Sunday]. He works 7 days a week for 15 hours a day, with no extra pay. Employees' passports are also being held by the company, and they stay in dirty accommodations full of bugs.

The boss said: "The interview damaged my reputation not to mention insulting. The salesman came to me before the interview and wanted $6,806 or he would ruin the reputation of my shop." The case was adjourned.

CHAPTER 14

WHEELS

To obtain a driver's license in Dubai, we needed to get an eye exam at an optical store. A "giant" chart with capital letters was held up in front of me. They asked what letters I "can't see" on the chart. I replied, "I can see all of them." In an instant they informed me I passed the eye exam.

As we headed over to an agency, equal to the D.M.V. to apply, and receive our license, my spouse is handed a piece of paper and a pen. The Emirati man asked him to write a statement which gave me his "permission" to drive. He is given a choice by the authorities "to let me" drive in all of the U.A.E., or just Dubai. We showed proof of a valid U.S. driver's license and the process was finished.

An interesting part of driving in the U.A.E. is the way speeding fines, parking tickets or any kind of moving violation is issued. Most likely you will not be stopped by a police officer who will write you a ticket on the spot. Instead, you are notified of your offense, and subsequent fine via text message. You may or may not recognize what you did wrong as was the case with my spouse.

He received a text message stating he had to appear at the police station, or our car will be impounded. When he showed up at the station, he is informed that he made an illegal turn and had to pay $54 in fines. When he questioned where the violation took place, they didn't know, other than a police officer spotted him make an illegal turn. He asked for proof showing he performed an illegal turn since he didn't realize he had. They proceeded to make him sit at the police station for two hours while they struggled to gather the proof.

When finally presented with the confirmation, the paper contained the make and model of our car, the color of it and the license plate number. They couldn't tell him what day and time it took place or the location, just that a police officer reported that he carried out an illegal turn. My spouse requested further proof, and they said he either pays the fine or goes to court. This way of dealing with tickets is typical in Dubai, and we have plenty of friends in similar situations.

The cost of taking off work to go to court far out weights the cost of paying the fine. For individuals in Dubai, paying a fine here or there is just a way of doing business in the city. Not recommended, but it's extremely common for people with speeding tickets to not pay until they renew their car registration, since no one comes after you for minor offenses.

Cops No-Show at Community Meeting

The first ever community meeting is scheduled with the police department to discuss traffic, and road related issues in the Emirates. The department was to explain how the roads are policed, but no one from the police department came. They apologized and said that urgent business prevented them from showing up. Everyone who did attend the meeting is disappointed, including a road safety activist.

The meeting went on as scheduled without the police there. The activist said: "Patience is the key and the police are working very hard and are spread between too many things. Our role is to help the police and not to beat them down." The activist said that questions gathered for the officers will be answered at a later time. Hot topics discussed were plans for a seatbelt law, pedestrian crossings and the law on window tinting. They will talk about truck drivers needing to be tested more and whether it is a violation if you don't use your blinker.

Clean your Car or Face a Fine

Residents are facing fines for having a dirty or dusty car. An expat in Abu Dhabi is pulled over by police and told to clean her car. The expat teacher was driving along a road during lunchtime when the police lights and siren came on behind her.

The officer asked for her license and registration. She gave him her license but was frantically searching for the registration. Her heart pounded, and she shook as she couldn't imagine what she had done wrong. The officer said stop looking for the registration and come with me. Walking over to the side of her car, he ran his finger along the side.

She said she was planning to clean it that day, and in all fairness said that it was dusty. The rules say that a car must be cleaned using a car wash. Police say this rule of keeping your car clean ensures that a car is not abandoned. It goes to show you how many vacated cars there are, as people try to get out of the U.A.E. quickly.

Vehicles are supposed to be tagged by police if they look like they have not moved. If they don't leave within a reasonable amount of time, the owners will have to pay $2 a day for impound fees with a cap of $544. If they are not claimed, they are auctioned. We have seen cars sit abandoned on the roads for over a year.

The Worst Woman Driver with Violations Reaching $252,654

A 28-year-old Arab housewife from the Middle East thought she was invincible. The woman's name popped up when the police did a computer sweep of unlicensed drivers. She had 1,551 unpaid fines and according to the police it was "only by accident" that they found her.

In the past four years, she had mainly speeding fines, and toll fines totaling $252,654. The woman racked up $98,012 on just one road alone. She got away with this since she never re-registered her car, or renewed her license.

The driver will appear in court, but has denied committing the offences. No further information available.

U.S. Cop Car Spotted in the U.A.E.

A classic American style police car went flying past an off-duty policeman with the sirens blaring. The officer is shocked to see the 1960s Chevrolet Impala with the word sheriff on the side of it. He called for an officer to follow the vehicle. The police car is stopped and seized.

The Emirati owner had documentation allowing him to register the car under a "classic car club." But, he did not have authorization to use the siren, or to paint the car black and white. He said that he used the car to race outside of the country.

The man is charged for driving a car that looked like a police car with a siren and changing the color of the car. He is fined $108 and another $108 for changing the color.

1,201 Cars Seized

There were 1,201 bad drivers that had their cars seized by the traffic police. They were speeding, running red lights, racing, failing to stop after an accident and driving in the wrong direction. Most of the motorists on the roads in Dubai are horrendous drivers. There is no regard to safety.

Cab Driver's Hair Matches the Top of his Taxi

A taxi cab driver has dyed the hair on his head and facial hair bright orange. He has lived in Dubai for more than 30 years. He's been doing this for 10 years. The man is from Pakistan and said the color he chose is for religious reasons, being a devout Muslim. He belongs to a community named Pashtun where they color their hair orange in "the practice of the prophet."

Here, the color matches the top of his taxi exactly. The driver pays just $6 for his dyed hair, $5 to trim his long beard and 80¢ for a splash of henna dye.

Cab Driver gets Clobbered

A British expat who had been out drinking was taking a cab home. He thought the driver was taking him the long way, so he punched him. The driver said the Brit accused him of taking a longer route to run up a bigger fare. The passenger told him to stop the car, and he yelled at him and then clobbered him.

The Brit admitted there was blood on the man's face, but said it may have come from his own hand because he cut himself on the driver's teeth. He said the driver called the police, and they detained him for several days before transferring him to a prison. The friends of the expat desperately tried to help their friend, and paid more than $816 in compensation to the cab driver. The expat apologized. No further information.

New Law Coming, Drivers have to Pass a Fitness Test

A new law is coming, it will require any commercial driver working in the U.A.E. to pass an annual fitness test. This will allow them to get a work permit. The law will make sure drivers are in good health so safety on the roads improve. This law says: "Any person who has heart ailments, diabetes or epilepsy could be prohibited from continuing with their jobs."

Drivers affected by the new law will be taxis, buses, heavy trucks and chauffeurs. Another law being introduced will make it mandatory that cars have fog lights, capable of penetrating the dense early morning fog.

Dubai Cabs Cash in

The Dubai cabs took in more than $272,000,000 in revenue back in 2012, and it continues to grow each year. Taxi drivers accommodated more than 74.5 million paying customers. The taxi company gives credit to their "training" and says they qualified 820 drivers. The company said they rehabilitated 3,055 cab drivers who previously "triggered" traffic accidents, or received complaints from customers.

Cabbies Face Jail and Fines for No License

The U.A.E. has had enough of illegal unlicensed taxis and an "Illegal Commuting Combatting Committee" is formed. More than 2,000 unlicensed taxis are stopped. Drivers caught during this campaign are given a fine anywhere from $1,361 to $2,722 and jail time up to 30 days.

But, they said that illegal cabbies will be given a chance to "change their ways" if they wish, and may register their vehicles with an online system.

Road Transportation Authority Bus Backs up on Highway

People are shocked to see a bus "backing" up on a highway. The bus is being driven by a Road and Transportation Authority employee who missed his turn. The right lane was completely blocked, so the bus driver tried to force the driver behind him to move so he could back up, and take the exit he missed.

This is not uncommon, but shame on that driver for risking people's lives and property.

Just Like the U.S., Really?
A motorist sets the record straight when an online consensus showed people thought that driving in the U.A.E. was just like driving in the United States. The motorist said: "Comparing the roads or traffic conditions to the U.S. is like apples and oranges. In the U.S. you have a system where traffic rules are respected, lane changes are orderly, speed limits are strictly enforced and fines are quick and steep for tailgating, or using a cell phone. Everything the U.A.E. doesn't have. The region falls short by miles and miles in comparison."

Motorists are being warned not to park your vehicle in the middle of the roads and freeways for no reason. They are being told by authorities that the only acceptable reason for leaving your vehicle in the middle of the road is an accident.

The city is also known for not having easy exits to where you want to go. If you make the wrong turn, it can mean driving a great distance to get back on track.

Car Pumped with Jet Fuel Yup, This Takes it to a Whole New Level
A person caught speeding is fined $108 for illegally modifying his car so he can use jet fuel. The guy took his car to a garage where it cost him $68,077 to illegally change his car. Not only is that dangerous to the public, but it has an environmental impact.

The price of a gallon of gasoline while we were there in 2013, was under $2. This person is under the illusion that if he changes his car to use jet fuel, he will go faster. Also, it will be cheaper. But, this does not give the car a magical power boost. Jet fuel is basically kerosene, closely related to diesel fuel. The question remaining is, how does he have access to jet fuel?

Expat Wins Finger-Flip Case
A U.S. expat executive is accused of giving an Emirati motorist the middle finger. The expat was parallel parking his car when the impatient Emirati repeatedly honked his car horn. The driver got out of his car to complain to the executive. The American spent a day in custody and is charged with making a lewd gesture. In court he strongly denied giving him the finger.

This ordeal surely could have led to 6 months in jail. The American is acquitted in a lower court, and he is finally cleared when the Emirati appealed the decision. The Appeals Court sided with the American. The expat said his friends told him to go home and don't come back. He said he doesn't want this experience to affect his view of the country.

This sort of thing happens every single day. So often lies are told to make it look like it's the expats fault.

The first time I took a trip to the mall alone, I was in a quieter area. I dressed appropriately and minded my business when a group of local women and children came walking towards me. When they got alongside me I ignored them, but could see out of the corner of my eye an elderly woman on the end. She wound up with her elbow and hit me in the arm. This took my breath away, and I felt immense pain in my upper arm as I stopped dead in my tracks. I turned around to look at the woman and watched her waddle away as if nothing happened. I felt this was done out of pure hatred.

I addressed the issue with my spouse as my arm swelled up and turned black and blue. New to the country, I was still learning, but told him surely this incident is caught on camera. I was convinced something can be done. Calmly he shook his head and said it is my word against theirs. Yes, it is on camera but they can easily say I swore at them. I didn't stand a chance in court and I could find myself in jail.

Another Finger-Flipping Case

A 45-year-old Russian tourist found herself in court when she was driving her car in a mall garage. She stopped to take a photo of a vintage car. There was a line of traffic building up behind her, and a Turkish motorist claimed he beeped his horn and she turned and gave him the middle finger.

She told the court she waved her hand. This is witnessed by her mother, and friend who were there. Her accuser offered no evidence other than his words, so the court did not convict her.

My husband and I were given advice when we moved to Dubai from someone who lived there. We were told never ever wave, or raise your hand when you are angry, as it can be construed as showing the middle finger.

No Seatbelt, I'm a Good Driver

A woman gave in to her child when she begged to go to her friend's house from class. When the mom picked her up, she asked her if she had a good time. The little girl said yes, and she didn't have to wear a seatbelt, because her friend's mother said she was a good driver. The mom was fuming and thinking about confronting the woman.

You will hear over and over the stupidity of people not using seatbelts on their children and putting small kids in danger. It isn't just the seatbelts though, people constantly text while driving at high speeds and take photos. The government just doesn't do enough to stop this.

A woman is spotted texting while her baby was in the car. The woman looked up only four times as she drove down a long stretch of a busy road. Another young child is seen sitting on the knee of their mother as the parents were both safely wearing their seatbelts. A pizza company was asking people to take photos of their delivery vehicles while on the road and send them to the company. This encouraged people to text and take photos while driving. When the company realized the foolishness of their request, the company took down the photos posted online.

A Jingle in the Morning Reminds People to Buckle up

A safety activist thought of a clever idea to get people to use seatbelts. She made up a nursery jingle to the tune of "If You're Happy and You Know It." The jingle plays on the radio in the morning and afternoon. It reminds "everyone" to wear their seatbelts. Among the lyrics are: "Use your seatbelt in the car, doesn't matter near or far, use your seatbelt in the car, buckle up, buckle up!"

The activist said: "The word is spreading, but much more needs to be done." She recalls meeting a Lebanese dad who informed her it isn't called a seatbelt, but rather a speed belt because you only put it on when you are speeding. The police are also airing young children on the radio to send messages that focus on traffic safety, crime prevention and child protection. They are "hoping" that parents will follow the traffic rules and regulations also.

CHAPTER 15
CUSTOMER SERVICE, ETC.

Customer service reaches a new low in Dubai so a weeklong conference is scheduled. The discussion will be on how businesses can improve on giving better customer service. A panel discussion had to be canceled when some of the leading companies just didn't show. They gave no prior cancellation notice, or explanation as to why they could not attend.

All over Dubai you will hear people grumbling how poor customer service is. A consumer went into a department store at a popular mall to look for a product. The store did not have it in stock. A representative at the store told the customer to pay for it, and the store will send the item in 3 days. The shopper agreed to pay since she trusted the name of the store.

Ten days passed and yet no product came. Eventually, she requested a refund and is informed she will have to wait 3 to 4 weeks to get her money back. The buyer was livid and announced she no longer will trust any customer service counter.

A male customer stepped into a motorcycle shop and asked the staff if they had "any customer service." Getting a blank look, the customer repeated the question, and one of the staff shifted to a colleague for advice. After a brief discussion, they came back and replied, "Sorry, we are out of stock." Finding that funny, the customer asked the staff to check with the floor manager.

The floor manager said: "I will go and check in the back to see if we have any left." She came back after looking and replied: "I could not locate any, but I could order some if you leave your details." The customer left his personal information. He is told by the floor manager that they would call once it arrived.

The shopper thought it will be best to share this experience with the manager sitting in his office. The manager first shook his head, then put his head in his hands and apologized.

Another shopper went to a huge electrical retailer with a friend to look for appliances for the kitchen. The buyer said: "The salesman's questioning technique was nothing more than technical babble with limited knowledge of the product. Customer service training leaves a lot to be desired." The shopper said the worst part is being followed around the store by the staff which was a real turn off and particularly annoying.

Rudeness Rises to New Levels

Many people talk about the rudeness that keeps circulating in Dubai and say people are focused on themselves and no one else. A woman was at a coffee shop having a nice peaceful cup of coffee at a mall. She was watching a group of ladies in the atrium attending a knitting workshop. A group of managers walking by, stopped and had an explosive confrontation with each other.

The woman said: "A blond lady clearly had a bone to pick with another manager. The blond shouted so loudly for a good 10 minutes that the knitting group had to stop since they could not hear the instructor. No one in the atrium had a choice but to listen to the woman shouting, and the customers in the mall became quite uncomfortable."

The woman could not believe that the blond woman's boss tolerates this behavior, since the boss did nothing to stop it. She believes that the blond woman with a chip on her shoulder should be deported back to her home country. She says it is an embarrassment to the rest of the expats.

No Chaperone, no Flight

A 37-year-old blind American businessman is humiliated when he is denied boarding a flight in Dubai. The staff at the counter refused to check him in for his trip to Jordan. He was on vacation for 3 weeks and wanted to visit relatives. The man is told the airline forbids anyone with a disability to fly unaccompanied. But, the man flew into Dubai unaccompanied on the same airline.

He asked to speak to a supervisor, he is told that there was no room for discussion, and is sent away. He said: "It was the staff in Dubai that had the problem." A champion of equality for blind people, he has flown around the world unaccompanied and has never encountered a problem like this. The only help he has ever asked anyone, was directions through a terminal.

The CEO of the airline issued an apology and said, "It should never have happened." As a "goodwill gesture," he is given a free ticket on the airline.

Bank gives Wrong Account Number

A customer opened a bank account and is given an IBAN [International

Bank Account Number], and a matching debit card. The customer needed this account so that his employer can direct deposit his pay checks into it, but now his first paycheck has gone astray. It turns out that the IBAN number on this account is not associated with the customer's name. In fact, it's not associated with any bank customer's name, so in effect the account doesn't exist.

His employer will not reissue the paycheck until he gets a letter from the bank confirming they had rejected his direct deposit because of the incorrect account number. He said: "I can't speak to anyone on the phone without having to remember 6, 8 and 10 digit pin numbers. I have to explain over and over again to various people what the problem is."

He has gone to the bank three times, explaining the whole story to customer service without getting a letter, a resolution or even an apology from them. He thought banking in the country had moved forward, he now believes it has regressed 20 years. He says he can't pay his bills online with no bank account, he can't direct deposit and his financial dealings have to be done in cash.

Bank Stupidity

A person tried to get a loan from a bank for a house and followed the proper steps. They provided an ID, salary documents, work letters and 4 hours of personal time at the bank. The customer received a phone call at 10:00pm one evening. He is told the loan is declined because his signature did not match up to one they had in the system from 3 years ago.

In Dubai, often bank documents are rejected. This is because the signature does not match what they have on file in the eyes of the person deciding, on whether you get a loan or not. People also have had their checks rejected by bank clerks not qualified to compare signatures, and they don't seem to understand that a person's signature over time may change. Banking problems are very common.

In a different story, a customer used a credit card from a bank based in a different emirate to buy an item. He paid the bill 2 days before the due date. The total came to $389. One month later the customer received a text message from the bank saying he owed $11 in late charges. He called customer service at the bank and told them he paid early and has the receipt. They told him that the entire amount isn't paid, and there was a balance of 11¢. They charged him $11 for the late payment.

The man then paid the late payment. Ten days later, he received another statement saying he had to pay $40 more. He called the bank again, and they told him the $40 was a fine for the late payment. The man spoke to a supervisor that lowered the fine and said that he could pay $14, and he'll arrange for everything to be OK. The man thought that was the end of it. Months later he received yet another statement saying he now owes $52! No further information.

This next story shows the bank being on the other side of the decimal point, where the bank owes you a few cents. A customer went to the bank to cash a check. He had given the cashier change so that the money given back will be bills, and no change. The cashier "refused" to take the coins.

After cashing the check she handed the customer his money, she didn't give him any coins, and short changed him. He questioned the cashier why he should accept being short changed when she refused to take the coins. The answer was "bank policy." The head cashier confirmed this and said, "We always round down." He wonders just how much money the bank is making off from everyone.

This bank customer had received several calls from their bank to pay the outstanding balance on their credit card. They received several text messages, and threats saying they will present the case to the legal department. The amount to be paid is 1¢. When it comes to money, size doesn't matter in Dubai!

A bank customer took out a loan and paid it off in monthly installments. After being paid off, he found his bank statements still showing the loan as active. He wondered why the statement still said this. The next day he went to the bank to inquire about the statement. He also wanted to get his "security check." back. The check he had to write in the full amount before he could get the loan. No one could explain why his statements still say the loan is active, but he is told it's paid off.

The bank informed the customer that they will automatically destroy the security check. They said in order for him to get the security check back, he will have to pay $13 for a letter. That letter will state that the loan is paid in full and confirm no outstanding balance.

This is a story that any expat who has a car loan in Dubai, will recognize. You are expected to continually pay.

Either Pay or the Pool Stays Shut

The real estate developer and management company that built and managed Shoreline apartments on Palm Jumeira said: "We will not maintain the facilities if we are not paid $4,083,911 in maintenance fees." This was a message to the individual owners of the apartments who have not paid.

Most of us rented these apartments with people paying in excessive of $3,600 per month. The problem was that the tenants were getting punished. The owners who sometimes don't even live in Dubai, were the ones who had not paid the maintenance fees they owed.

All the swimming pools were closed, and they even threatened to close the gyms and shut down the elevators if the unpaid balances are not settled. Residents living in the apartments were not allowed on the beach if their apartment owners had outstanding balances. We were fortunate since the owner of our apartment had always paid his bills.

The management company posted the names of the owners who owed the fees in the lobby of each building. It also reflected the amount needed to be paid. Many owners who still would not pay, lost their tenants since they did not have access to any of the amenities. They even took it a step further and made it very difficult for visitors to come to the apartments.

The guests not only had to sign in [not uncommon], but they were required to have a guest pass. This pass needed to be obtained at a facility, located off-site. It was not even acceptable for the tenant to come to the lobby to accompany their guest since security was there to stop them. The housemaids were no exception.

Another rule that went into effect was that they did not allow people to "walk on the sidewalk" next to the beach after 10:00pm. This rule affected many people since it is common to walk after a late dinner, or before bed. It seems the developer and management was out to punish everyone. With the headaches people went through, many laughed at a radio advertisement. The ad said: "New apartments went on sale that would appeal to anyone who still valued living at the most prestigious address in Dubai."

Pathetic Postal System

The U.A.E. does not have a postal system with a home delivery service. You can't receive your mail at home. They are however setting up a trial phase, but the recipient will have to "pay a small fortune" for the convenience of having their mail delivered to their doorstep. It is upsetting to the public that the government doesn't offer a service without gouging their residents.

In the meantime, people have a post office box while some use their work address. A letter went out informing people that when it comes time to renew your box, you need to bring your renewal letter to the post office. They also said to bring your government issued ID card [new to Dubai at the time] since they needed to scan the card.

The post office "forgot" to install the special scanner that reads the ID cards. The announcement was made at the post office to the gobs of people standing in line. They said the scanner will not be installed for a while, and they will have to come back. This wasted peoples' time, and they were enraged especially since no apology came with it..

Another thing the U.A.E. doesn't technically have is a zip code system. This presented a problem when I needed to mail documents to my spouse while I was in the U.S., and he was in the U.A.E. I shipped the paperwork through a service who informed me it cannot go without a zip code. I knew there wasn't a zip code, so I elected to use 5 zeros which worked.

The address my spouse gave me was his work address. The first part started with a post office box number. After that I needed to write the "name and description" of the buildings near his work place, to identify the area. This is how it works all over Dubai since it gives the delivery guy an idea of where to go.

Charged to use a Wheelchair

A senior citizen flying into Dubai was very disappointed at the airport when they could not get a wheelchair without having to pay first. They said: "Nowhere else in the world does this happen, and it doesn't give a good first impression."

Upset over Fireworks

A family got into their car very excited to watch the fireworks during a holiday. Radio and internet searches confirmed that the firework show will start promptly at 9:00pm, and they will be fabulous.

The only problem was the fireworks ended at 8:30pm. This family does not understand why you would advertise a different time than the actual time of the event. That's Dubai.

Management of New Year's Eve Crowd was a Disaster

People hurried like mad as they tried to get to their New Year's Eve parties, on Palm Jumeira. A firework record was about to be attempted.

Complaints later poured in from the public. They said how dangerous it was in the street when massive amounts of people were corralled like cattle. Many were trampled on in pedestrian traffic with one person fighting to rescue a child in a stroller. The buggy rolled away and was about to crash into a building at a train station.

Thousands and thousands of people stood in line for many hours at one train station trying to get to their destinations. Crowd control separated families and put single people in groups of 150 people. Several hundred stood in line at another train station where they boarded the women and children first. This made it very difficult for the women and children to maneuver their way through the impatient, pushing crowds. They were not only pushed, but touched and pinched.

The methods used to control crowds were in complete shambles, and most people agreed that they should have just stayed home.

Ticket Holders better not Miss Bus on New Year's Eve

A concert and party was held on the beach at a resort on Palm Jumeira. The amount of people attending was huge since the world record for the most fireworks was being attempted. The access to the palm shut down at 10:30pm for safety reasons. Double-decker buses that were transporting people to the resort had its last bus run out to the palm at 9:00pm. The public was encouraged by the event organizers not to be late, since they won't be able to get there by any other means.

Ticket holders for the concert are told they must go and exchange their tickets for wristbands. The organizers decided "after" the paper tickets were issued, wristbands will make it easier to get into the concert. There are only a few designated areas throughout the city that can make the exchange. This left people scrambling to get their wristbands. Next, thousands of outraged people missed the concert and party due to being stranded on buses, and sitting in traffic for more than 5 hours.

An irate man spent 9 hours between the stampedes, and a bus that never moved. He ultimately began the endless walking as he tried to get to his $5,445 table that he paid for. He totally ended up missing the concert, and firework attempt. The event planners eventually apologized for the "inconvenience" to the thousands of people that missed the concert. They are told they will get a "full refund." But, they were only given 50% back of what they paid.

The irate man received a letter saying that the organizers understand the frustrating situation. With that in mind they were reimbursing him 50% too and the process will take 7 working days.

Another problem was to get your money back, you had to show your wristband. Many threw the band out. It was ironic that the people actually lucky enough to have made it to the concert, somehow received a full refund. Many are saying this is "not fair." A spokesperson for the event said: "Anyone who purchased a table would be contacted and dealt with on a case to case basis."

Homer Simpson Doll Banned in Iran

All figurines of the cartoon characters "The Simpson's" are added to a list of ongoing banned toys in Iran. It isn't specified why the Simpson's had made the list, but adult dolls are banned. The Institute for the Intellectual Development of Children and Young Adults in Iran had made this decision. Barbie dolls are also banned, and police had closed dozens of toy shops for selling the dolls. Doh!

CHAPTER 16

FOOD AND SHOP

A grocery store and deli was opened in Dubai by a well-known chef who taught at culinary colleges across the United States. He contributed to many cookbooks and will serve wholesome food for any homesick American. This is predicted to be a place you can breathe fresh air, away from other restaurants.

The chef who counts American Presidents and celebrities as his earlier customers, started a culinary school in Dubai. He said: "The image that has stuck with America being only fast food is wrong, even though people talk about stepping off a plane, you will more than likely see a pizza parlor, fried chicken restaurant or a corner shop selling fizzy drinks." He also added: "Americans don't eat like this all the time and the main cuisine Americans are looking for is natural or organic."

So often in Dubai you come across angry customers who feel the need to shout and yell at restaurant staff and management. For example, a patron who sat at an extremely busy restaurant during lunchtime, saw an awkward scene unfold.

A husband with his wife and children, is flustered with management for not bringing him an extra plate. The manager was struggling to reason with the customer, he grew angrier and more agitated which led to a gigantic scene, as the customer bawled out the manager.

The customer could have simply got up, walked over to the counter and asked for a plate, but instead he caused drama. This left everyone in the room uneasy.

I saw many similar episodes, but one in particular was at an ice cream parlor. A Filipino staff member accidentally put the wrong flavor of ice cream into a cup for a customer. Instead of the Arab pointing out the mistake, he yelled and shouted at the worker for a good five minutes. Many of his family members chimed in as well, embarrassing and belittling the employee. The racket echoed throughout the mall.

Another incident was at a restaurant. An Arab customer refused to stretch his arm out to grab the ketchup bottle at his table. Instead, he slammed his fist down and yelled for the waiter to come hand him the bottle of ketchup. This sudden outburst startled everyone in the restaurant.

A survey is taken on how long a customer will wait for a dinner table at a new restaurant in Dubai:
49% not more than 15 minutes.
18% not more than 30minutes.
1% as long as it takes.
32% I wouldn't wait.

Restaurant Rip off

A couple went into a restaurant and is charged for an extra item on their bill. They refused to pay for it and encouraged the staff to look at the CCTV, but the staff stated they did not have cameras. The table became surrounded by not merely the staff, but an enormous security man.

The customers then threatened to call the police at which point, the restaurant removed the item from the bill. The couple was so embarrassed and humiliated over the incident, and said the restaurant didn't care. The couple said: "We don't expect good customer service in Dubai, but stealing from customers just took it over the top."

Restaurants must have an Arabic Menu

The restaurant menus in Dubai are all printed in English. The U.A.E. Ministry of Economy is fed up with English only. They said: "All the restaurants need to now use Arabic language on their menus. This decision is in line with plans by the U.A.E. to make Arabic the basic language in all trade and official dealings."

Surprise visits are being made to different restaurants, and anyone not following the new law is given a fine up to $27,224.

Restaurant Ceiling Caved in

An Emirati man said his son was in a restaurant at a shopping mall in Abu Dhabi. He is injured after the ceiling caved in on him. The boy is accompanied to the restaurant by their nanny, and while he was eating the ceiling came crashing down. He was taken to the hospital for head injuries.

The father claimed negligence and has filed a complaint with the police against the management. He said: "My son is now suffering from panic attacks and fear." No further information available.

Chef Stabbed after Argument over Office Phone

A hotel chef from Sri Lanka was running for his life toward an elevator with blood dripping from his hand, screaming for help. He is stabbed by his Syrian manager. The manager was in charge of the banquet staff at a hotel when he, and the chef became involved in a dispute. This was over the usage of the manager's office phone.

The chef explained to a court he had been preparing for an event, and he needed the phone to tell the staff to bring the food to the guests. The manager walked in and saw the chef talking on the phone with his assistant there. The assistant is asked to leave, and the manager then lunged at the chef with a knife he kept in his desk drawer. He denies the charges and said: "The chef was angry with me about not being allowed in the office and stabbed himself." No further information available.

Charity at a Table

A customer seated at a table in a restaurant was not happy when trying to enjoy a meal with family. A card that had a picture of a starving African boy holding a bowl in his hand sat in the middle of the table. The card read $1.36 is added to your bill for a donation. If you choose not to give, kindly tell your waiter before you get your bill.

This customer isn't upset because the card was on the table, but how the restaurant went about asking for donations. They said: "It is not up to anyone else but the customer as to how much they should donate. No one should have to feel guilty about spending money at a restaurant when they want to enjoy a meal. If the owner feels the need to donate, why don't they take it out of the money charged to the customer, or the profits they are making without spoiling the dining experience of the customers."

A Message to Dishonest Diners

A waiter at a restaurant wants to remind people they make less than $27 a day. They said: "Unlike you people, our job is not easy. Some treat us with no respect, and yet we put on a smile. Unfortunately we make mistakes, because we have more problems than you do, that's why if you get excess in your change give it back, because we are the ones who will suffer paying for it."

Appetizer Disputes

A large group of people are angry when they went to a Greek restaurant at a resort and spa. At the end of the evening when the bill came, they are asked to pay an additional $87 to cover the appetizers. They tried to explain to the staff they didn't ask for them. It was the manager who came with plates to enjoy. They actually thought it was part of the entertainment.

The manager doesn't understand how they thought they didn't have to pay for the appetizers. Eventually the charge is waived.

Store Employee Abused

A customer is at a grocery store shopping when she observed several young workers busy stacking vegetables on a display. A supervisor quickly ran across the store to the workers, yelling at them. He then punched one worker in the neck. The young boy complied with the supervisor's orders, but was yelled at several more times.

In shock, the customer asked a female worker who the abusive manager was. She pretended not to hear. The customer asked her again, the worker turned and quickly walked away. She gathered that this abuse was common, and the female worker knew the consequences of speaking out.

Workplace violence is inexcusable, and no worker should ever have to live his or her life under physical or verbal abuse.

Supermarket Arrogance

People standing in line at the grocery store had to move over to another line, while the cashier cleaned up a spill, at his register. While they were waiting in the next line, an Arabic man came pushing his way through with his cart, right up to the closed counter. He is told the line is closed. He then became angry and refused to move as he began to put his items on the belt.

The cashier quickly opened and checked him out. Customers that had to move asked the cashier why he opened when he wasn't finished cleaning the floor. He said: "The man was unwilling to listen, and since he was at the counter, I had to open." It is far too common for workers to drop what they are doing, or drop other customers to appease the local Arabic people in Dubai. This happens out of fear of losing their jobs.

In a different story, a lady was shopping at a supermarket. She was ready to move out of the way of a woman and her daughter when the woman screamed "MOVE."

Being put off, the lady purposely didn't move. The woman screamed "MOVE" again then took the cart and pushed her way through. The lady said: "It was a poor example set for the woman's daughter, and I would like to see her try and do that in a civilized country."

Thousands of Dirty Stores are fined

In Al Ain, a city within Abu Dhabi, 4,865 outlets are fined in the prior year for violating hygiene laws. The hair salon equipment is not sterilized, face towels and shaving sets are reused many times. Some of the women's salons were using questionable henna [body paint]. Fake cosmetic products were also found being used on customers.

The public health authorities gave out fines to 641 men's salons and 385 women's beauty salons. Fines are given to grocery stores, dry cleaners, car washes, butchers and garages. Some food establishments were dumping waste near their premises. Others were selling expired and illegal products. Yet others were employing workers without a health card.

In Abu Dhabi, 401 restaurants violated the rules and 5,205 warnings were issued. Those found in violation, or caught carrying out illegal practices are fined anywhere from $54 to $1,361.

53 Food Outlets Forced to Close in Dubai

Dubai has done their own investigation on subpar eateries, closing 53 outlets in six months. The establishments are closed temporarily for not adhering to rules on proper food storage, preparation and transporting. Inspectors went into 12,910 eateries.

Twenty-five establishments received an A grade of excellent, 1,591 received a B grade for very good, 5,557 received a C grade for good, 359 received a D grade for medium and 29 received an E grade for poor.

Laundry Goes Black

A unique new laundry detergent is claiming to keep your "black clothes black," by locking in the color to help in fading. The detergent is geared towards the millions of black Abayas worn in the region by the ladies. A yearlong test is done on the detergent, where many women took part. One woman said: "It's been a year since I bought my Abayas, and they still look as black as new."

Fish Eggs on your Face

A cosmetic firm is shifting pearls and caviar, towards a skincare product, that claims to "tighten your skin by 82%." They say caviar is a very important beauty treatment especially beneficial to dark circles around the eyes.

Using caviar as a beauty aid in the U.A.E. is low. However, caviar as food is 100 times higher.

No Place to Sit at the Mall and No First Aid

Residents are in agreement that Dubai offers the best malls in the world, but the malls lack seating. The only real good places to sit are at the food courts and cafes, usually jam-packed. For people who might be sick, the elderly or a handicapped person, they will have a hard time finding a place to sit. Malls should not only be for active young people who can walk miles without resting.

A woman was with her son at a mall when her toddler fell flat on his face, and bit through his tongue. There was blood everywhere, and her son was screaming. She is surprised that no one within the mall came to help [possibly because of the Good Samaritan Law or lack thereof].

She asked a security guard where a first aid station was, and is told there wasn't one. In the beginning the guard didn't know what to do or who to call, so it's obvious they are not briefed on medical issues. He then suggested calling an ambulance. The woman is angry at how a mall welcomes thousands of visitors and doesn't offer first aid.

Staff needs to Back off

For people shopping in Dubai, there isn't a place you can shop in peace. You are constantly being stalked by staff. One woman said: "From the moment you step in you are greeted by a herd of eager sales clerks who follow you around, stand next to you or behind you. They focus on your every move. You almost feel like you are being harassed, and your shopping experience is spoiled. These assistants need to understand that not everyone enjoys having five assistants doing everything for them, and their eagerness may just drive the customer away."

She now prefers to shop online, rather than being chased around the store.

Web of Excuses

A customer purchased a birthday gift from an online Dubai based company. They are told the item will be delivered in five days. When eight days passed, and the gift still didn't come, she called to speak to a customer service representative at the online store. The representative said they had nothing to do with the delay and suggested calling the merchant directly. The customer called the merchant who reassured that the gift will come soon.

Twenty days passed, it was now time for the birthday party. There still is no gift, and nobody knows what happened to it. The company blamed the merchant, and the merchant blamed the courier and the courier said they haven't received anything.

The customer said: "Online shopping in Dubai certainly doesn't make life easier."

Skimpy Clothes Show you are Uncivilized

A Dubai resident voiced their opinion for anyone who dresses in skimpy clothes. They have a few words for you and said: "Mark Twain wrote, clothes make the man. Naked people have little or no influence on society." Another person allowed for the observation and said:

> *This is very true, but the sparsely dressed men and woman seem to be liked by all. By wearing little clothes, this makes people resemble the early man and hunter gatherers whose intellect has not yet evolved. Everywhere we look we see indecency, and vulgarity, such as at universities, malls and on the streets. There is no religion or culture in this world which directs people to shed their clothes, because this would cause them to commit unlawful legal acts. If people wore decent clothes, society would be a much better place.*

Cancer Risk Found on New Bed

An Emirati man shopping for a new bed found one at a well-known store. He paid $7,623 for the set. While the delivery people were setting it up in his home, he noticed a sticker on the mattress. The sticker said that it might contain a chemical known to the state of California to cause cancer, or birth defects. He told the delivery guys to take it away.

The store refunded his money, but he said this incident isn't about the money. He wonders how a bed that causes cancer can be sold. Also puzzled over why the store never informed him. He worries for other consumers. He said: "Every buyer should ask before buying furniture if it is safe, or not."

The attorney for the store said they don't have to warn the customer, or even place a warning sticker on the bed. He said: "We could have removed the sticker. These are regulations by the state of California only, to have the sticker on. It is not followed by any other country, even other states in the United States."

The consumer protection department at the Ministry of Economy said samples of the bed are being tested. If unsafe the bed will be "confiscated," and the retailer will face charges.

CHAPTER 17
SCHOOL, YOUNGSTERS & PAMPERED

Public schooling, primary and secondary education is mandatory for both boys and girls in Dubai and is free of cost for all Emiratis. But, most expat parents prefer to send their children to one of the many for-profit, private schools. The competition and fees for the international schools are high. Some fees are the equivalent to a college tuition in the United States.

The fees differ by each school with many charging for each age group. Additional fees are payable for registration, transportation, uniforms, extra-curricular activities and other expenses. The fees and deposits that parents have to pay are a disgrace. The deposit for each child can be $680 on top of a school fee of $272, which often is non-refundable. You are not even guaranteed a slot since there may be only 20 available. But, the school will continue to take in 400 applications. This process is not only done with one school, but you need to do it with three or four different schools to assure your child gets in. This can quickly become unaffordable if you have more than one child.

It's an endless headache for expat parents to ensure their kids are in the best schools, and within their means. It's not entirely the child's academic achievements that dictates where he or she can go, but the income of the parents. Again, because these schools are not cheap. Where you work also impacts where you will put your child. The better companies will give expat parents a school allowance to help pay for your child's education. But, the higher up you are in the pecking order of your job, the bigger the allowance your company will give. Many of the schools have entrance examinations with most having a uniform, or dress code.

Every year the schools have to go through an inspection. From what I know, inspectors are hired through an outside company. They will never suggest a school is doing excellent since they want their business every single year. Nor would they ever suggest a school that is not doing well be mentored by one that is. Because all private schools in Dubai compete with each other.

From the schools side, when the inspectors arrive it becomes a game of impressing them, and not so much showing off the school's academic capabilities and achievements. It is important to get a high score from the inspectors because this attracts the more affluent students and allows them to charge a high fee for the next school year.

During inspection times, schools are stricter with their dress codes. For example, after physical education the students must change back to their school uniform. Any activity the kids do outside of the classroom that requires them to leave the room is cut back. It is important to show all classrooms are full when the inspectors come. The children are told to be on their best behavior.

The teachers are stressed as they try to achieve a good report from the inspectors, and again for raising school fees. Roses are placed on tables in the bathrooms, Arabic tents are set up, equipment is flown in and back out after the inspectors leave. This list is ongoing.

Parents are fed up and think it has gone too far. Children first, profit second. A teacher who has been through the inspection in Dubai for 4 years said: "Even though the process is not unique as countries around the world do inspect schools, it is the way Dubai goes about doing it."

An ex-teacher talks about the education system and puts it bluntly. The teacher said:

> *It is all about the money in the U.A.E. and the majority of the schools don't care about the education. To run a successful school you need passion for education, and the culture for profit education has created ruthless, greedy management that has long forgotten their passion for teaching. The management will tell the teachers to think of ways to justify a pack of pencils and paper for $544 when in reality it costs less than $13 in supermarkets.*

An immense problem in Dubai is that there just isn't enough English schools around for all the students. It has become difficult to secure a spot for your child. Some of the parents are on a "2 year wait list." Unless you somehow "bribe" the school which has been done, a personal visit, or a telephone call just doesn't work. Some suggest that you need to register your child while the baby is still in your womb!

DUBAI, 1 CITY 2 DIFFERENT TALES

An English school is set to close its doors due to financial reasons, and possibly over the land the school is built on. The parents are already paying around $2,450 per term, but say they are willing to increase the fee up to 20% in order for the school to stay open. They are aware the school is considerably cheaper than other English schools in Dubai, and they are pleading for them not to close. Ultimately the parents proposal had been rejected, and the board has closed it.

The end of the school year is usually in June, and most of the moms pack up their children and go back to their home countries for the summer. Dubai is left silent, and a lot less traffic on the roads. The school week runs Sunday to Thursday, and so does the work week. Weekends are Friday and Saturday.

A 16-Year-Old Expat Boy Whipped for Drinking Alcohol

Foreign Embassies are speaking out to students from their countries warning them of the dangers of breaking the U.A.E. laws. While the British embassy was visiting a school talking about the laws in the U.A.E., one student said: "Dubai's just like an upper class Spain isn't it?" She was told, "No, it isn't." This student was under the wrong impression. She was then told that even though Dubai has gone through amazing transformations; traditions, values and especially the religion remains intact 100%.

The embassy told the story of a 16-year-old British Muslim boy who was offered alcohol, and he took it. He was arrested and detained, but after he was sentenced to be whipped, it became a human rights issue. The British Embassy through the foreign office in London put pressure on the U.A.E. authorities to not punish him, but to no avail. Punishment was carried out. The embassy had their hands tied as they have no authority to intervene in local Emirati law.

Bring Back Caning

A person voiced their concern about teachers slapping children and referred to it as child abuse. Another person responded by saying they are all in for corporal punishment. They said: "That is exactly what the U.A.E. needs. Just a slap is not enough. The cane needs to come out of retirement. Fear is a motivator, caning a misbehaved child would make the number of misbehaving children stop."

Kids and Sports

There are many opinions about children involved in activities. Some have said, the kids in Dubai have everything handed to them on a platter. While others say, getting to the top is much easier for them than in a lot of other countries because of the little bubble they live in. The problem many believe is the lack of competition they have to enable themselves to becoming better, especially if they ever want to compete on a world level. They also feel more funding for sports in Dubai is important.

A group of mothers at a soccer tournament watching their daughters play, saw the referee blow the whistle for something the mothers believe was wrong. The female referee didn't stop the clock, and she gave the ball to the other team who ultimately scored. All the mothers thought it was important enough to bring it to the "organizers" attention. They were told that the referee was only a classroom teacher who volunteered her own time.

The organizers said because of behavior like theirs, nobody wanted to coordinate and referee the tournaments. The women were not happy being told off since they believe, it is important for the children to stand their ground, including the right to be heard. What they don't want their children to learn is, if you don't like it, keep quiet or there won't be a tournament. They don't want the girls to think they have no right to complain, and they should accept their fate in life since their opinion is not valued.

Teachers Need a Voice

Teachers are tired, over worked, have way too many extra-curricular activities, and no half term break. The parents say, since teachers are unhappy, the child bears the brunt of the teacher's anger. Any parent who complains is branded as the problem parent. Many of the parents wonder why teachers in Dubai accept what is put forth in front of them without standing up for themselves in front of the Administrative Board. They believe if the teachers don't have a voice, then how can they expect the children to learn from their example?

No Student Unions

Eight Kuwaiti students were expelled from a university in Dubai for trying to start a union. The college said, "The students didn't ask for permission." This probably would not have mattered either way. The students had also broken a U.A.E. law by raising unauthorized donations.

U.A.E. Kids are Fatter than in the U.S.

A new study has shown that U.A.E. children and adolescents are fatter than Americans. 1,440 students were randomly selected from 23 public schools, ranging from grades 1 to 12. They found 20% of the young people were obese, and 14% overweight. What they have learned was that young Emiratis were not getting enough fruit, vegetables or exercise.

Researchers were very concerned about the lack of exercise, and a "sugar-laden western diet." They said there was a link between children with weight issues, and their "bulky" parent's. They noticed the body mass index of young Emiratis was greater than in the U.S. too.

Lots of people spoke out on this issue. Many said poor lifestyles, unhealthy eating habits, lack of exercise and eating out late contributes to the obesity. It was said it's not just limited to the young Emiratis. It affects the majority of the population in the U.A.E., not to mention the health-related issues that go along with obesity.

A resident made suggestions to control eating habits. They said: "Add photos of starving kids on fast food boxes." This person had ideas for other habits too. They claimed: "You could also add photos of tortured animals on cosmetic products and photos of victims in tragic car accidents can go on liquor bottles and beer cans."

The researchers also saw a lot of underweight teenagers among the girls. They think it could be because the girls want to "copy the western ideal of a slim body."

When visiting any mall in Dubai, you will see a parade of golf carts whizzing by you, as if you were in an airport. Some of the people appear to not be hindered from walking in any way, seems they plain don't want to. If that isn't enough, people often hire someone to carry their shopping bags. These people are dressed like a bellhop as they hold onto the shopping bags while waiting outside of the store for the person who hired them.

The West is to Blame for Eating Disorders

It has been concluded in another study that the west is at fault for the body image in the U.A.E. The "western cultural invasion" is strongly blamed for making teenagers, mainly girls, unhappy with their bodies. It is described as "West Goes East Syndrome." The study showed that 73% of students in the U.A.E. are becoming far more self-conscious about their bodies. It has been said this is due to the advertisements, pop music, film and "general baggage" of the west. But, one professor of the study said:

> *The west cannot be blamed entirely as the problem can be found in different cultures around the world. Unfortunately, some women become obsessed with their looks and diet way too much, and that is not the fault of the west. We do not copy everything you do, we can come up with our own problems ourselves.*

Pastries offered as a Healthy Snack in Schools

A study has found that health officials are encouraging school children to eat chocolate croissants as a healthy, nutritious snack. Some schools were offering donuts to children at break time. The teachers have openly admitted that they were not a good role model for the children because "they were too lazy to exercise."

A research team observed schools by walking around and found most children were consuming soda, chocolates and other sweets while a few were eating fruit and vegetables. Because most parents do not want their children eating fruit, a school was forced to shut down a "healthy fruit campaign." But yet a parent said: "Being fat is bad, because having a big belly might cause problems driving a car. It would get in the way of the steering wheel."

Some parents also thought that "fat children do not grow tall." The U.A.E. has one of the highest rates of obesity and diabetes in the world. A resident said: "As long as local culture allows young boys to tell their mothers and maids what they will eat and do, unhealthy eating practices will continue." Ironically, there is an advertisement for a 3 year university course on how to make better mothers.

Athlete says Fat Teachers are a Bad Influence

An Emirati marathon runner looks back at her former teachers. She said:

> *Every single physical education teacher I have ever had in school has been overweight and ate like a whale. Tubby teachers, snacking on junk food in school need to get in shape for the students, so they can be good role models. I don't know how, or why they were employed. They would wear jumpsuits, and you could see their fat bellies.*

She explains every teacher needs to be healthy to set a good example for the children. She stressed she's talking about healthy, since there are skinny people who eat unhealthy and have high cholesterol.

Teacher Guilty of Drinking Alcohol

A teacher went to a Syrian man's home with a friend for lunch. Her friend eventually left the home while the teacher remained at the dinner table enjoying a glass of wine with the guy. The teacher was unaware he is married and just kicked his wife out of the house the day before.

The day he kicked out his wife, she called the police, but the police didn't respond until the following day. The next day, police walked in and saw the teacher drinking. Both are arrested.

The teacher is led in front of the prosecutors wearing a "green prison uniform." She's told she is being investigated for "being alone in the company of a man who was not her husband." She is charged with drinking without a license and is released several days later on bail. No further information.

Teenager Dies after Caught Cheating on a Test

A 14-year-old Indian girl jumped to her death from the 17th-floor of a skyscraper. The girl arrived home early from school and had been crying and feeling embarrassed when she is caught by her teacher cheating on an exam. A letter was sent to her family by her teacher. When her father read it, he scolded her.

The daughter ran to her bedroom and locked the door. She then sprang from her bedroom window, and was found in a pool of blood, on the ground next to her building. The police think it is a suicide.

Student Ordered to Pay Back Scholarship Money

A female Emirati college student was studying in the U.S. on a U.A.E. government scholarship. She and her father are ordered by the court to pay back over $176,969 in scholarship money. Her grade point average was 1.68

which is below the acceptable grade a student needs to have, while being on a U.A.E. government scholarship.

A lower court first dismissed the case, but the Appeal Court convicted them and order them to pay back the money.

Child is Bullied in School by Mistake

When a mother found out her child was being bullied she took her child with her and confronted the school administrators. The school conducted their own investigation into the matter and asked the bullies point blank, in front of the child, if they did this.

The mother then received an email from the school. It said: "The children cannot recall any incident involving your child, and as they are good children, your child must have been mistaken. We are very experienced as a school and do not tolerate bullying." The child continued to be bullied from the "good children."

School Mom was a Sight for all

The parents at a school were unhappy watching an overweight expat mom parade around in a mid-thigh loose tunic blouse. The bottom 10 inches of the tunic is made of transparent fabric, and she wore no pants. The moms claim, not only did they endure the sight, but shorter children saw much more. They said if she walked around like that at the mall, she would be arrested immediately for indecent exposure.

They are pleading for her to buy clothes that cover her, and they think she needs a mirror. It's suggested, if she wants to walk around half naked she should do it in her home, since the decency laws are there for a reason.

School Bus Runs Red Lights

A motorist noticed a bus passed them going 62mph. The reason for speeding was the driver tried getting through all the traffic lights on green. Though he still went through some red lights. The motorist caught up with the school bus and saw several children jumping around. The driver ran more red lights near a school.

Concerned, the motorist tried to remember the phone number on the bus to report it, but unfortunately could not. The motorist knows this kind of driving happens all the time in Dubai and says this should not be tolerated. But, the resident also knows most people have the attitude of, it's Dubai, it happens, get over it.

Child Seats in Taxis?

The Dubai Roads and Transport Authority or R.T.A. advertised they now have child seats available in taxis with the "lady drivers." Upon request, you may ask for a pink lady driver to pick you up if you do not feel comfortable getting into a taxi with a male.

A woman called the taxi company to ask for a child seat with a lady driver for the next day. But, the company does not pre-book, and is told to call 20 minutes before being picked up. She is informed that it was doubtful she will get a lady driver, and she will have a regular taxi with no child seat. The woman tried explaining how unsafe it is when you don't have a child seat, and the company "seemed" to then understand and said it will not be a problem.

The woman called the next day, and they said: "No lady driver can be sent, we shall send normal taxi." Again, the woman explained the safety issues. The girl spoke with her supervisor, who said she could have a lady driver with a car seat. She had the "choice" of waiting either 3 hours, or she could wait all day. This story is typical in Dubai. If it sounds too good to be true, it usually isn't.

Children Hanging out of Cars going 75mph

Photos by motorists are taken of 2 children standing up inside a car. Their heads are sticking out of a sunroof as they zipped down a highway going 75mph. The woman driver is "safely" buckled up, and oblivious to what is going on, as she drives away in her expensive car.

This caught the attention of the road safety campaigners, and they are furious. They said: "Just when we think we have seen it all, more stories come rolling in." A photo is taken of a "Roads and Transport Authority" car with 2 children in the back seat wearing no seatbelts. The campaigners said of all people, they should know better.

Another photo is taken of a child not strapped in and jumping around while the parent was traveling at 62mph. A woman motorist was spotted driving a classy car with 3 young boys. Two boys are standing in the back seat, a third is in the front seat opening and closing the door multiple times, while the mother is texting. Yet another witness saw a small girl sitting on the "edge" of a car window as the car was speeding, and the boy is sticking his head out of the sunroof. A parent dropping off a child at a day care for infants and toddlers, found 3 cars not having any car seats in them.

The road safety ambassador said: "This behavior could not be excused as a cultural mindset. They are just not aware of the consequences of unrestrained children on high-speed roads."

Tailgating is constant in Dubai and I mean 2 inches away from your bumper! Most people know this is dangerous, but at 7am when parents are bringing their children to school it becomes terrifying.

A father was driving recklessly around a school as children and parents were in the crosswalk. He parked his SUV on the "sidewalk" near the school gate as he dropped off his child at school. Children were everywhere, and if the man had waited just a few minutes, he could have found a parking spot, rather than endangering the children.

Limo Pick up for the Children

A parent really doesn't understand why other parents feel the need for scheduling limos to pick up their children in front of the school. She is unimpressed. She believes that this is tacky, showing off and puts peer pressure on the parents to do the same for their children.

The parent wonders if it's not enough that everyone in Dubai is constantly competing. She says they compete over the nicest cars, biggest house, newest beach club membership and whose children are in the best schools. She said how quickly people forget where they came from.

Opinions varied with a lot of backlash against the parent that voiced this negative view of children picked up by limos. One parent defended the limos. She said: "We should understand that it is a happy feeling for the parent who created excitement for their child and the convenience the limo provides." Another said: "If you got it flaunt it, then sit back and relax, while watching others gnash their teeth in jealousy." Still another said: "It's nobody's business how other folks live and what vehicles they go to school in. Green-eyed monster, jealousy."

Pampered Kids can't Solve Real Problems

A Dubai expat resident puts things in perspective. They said:

> *If you were born after 1978 this has nothing to do with you but if you grew up in the fifties, sixties and seventies; Our beds were painted in bright colors full of lead. Bottles from the pharmacy were easy to open. Doors were a constant danger for our fingers. We never had a helmet when riding a bicycle. We drank water from the tap, and not from bottles. We left the house in the morning and returned when the street lights came on. We broke bones, and nobody was sued – these were simple accident's and nobody's fault. We ate cookies and bread with lots of butter. Drank gallons of liquids and still did not get too fat. We did not have video games, but we had friends who we met on the street. Nobody brought us and nobody picked us up. Some kids were not as smart as others, and they failed exams and repeated class. This did not lead to emotional parent-teacher evenings, or even to an adjusted grading system. Our actions sometimes had consequences, if someone broke the law, parents would not pull you out of the mess. They had the same opinion as the police. Our generation brought about a vast number of innovative problem solvers and inventors with the ability to deal with risks. We had freedom, failure, disappointments, success and responsibilities. We knew how to deal with everything and anything not like today.*

Good Parenting as Kids Cut in Front of a Line

A customer was at a food court and watched in amazement as two kids grabbed money from their parents. They ran over to a donut counter where three people were waiting in line to be served. The children looked over the donuts at the counter, then turned to look at their mom, as to question what they should do next.

The polite thing is to tell them to get in the back of the line. Instead, she waved and gestured for them to push to the front of the counter. The customer says: "Really, she must be so proud of herself to have taught her children this way."

Mother Angry for Woman not Giving Food to her Child

A woman was out having a very nice peaceful lunch with friends. She watched a cute little 5-year-old boy, playing rambunctiously around the tables. She wondered how these children could be so undisciplined. The little boy walked up to the table where the women sat and took food off their plates. He left, but to the woman's amazement came back for more food.

She asked the waiter if he knew where the parents of the little boy were. He shyly pointed to a big noisy table. The boy's mother came running up to the women screaming at the top of her lungs. She said: "What sort of people are you not to feed the child [sic]? Why all expats are so greedy even when you can afford to go to a place like this [sic]?"

The woman was speechless and looked at her in shock. She didn't say anything, but thought the audacity of that lady.

In-Flight Childcare on Long Haul Flights

Nannies are set and ready to go. Hundreds are placed on flights to help take the pressure off parents while they travel with their restless youngsters on long flights. This will be a free airline service as the nannies will entertain the children and even serve them food so the parents can enjoy their meal in peace.

The nannies are trained at a famous nanny college in the U.K. The passengers are warned the nannies "will not" be changing diapers. It is believed that the service will not only help the parents, but children traveling alone will also benefit.

Most parents welcome the new idea. But, one parent says they could entertain their own child, since it is about preparedness. She said: "Shame on the parents who can't even look after their own child on a flight. The same parents who probably left their maid at home and has already booked the children into the kids club the second they land."

Tourist Leaves Son at Airport

A family from a Gulf country were in Dubai on vacation. A taxi dropped them off at the airport as they hurried to catch their flight back home. The couple forgot to take their 5-year-old son who was fast asleep in the backseat of the cab. The parents said they were too busy with their bags, and in a big hurry to catch their flight to realize the boy wasn't there.

While inside the terminal, the father pleaded for help from a policeman, once he realized his son was missing. The officer then retrieved the CCTV footage to track down the plate number from the taxi and inform the company. When the taxi company contacted the driver, he said he did not even realize the boy was in the backseat. When he looked, he saw the boy sound asleep.

Two hours later the family is reunited, and the boy was still sleeping. The father thanked the taxi driver and the police before the family flew home together.

U.A.E. Youths Advised not to Copy Westerners

Young Emiratis are being taught to use the computer to "reflect the U.A.E. heritage and culture, instead of imitating the west." They are being encouraged to post patriotic messages. A class is put in place teaching the youths about cybercrime, bank theft, avoiding piracy, and the proper use of Facebook and other social networks.

Kids Shop and Skate Around the Clock

When Ramadan ends another celebration begins, called Eid. The Dubai Mall stays open for 24-hours on certain days, and festivities go throughout the night. Activities include, arts and crafts for kids that continue on until "3am." The mall is crammed.

Residents don't understand how all these parents can keep their children up the entire night playing while they shop. They said parents don't seem to understand children have to get a good night's sleep. Many noticed unruly, and whining children the next day, because of the lack of rest.

Father Loses Job over Hurt Child

A well liked Pakistani man who spoke little English worked as a runner and assistant for a television production company. The man received horrible news saying his 16-year-old daughter had fallen into a "pit of hot coals," and is burned badly, needing an operation.

When the father asked his employer if he could go back to his country to see his daughter, they said no, and refused to let him go. He eventually went, but his work visa was canceled by the employer, and he no longer can come back to Dubai. This left him no way to pay the medical bills. A collection was set up for him.

CHAPTER 18

OVER THE TOP

The practices on the other side of the world differs greatly from what most of us are accustomed to. If you ever wondered what it would be like to be treated as if you were "famous," Dubai will give you a good idea. Not only is everything at your fingertips, but a barrage of staff is constantly around to accommodate you.

Delivery service for almost anything is usually always available. When it's sweltering outside, and you don't feel like going to the grocery store, or perhaps ran out of milk and bread, your items are a phone call away. If you are too sick to go to the pharmacy, the pharmacy will come to you. If you crave a cup of coffee, donut and a paper in the morning, the restaurant chains will be on their way.

At anytime of the day or night you can have a cheeseburger from McDonald's, a sandwich from Subway or any other variety of food. This is delivered right to your door. It may be brought to you on a motorcycle or a bicycle, but none-the-less it's still hot.

Maybe you need a massage, or hair and nails done, the professionals will be on your doorstep. There is even a beach butler to move your chair on the beach, or set up a cabana with fresh, cold fruit.

It's a strange feeling to never open a soda can, or to never throw fast food trash away. There is someone always standing there watching over you eager to do it for you and it is usually always the migrant workers. By doing some of these things yourself, you have now taken a job away from someone who can no longer support their family in their home country. So, you follow suit and adjust.

Dubai also has an abundance of taxis that are everywhere if you don't feel like driving. The fares are consistently always cheap. Anytime we stepped outside the door of our apartment, one was always waiting.

Luxurious Police Cars

The police department in Dubai now has a Bugatti Veyron which adds a splash to their glamorous collection. They currently have a Lamborghini Aventador, Ferrari FF, Mercedes SLS & AMG, Bentley Continental JT, Aston Martin One-77, McLaren MP4-12C, Nissan GT-R and BMW's.

The fastest production car ever made is the Bugatti Veyron and is capable of speeds more than 250mph. The Aston Martin One-77 is worth $2,994,868 and there are only 10 in the world. It can go from 0 to 62mph in just 3.5 seconds and reach speeds up to 220mph. The police department had secured a "second batch" of luxury cars which will include another Audi R8, Mercedes SL63, Mercedes G-Class Brabus and a Nissan GTR.

A brigadier from the department said: "This is promoting the image of Dubai to the world. The supercars will patrol tourist hotspots in the city to show off how classy Dubai is to visitors." Police officers stated: "People are asking to be arrested so they can have a ride in the supercars." The public knows the places and times the officers will be on patrol so they line up and wait for them.

A female officer said: "A special instructor came to Dubai to teach me and my female colleague how to drive the Ferrari." She loves the car but says, "I can't speed or I will be fined." The police are warning drivers not to take pictures of them while driving since taking your hands off the wheel could cause serious accidents.

Plates Auctioned off

Dubai is crazy about their license plates and often spend more on the plate then they do on the actual car. The Dubai Roads and Transportation Authority has given the green light for old cars to be registered as vintage cars with a special license plate. An event auctioning off license plates for the vintage cars was held. Almost $544,522 was raised and 63 plates were auctioned off. The plate with the number 13 sold for $83,039. The number 444 sold for $33,488 and 99999 sold for $24,503.

Other auctions were held as well for anyone who wants to acquire a distinctive number. A series of 4 and 5 numbers were up for grabs including the popular numbers 20102, 25052 and 4546 which are paired with a letter. The bids started from $272 to $544 and a refundable deposit of $1,351 was required.

People who believe in having the right numbers have already spent huge sums of money in the second auction. The K12333 sold for $5,581 and the K69699 went for $5,036. The total sales for the second auction in just one month netted the Roads and Transportation Authority $6,806,523.

A third auction is scheduled where they will auction off 101 license plate

numbers.
Calling all Taxi Plate Owners
All Emiratis who own taxi plates, roughly 6,597 people will be given a check for $7,185,490 to be split. This bonus comes from the Sheikh, Vice President of U.A.E. and Ruler of Dubai.

Before a taxi corporation was ever created in Dubai, the families were awarded taxi plates and they rented the plates out to drivers. A taxi company was then established and the plates were leased to the taxi company. Eventually the plates still owned by the Emiratis, were leased to the Roads and Transport Authority that was created in 2005, for $272 a month.

The Roads and Transport Authority then turned around and leased the plates to 6 taxi companies for $980 per plate, per month. An RTA chairman said: "The bonus the Emiratis received would help them better cope with the requirements of life and earn a decent living for them and their families."

Upscale and Ritzy Valentine's Day Experiences
For anyone who wants an evening of romance on Valentine's Day, it can be costly. Packages costing as much as $27,230 are offered to wealthier romantic couples by resorts.

The valentine's date through Madinat Jumeira resort will start out fantastic. They will ride in a Rolls Royce to the Burj Al Arab [the hotel in the shape of a sail on a ship]. This is followed by a helicopter ride through the evening skies.

They will end up at the fabulous Madinat Jumeira resort where the couple will embark on a private dinner on the executive terrace. The terrace will be decorated in red and white roses especially flown in from the Netherlands. A photographer will be on hand to capture the memories along with a trio to provide music. The lovebirds will then turn in for a good night's sleep in a Presidential Suite fit for a king and queen. This has been said to be one of the most exclusive dates ever for $27,230 and is available to whoever grabs it first.

Any valentine couple wanting to stay at the Sheraton is offered a package for $13,615. This includes a 5-course rooftop meal, a 1 night stay in their Royal Suite with breakfast in the morning. The pair will also receive a couple's massage, a shopping voucher worth $2,723 and customized amenities upon arrival.

If that doesn't suit you, here is what others are offering. A resort on Palm Jumeira named Zabeel Saray has a package which goes for $10,892. A limousine will pick up the couple for a 1 night stay in a 5-bedroom villa. Inside the villa includes a private butler and fabulous swimming pool. A spa treatment and a makeover is reserved for the lady. The couple will walk on a red carpet from their villa to a private dining table under a gazebo on the beach. There, a 5-course meal and champagne [remember, hotels may offer alcohol] will be served. In the morning breakfast will be in the villa garden and then it's on to a private cooking class.

The Waldorf Astoria resort is letting any couple customize their own package. If the couple has to travel a distance to get to the resort, a helicopter or seaplane will be arranged. They can stay in the Imperial Suite fitted with a grand piano and enjoy a private dinner if they choose. Cupid's little helper [a personal concierge] will be available, and a private section of the beach where the couple can have lunch. A package price isn't given as it depends on how you customize it.

In Abu Dhabi, the Jumeira Etihad Towers has an offer for $8,169. A limousine will transport the couple to the hotel for a dinner. The meal includes oysters, octopus carpaccio, shellfish bisque and seared scallops with butternut squash puree. The couple will get to enjoy a spa treatment, a 1 night stay at the Club Suite and breakfast to be served by a butler on the beach. Now that's a valentine's gift!

Best Drivers Rewarded

There are 700 people who did not commit any driving offenses in a year and have been chosen by the chief of police to be awarded gifts. Prizes will include meals at posh restaurants, shopping vouchers and hotel stays. Winners were from various nationalities with the largest group being Emiratis which totaled 220 people.

This list is made up of 173 women, 97 Indians, 56 Pakistanis and 44 Brits. The winners were informed by receiving a text message on their phone saying they were a winner and that they were the best driver out of 1.2 million motorists. A follow-up phone call was then made by the police department to make sure they received the text message. The police said: "We were surprised that some of them were dead."

$350,000 Finder's Fee

The world's most expensive model car was unveiled with a whopping price tag of $2,015,031. It was announced that if someone could find a buyer for the model car, they would be given a reward of $350,000. This little Lamborghini Aventador LP 700-4 had made it into the Guinness Book of Records. The imitation car is clocked at being the priciest. The model is 25 inches long and is protected in a "bulletproof" display case. The car is made of gold, sterling silver and platinum. It is set with many large carat gemstones.

The German artist is trying to find potential buyers for the model car and said: "I will make a full-size car when I sell the model." If the model sells, $650,000 of the profit will go to a charity chosen by the buyer and himself. If the model doesn't sell, it will return to Abu Dhabi to be auctioned off. The car was scheduled to travel to New York, Singapore, Beijing, Macau and St. Petersburg to search for a buyer.

Fans can Elect Gold

The Rolls Royce Motor Company of Abu Dhabi made a special announcement. They said the little iconic figurine that sits on the front hood of the car will now be available in "24-carat gold." This choice is only available to Middle Eastern clients.

The graceful figure first made its appearance in 1911. The car with the 24-caret gold figurine on the hood will be displayed in the showroom in Abu Dhabi. This is the largest Rolls Royce Motor Showroom in the world.

A New must have Accessory is a Body Guard

Dubai residents are out to impress in a big way and it's not with a new designer handbag or flashy diamonds. They are hiring bodyguards. There are many people in Dubai that hire bodyguards for security reasons. But, a security company has said there has been a growing trend in "hiring beefed up men just to enhance their social status."

A Posh New Cinema

A "9D" movie theater just opened and was the first in the Middle East. The new cinema has scores of interaction. You can see, hear, smell, touch and interact with the props that allows the audiences to take part and throw themselves into the movie. The 9D also allows you to be met with rain, wind, lightning, fog and other scenes in the movie.

A person can even have actual contact with dinosaurs or experience Space Odyssey fun. The seat and environmental effects, along with the lifelike picture can make the movie a surreal experience.

Another new cinema opened in Dubai that features 7 standard movie screens and 3 platinum movie "suites." Five of the movie screens are set up for 3D movies. The entire venue has almost 900 seats and is located alongside a "platinum lounge" that offers a full kitchen to serve their guests. A gourmet popcorn shop has also been added.

The World Islands

The developer who created the World Islands, the group of islands made to look like a map out in the sea, blocked crazy ideas from potential buyers. A wealthy customer wanted to make his island look like "Darth Vader's helmet" from the movie Star Wars. While another wacky idea from a possible buyer was to have his island shaped into a mermaid.

The developer said, "None of these ideas are permitted." But, they could however reshape their islands as long as it wasn't too drastic and did not affect the surrounding environment. Another stipulation is that 50% to 60% of the islands must remain beach and they can't pour "concrete over the island."

Underwater Hotel Surfaces

Replicas like the Pyramids of Egypt and the Eiffel Tower are being built in Dubai. It's no surprise that an underwater hotel named Hydropolis is being constructed. This project is underway and has been collaborated with a European company. The "water discus hotel" will eventually move to an array of locations around the world. These places will include the Maldives, Caribbean island of Martinique and several places in China.

The design will have one disc suspended above the water and the other disc beneath the waves. A Dubai chairman said: "The process had to be thought of in the same way an oil platform would be built. How it's built, how you jack it up, how you anchor it and how you create it. It will look very futuristic. The reefs that typically form around similar designed oil rigs will mean the hotels will have a host of marine life."

Dubai is often accused of "copying" other countries, never truly taking on a project by coming up with ideas themselves. There are individuals that indicated that Dubai had gotten this inspiration from the classic tv cartoon "The Jetsons," but they have denied it. The underwater hotel has a remarkable resemblance to the Jetson house. The project is estimated to cost $50 million to build.

Giant Hotels Duke it out

High profile resorts are in fierce competition with each other over the best waterpark, firework display and number of new guests. The Atlantis resort on Palm Jumeira will ultimately spend $26 million to upgrade their Aquaventure waterpark. They will reveal a third resort location and possibly a fourth.

One New Year's Eve, the Atlantis resort and the Burj Al Arab resort tried to surpass each other for New Year's Eve fireworks. The Atlantis purposely started their spectacular show over the sea "5" seconds before midnight to capture everyone's attention first.

The average cost per night to stay on the Palm Jumeira is around $900. The One & Only Resort averaged a room rate of $975 a night. With prices like these, you can understand why they strive to be the finest. In 2014, Dubai claimed to have had more than "10 million tourists." The goal for Dubai is to have "100,000 hotel accommodations" and "15 million" tourists by 2015.

World's Biggest Ferris Wheel

The soon to be "world's biggest Ferris wheel" will dominate the skyline of Dubai. It is being developed off the coast of Dubai. Ironically, named the "Dubai Eye." London has a giant Ferris wheel as well called the "London Eye" built in 2000. This entire entertainment project will cost $1.6 billion with the Ferris wheel alone costing $272,301,492.

The project will sit on an island and stand at 689 ft. The current record is set in Singapore where their Ferris wheel stands at 541 ft. Developers are predicting to attract 3 million visitors per year and aiming to have all of it finished in 3 years. Retail and entertainment zones will be complete in 2 years.

This entire project will include a promenade, restaurants, a food hall offering fresh produce and a 5-star hotel. Included will be private low-rise residential buildings. All areas will connect by a cable car and monorail. The island itself will attach to the mainland by a bridge. A chairman said: "This project will continue to build on the emirates reputation as a leader in the global entertainment and retail landscape."

The Sheikh and Ruler of Dubai has approved several projects that will consist of five theme parks linked together and is estimated to cost $2.7 billion. A Universal Studio Theme Park is on the list and another shopping mall dubbed to be the "world's biggest."

Millionaires Head for the Yacht Show in Dubai

Dubai and Abu Dhabi together hold an International Yacht and Boat Show each year in March. These clients come from all over since there isn't another show for a radius of 2,484 miles. This is an elite event, you can meet the who's who of the maritime society.

The Middle East is home to 60% of the world's super yachts. More than 750 firms will be on hand to try and sell their beauties to millionaires who will be attending. A European builder launched his latest vessel in Dubai rather than in Florida. He said:

> *The vessels are not cheap and we know there are few boat shows in the world where you can find people who fit our target group. I know that the people we are looking for are coming to the Dubai Boat Show. Middle East customers can be demanding. It can be difficult to know precisely what they are after in a yacht. But, when they fall in love, they pay.*

An executive from a yacht company said: "If you can buy a car, you can buy a boat." he denied that the show is for those who have deep pockets. The smallest boat he will showcase will sell for just over $27,226. If you throw in up-grades, the number could easily rise to $54,452. The largest vessel his firm sells comes with a price tag of $6 million.

The executive said: "You can't forget to also factor in 10% of the yacht's price per year for fuel and other costs. Many people who have saved money to buy a house often end up blowing the money they saved on a yacht. These customers share something with most of the homebuyers in the U.A.E., they like to pay in cash!"

The vessels showcased are worth a total of $272,000,000 and 19 super yachts measuring over 78 ft. in length are being welcomed.

Plans for a New Flight Experience

An event in Dubai given by an Airbus representative gave a glimpse into what flying in a futuristic plane will look like. The project is only in the theoretical phase with a potential launch date of 2050. The Airbus concept officer said they would be focusing on the passenger's needs.

The aircraft would present a panoramic view and personalized services. The cabins will offer gaming, shopping and relaxation services. An interactive zone would feature "holographic projections" that can allow passengers to go on a shopping spree in the sky and use "virtual fitting rooms." For gamers there would be "holographic gaming scenes." A "smart tech zone" would be available for anyone who wants to work.

Passengers who are nervous or stressed out, a "vitalizing zone" will be available aimed at helping them relax with vitamin and antioxidant-enriched air, aromatherapy and mood lighting. The seats of the airbus will fit the passengers "body shape." They are equipped with "interactive conferences" where the cabin will identify and respond to the passenger's needs.

Feelings at the event were mixed, some were welcoming while others were nervous over safety concerns. This project will cost more than $5 billion and the company is already offering small parts of the concept.

Pod off

Passengers at the Abu Dhabi Airport now will be able to rest at the airport in a pod. The pod is called a "GoSleep" and is a Finnish design chair. This pod converts into a flat bed with a partially or fully enclosed sliding shade that will isolate the passenger from noise, lights and crowds. It will eventually be upgraded to include internet access, a secure storage for luggage or valuables and a charging system for electronic devices. These pods accept credit cards and cost $12 per hour. The airport is "first in the world" to install the "GoSleep" pod.

22-Carat Tea

A cafe has introduced a tea made from gold plated tea leaves imported from overseas. This cup of tea goes for $15. A cafe managing partner, an Egyptian national is quoted as saying: "The tea is beneficial to health as it is very relaxing." The partner had since retracted that statement when it had caused controversy.

A director of the Dubai Food Control Department strongly came out and said: "Such health claims are propaganda and commercial lies. A publicity trick to justify high prices for cheap products." But, customers are going out of their way to have a sip of the brew and describe it as sweet, tangy and fruity.

Bomb Proof Underwear

A pair of lightweight long johns survived a grenade attack and gunfire in a Dutch lab and passed the test with flying colors. The underwear went on sale in Dubai and is aimed at protecting the private parts of troops in conflict zones. In addition, to politicians or business executives from would-be assassins.

A salesman for the manufacturer said they are "comfortable" and could be "worn under any clothing." The underwear is made from ultra-strong Polyethylene material. He also said: "The underwear could withstand an

IED [improvised explosive device] in a conflict zone since most IED's tend to come from the ground up. You need the protection in the groin area. Certain cultures may be embarrassed to discuss matters regarding their lower body parts, but once they see the dangers of explosives, they are more willing to discuss it."

The underwear is new on the market so the company was reluctant to discuss the price.

Santa Clause is Mobbed by Children

A Santa who appeared at Ski Dubai in the Mall of the Emirates is attacked by children. They are "not" patiently waiting to see him, but rather pulling at him and holding their hands out for gifts such as iPhones and tablets. Ski Dubai, inside the mall was not the only place in the desert to experience snow flurries. A family woke up one morning, peeked out their window and saw flakes falling, snow piled on their lawn, a snowman, frosted plants, icicles and penguins. The family shelled out over $1,361 to a company to make it happen. Oh, the penguins that were used, they were only toys from their swimming pool.

Since it has never ever snowed for real in Dubai, six families handed over money to the company to create a winter wonderland. An expat man who has lived in Dubai for 10 years said: "None of my children has ever seen real snow. They are in amazement when they see the fake snow." The owner of the company said: "It takes 90 minutes to set up a snow scene at someone's house." The snow will last up to one week and then, they return to clean up the mess. He also said: "The snow looks real and is made out of paper from plant material and you can easily make snowballs with it."

New Houses Handed out to U.A.E. Nationals

The U.A.E. Vice President has ordered the first phase of 114 houses worth $43,017,196 to be "distributed" to U.A.E. citizens. The reason for the giveaway was to provide modern housing and ensure family stability and decent living conditions to Emiratis. It is aimed at replacing old buildings.

Another phase will be to renovate and build "10,000 homes" for the locals at a cost of $408,000,000. The design of these homes will take into consideration the "lifestyle of the Emirati families, functionality, comfort and privacy." The project will be complete by the end of 2017.

Nail Filing Record Attempt

A beauty salon attempted to set a Guinness World Record for the most nails filed and painted in an 8-hour period. The goal is to manicure "50,000 nails" between the hours of 2:00pm and 10:00pm at a mall. One hundred beauty technicians will work on attempting the record. The manicures are free and for anyone who donates, the money will go to charity. No further information.

Record Attempt with Smallest Parachute

A Guinness World Record is about be to being attempted by a test pilot and professional stuntman who will skydive with the "world's smallest" parachute. The parachute will measure only 35 square feet. Most expert skydivers use 80 to 200 square feet. The smallest ever used in the last 10 years averaged between 70 and 90 square feet. A previous "unofficial" record was set in 2008 using a 37 square foot parachute. The public has been asked to be present to cheer for the man.

The record was broken, and the stunt was successful. The professional stuntman said: "I'm sure my wife doesn't want me to do another stunt like this anytime soon."

World Record Fireworks

A world record for the most fireworks was set off and is accomplished. This attempt was made during New Year's Eve going into 2014 on Palm Jumeira and the World Islands. Dubai set off "500,000 fireworks" in a "6 minute" display that traveled 62 miles and rose higher than 2/3 of a mile. The current record was set by Kuwait when they set off 77,282 for their 50th anniversary of their constitution.

A company who organized the event in Dubai said in previous years, they saw as many as "1.7 million visitors" from all over the world come to downtown Dubai for New Year's Eve. He also said: "That is more than at the New Year's Eve galas in New York, London and Sydney."

Dubai has since lost their title to the Philippines when they had set off 810,904 fireworks in the pouring rain on New Year's Eve going into 2016. Their display lasted for 1 hour, 1 minute and 32.35 seconds.

Dubai Mall, the World's Most Popular Mall

In 2013 the Dubai Mall claims to have attracted 75 million visitors and is growing by 15% a year. An average of 6.25 million shoppers a month made it the most popular shopping mall in the world for a third consecutive year. The mall said "their stats" showed it is significantly more popular than the Mall of America in the U.S. and the Bullring Mall in the U.K. They claim each mall pulled in 40 million visitors in 2012.

The more than 1,200 retailers were up 26% in sales for the year 2013 and half of all luxury goods sold in Dubai are purchased at the mall. Dubai Shopping Festival attracted 4.36 million visitors and brought in $1 billion a week to Dubai's economy during the entire time of the festival.

The giveaways, especially during the festival are superb. Some of the prizes you can win are many shopping sprees in Dubai and Paris. Multiple trips with spa treatments to the Maldives are given away and once there, the resort will carve a table and chair out of sand on the beach for you. Some other trips are family holidays to Disneyland Hong Kong and 2-night family packages at the Atlantis Resort. These are just to name a few.

If you spend $54 at the Dubai Mall in a month [easy to do if you grocery shop there], you could win a brand new Mercedes-Benz 200. You can also win a Sea-Doo GTI 130. Raffle tickets to win other new cars can easily be purchased at every gas station in town and cost little to buy. Some stations give out 7 cars every day!

Through this thought-provoking book, I hope you have been able to see just how fortunate most of us are, coming from fair-minded countries and understand the need to want to share these stories. Even though this is the end of the book, unfortunately it is not the end of the more serious issues. They will likely continue for many more years to come.

The author supports the work of Amnesty International.
For information visit, www.amnesty.org

The author supports the work of Humane Society International.
For information visit, www.hsi.org

The End

REFERENCES

I have compiled these stories for 3½ years while residing in Dubai. This book can be corroborated with:

[Unattributed]: Citing Sources:
[http://worldpopulationreview.com]: [2015]
[Unattributed]: Citing Sources:
[http://en.mwikipedia.org/wiki/Dubai]: [2015]
[Unattributed]: Citing Sources:
[http://en.mwikipedia.org/wiki/Burj_Khalifa]: [2015]
[Unattributed]: Citing Sources:
[http://worldweatheronline.com]: [2015]
[Unattributed]: Citing Sources:
[http://metric-conversions.org]: [2015]
[Unattributed]: Citing Sources:
[http://en.wikipedia.org/wiki/Deira, Dubai]: [2015]
7days, Idea, 2011, 2012, 2013, 2014
[Unattributed]: Citing Sources:
[http://Dubai-online.com]: [2015]
[Unattributed]: Citing Sources:
[http://en.m.wikipedia.org/wiki/list_of_hotels_in_Dubai]: [2015]
[Unattributed]: Citing Sources:
The National, Idea, 2011, 2012, 2013, 2014
[http://jumeira.com]: [2015]
Abudhabi is an informative website
(http://abudhabi.com)
[Unattributed]: Citing Sources:
[http://passion4luxury.com]: [2015]
Gulf, Idea, 2011, 2012, 2013, 2014
Wikipedia is an informative website
(http://Wikipedia.org)
[Unattributed]: Citing Sources:
[http://xe.com/currancyconverter]: [2015-2016]
All dollar values are based on exchange rate at the time of writing.

ABOUT THE AUTHOR

Northern Empress is born and raised in Minnesota and concluded her education there. She is married to an airline captain and was a former flight attendant. They lived in Dubai, United Arab Emirates for 3½ years. Further residing in Shenzhen, China for slightly over 2 years while her spouse worked for an airline.

This novel is her first significant launch in writing and was in the works for many months. She has however written for travel forums with a mass of individuals reading her advice.

Northern Empress and her spouse has traveled the world extensively having spent a lot of time on all the continents except for two. She has many adventures in these diverse countries. Her desire is to share what she saw and experienced in the Middle East.

Made in the USA
Lexington, KY
09 April 2016